Disney's
Kim Possible

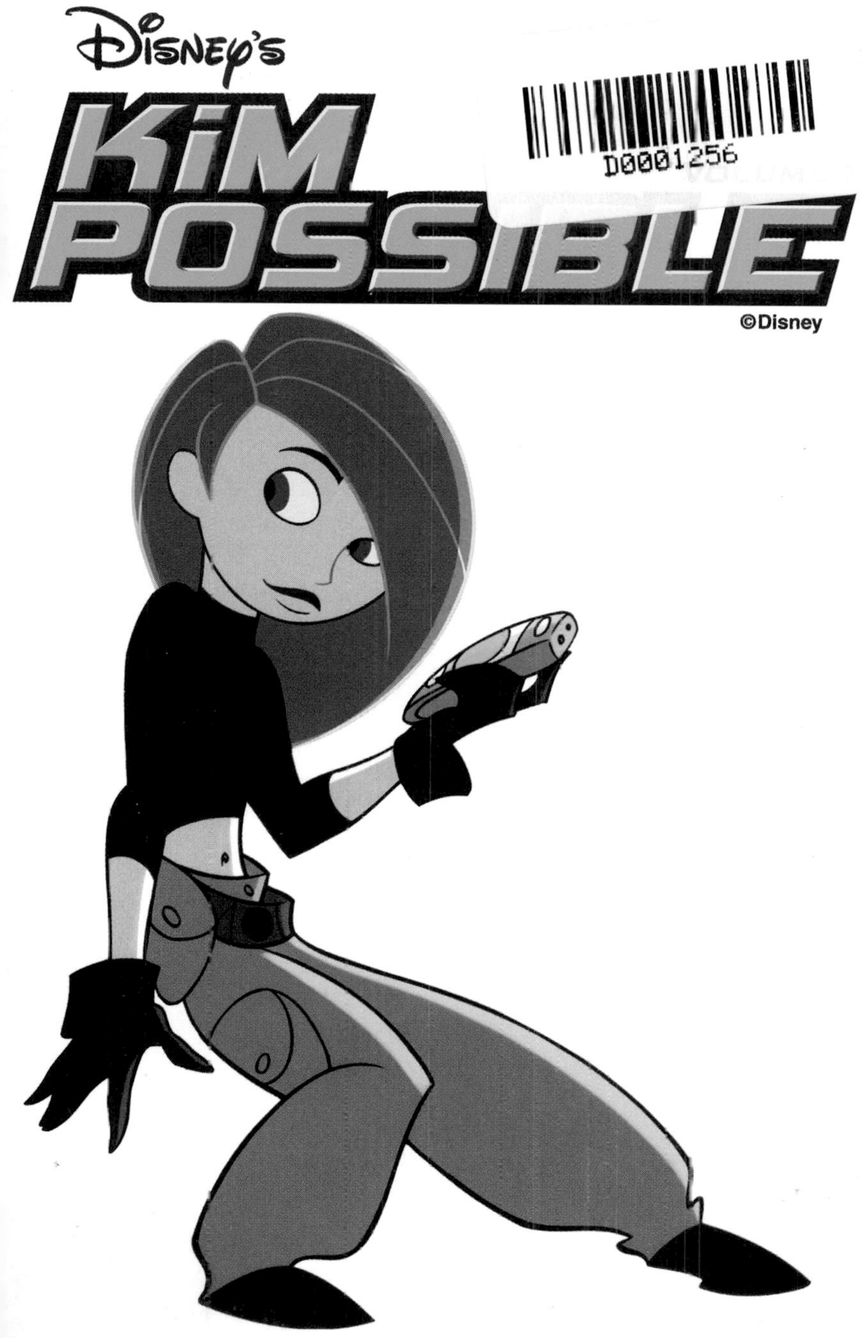

ALSO AVAILABLE FROM 🐾 TOKYOPOP®

MANGA

*INDICATES TITLE IS IN THE RIGHT-TO-LEFT FORMAT

ACTION

ANGELIC LAYER*
CLAMP SCHOOL DETECTIVES* (April 2003)
DIGIMON (March 2003)
DUKLYON: CLAMP SCHOOL DEFENDERS* (September 2003)
GATEKEEPERS* (March 2003)
GTO*
HARLEM BEAT
INITIAL D*
ISLAND
JING: KING OF BANDITS* (June 2003)
JULINE
LUPIN III*
MONSTERS, INC.
PRIEST
RAVE*
REAL BOUT HIGH SCHOOL*
REBOUND* (April 2003)
SAMURAI DEEPER KYO* (June 2003)
SCRYED* (March 2003)
SHAOLIN SISTERS* (February 2003)
THE SKULL MAN*

FANTASY

CHRONICLES OF THE CURSED SWORD (July 2003)
DEMON DIARY (May 2003)
DRAGON HUNTER (June 2003)
DRAGON KNIGHTS*
KING OF HELL (June 2003)
PLANET LADDER*
RAGNAROK
REBIRTH (March 2003)
SHIRAHIME: TALES OF THE SNOW PRINCESS* (December 2003)
SORCERER HUNTERS
WISH*

CINE-MANGA™

AKIRA*
CARDCAPTORS
KIM POSSIBLE (March 2003)
LIZZIE McGUIRE (March 2003)
POWER RANGERS (May 2003)
SPY KIDS 2 (March 2003)

ANIME GUIDES

GUNDAM TECHNICAL MANUALS
COWBOY BEBOP
SAILOR MOON SCOUT GUIDES

ROMANCE

HAPPY MANIA* (April 2003)
I.N.V.U. (February 2003)
LOVE HINA*
KARE KANO*
KODOCHA*
MAN OF MANY FACES* (May 2003)
MARMALADE BOY*
MARS*
PARADISE KISS*
PEACH GIRL
UNDER A GLASS MOON (June 2003)

SCIENCE FICTION

CHOBITS*
CLOVER
COWBOY BEBOP*
COWBOY BEBOP: SHOOTING STAR* (June 2003)
G-GUNDAM*
GUNDAM WING
GUNDAM WING: ENDLESS WALTZ*
GUNDAM: THE LAST OUTPOST*
PARASYTE
REALITY CHECK (March 2003)

MAGICAL GIRLS

CARDCAPTOR SAKURA
CARDCAPTOR SAKURA: MASTER OF THE CLOW*
CORRECTOR YUI
MAGIC KNIGHT RAYEARTH* (August 2003)
MIRACLE GIRLS
SAILOR MOON
SAINT TAIL
TOKYO MEW MEW* (April 2003)

NOVELS

SAILOR MOON
SUSHI SQUAD (April 2003)

ART BOOKS

CARDCAPTOR SAKURA*
MAGIC KNIGHT RAYEARTH*

TOKYOPOP KIDS

STRAY SHEEP (September 2003)

Disney's

Kim Possible

Volume 1

©Disney

Series created by
Bob Schooley and Mark McCorkle

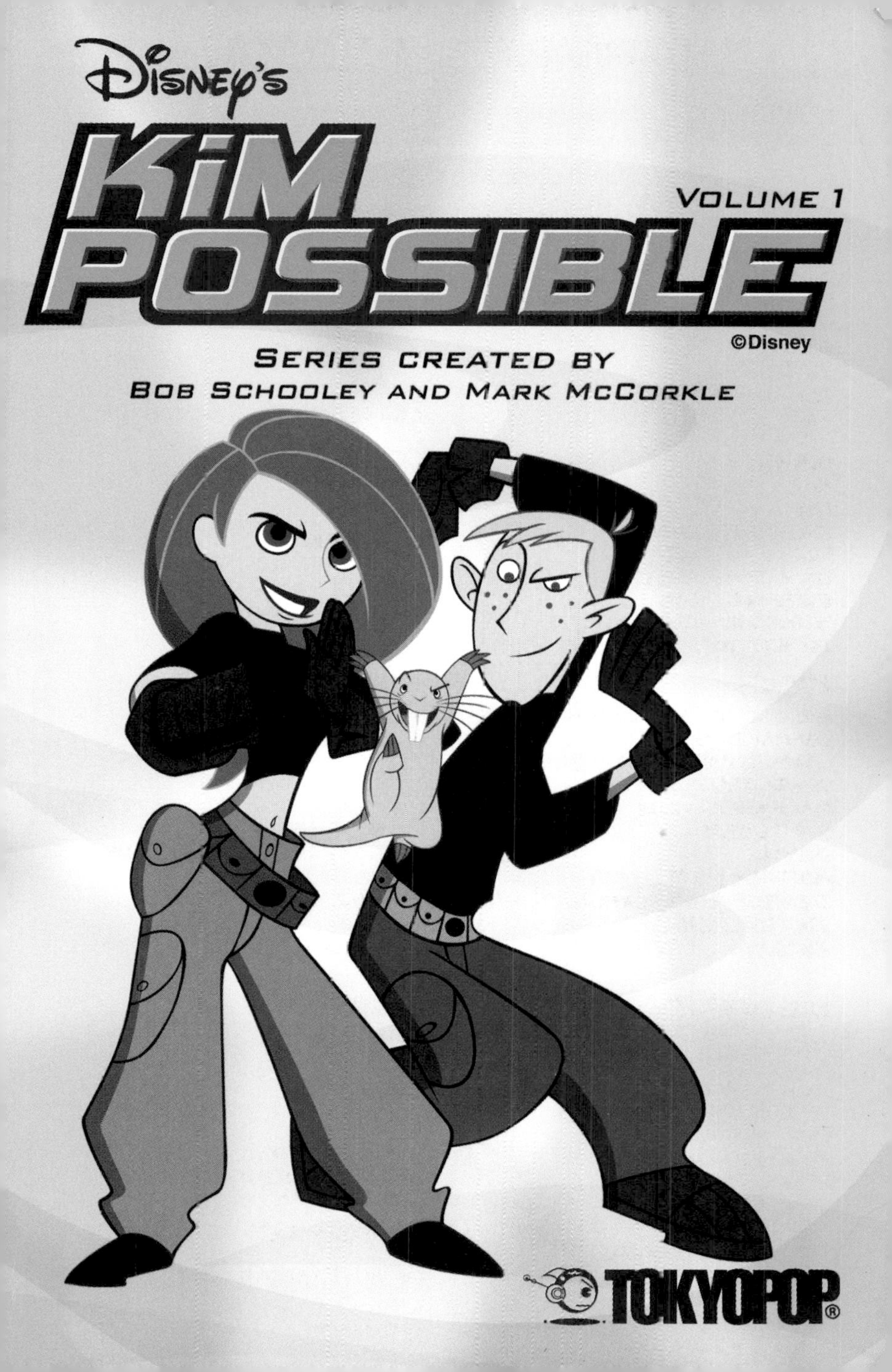

TOKYOPOP®

Editor - Jodi Bryson
Contributing Editor - Amy Court Kaemon
Graphic Design & Lettering - Marcus Lindlahr
Production Specialists - Monalisa de Asis, Anna Kernbaum, Paul Morrissey
Additional Layout - Raymond Makowski
Cover Layout - Patrick Hook

Senior Editor - Julie Taylor
Managing Editor - Jill Freshney
Production Manager - Jennifer Miller
Art Director - Matt Alford
VP of Production & Manufacturing - Ron Klamert
President & C.O.O. - John Parker
Publisher - Stuart Levy

Email: editor@TOKYOPOP.com
Come visit us online at www.TOKYOPOP.com

A ⦿ **TOKYOPOP**® Manga

TOKYOPOP® is an imprint of Mixx Entertainment, Inc.
5900 Wilshire Blvd. Suite 2000, Los Angeles, CA, 90036

© 2003 Disney Enterprises, Inc.

TOKYOPOP is a registered trademark of Mixx Entertainment, Inc.

All rights reserved. No portion of this book may be reproduced or
transmitted in any form or by any means without written permission
from the copyright holders. This manga is a work of fiction.
Any resemblance to actual events or locales or persons,
living or dead, is entirely coincidental.

ISBN: 1-59182-145-2

First TOKYOPOP® printing: February 2003

10 9 8 7 6 5 4 3

Printed in Canada

Disney's

Kim Possible

Volume 1

CONTENTS:

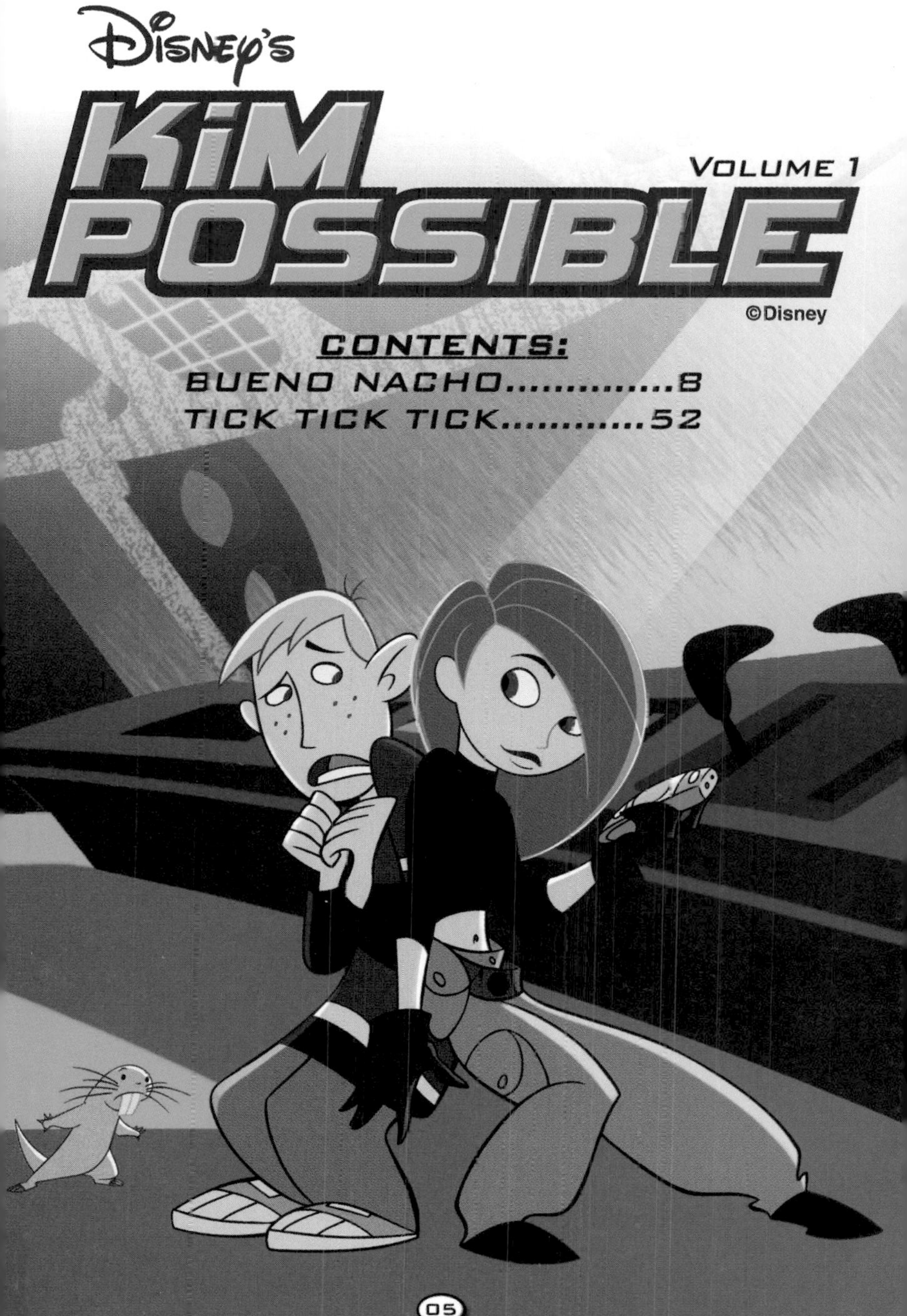

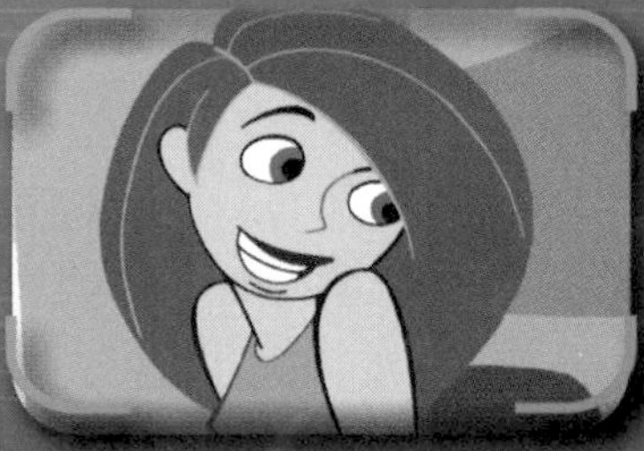

KIM POSSIBLE

A STUDENT AT MIDDLETON HIGH SCHOOL WHO LOVES CHEERLEADING, SHOPPING AND HANGING OUT WITH HER BEST FRIEND RON. BUT KIM'S NO ORDINARY GIRL–SHE CAN DO ANYTHING, INCLUDING SAVING THE WORLD IN HER SPARE TIME.

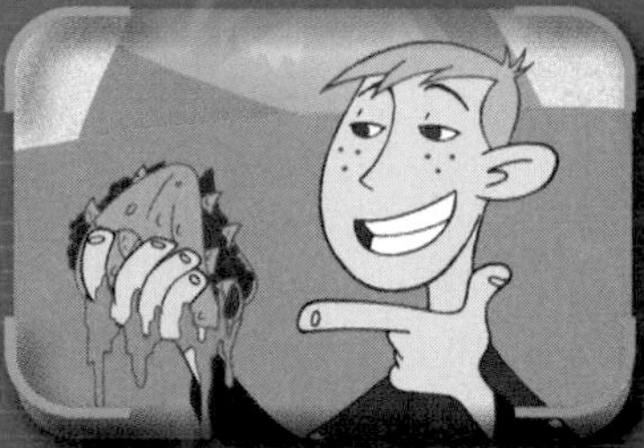

RON STOPPABLE

KIM'S BEST FRIEND AND SIDEKICK.

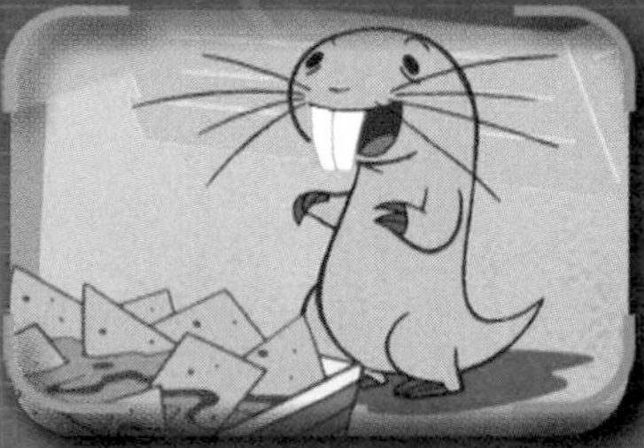

RUFUS

RON'S PET NAKED MOLE RAT.

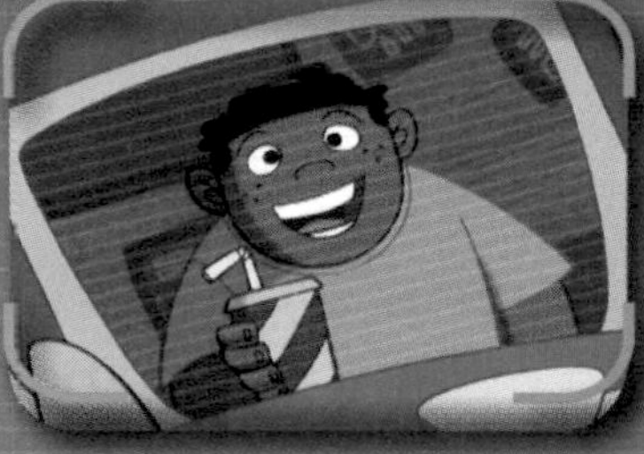

WADE

THE 10-YEAR-OLD GENIUS WHO RUNS KIM'S WEBSITE AND KEEPS HER UPDATED ON EVIL SCHEME DEVELOPMENTS.

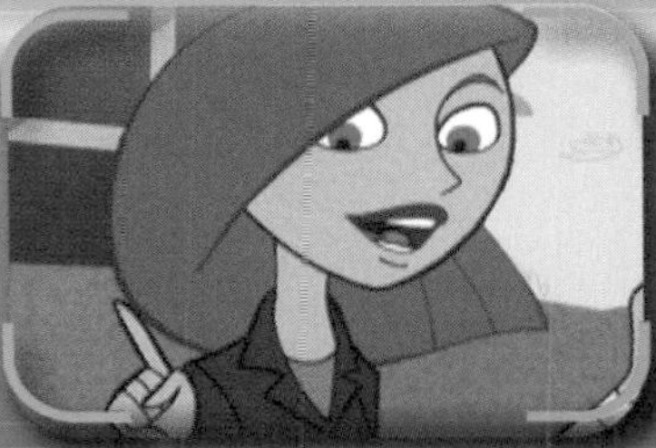

Kim's mom

A brain surgeon.

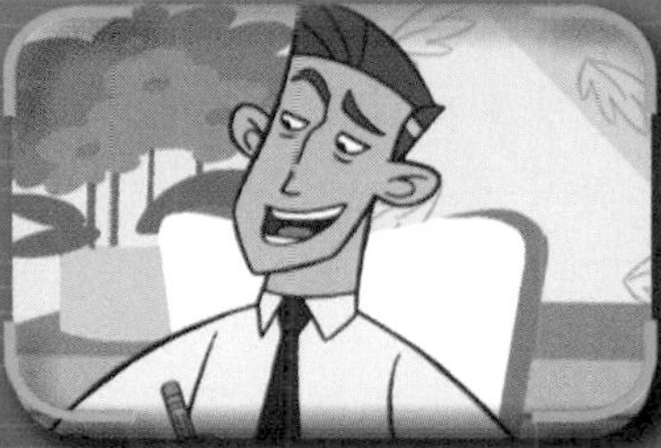

Kim's dad

A rocket scientist.

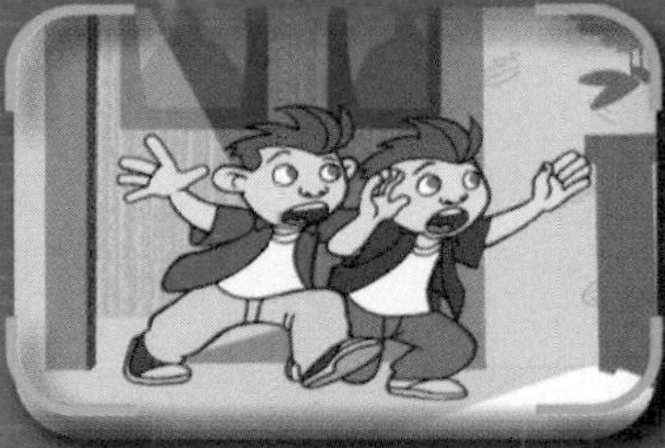

Jim and Tim Possible

Kim's younger twin brothers who are constantly causing Kim double trouble.

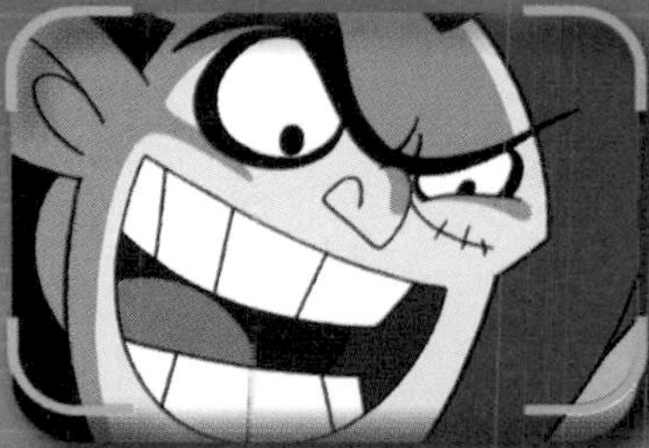

Drakken

A bad guy who wants to take over the world.

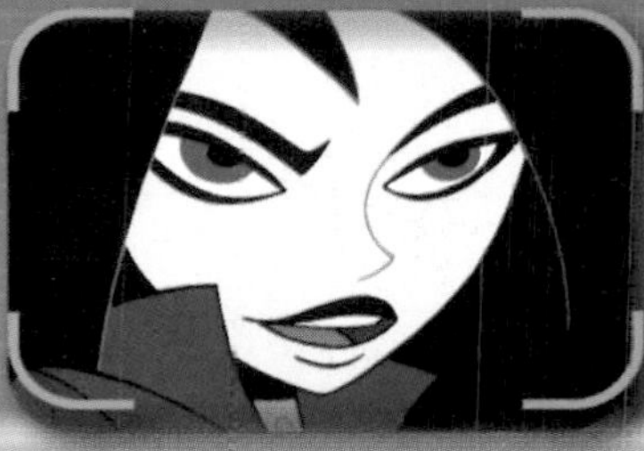

Shego

Drakken's glamorous henchgirl.

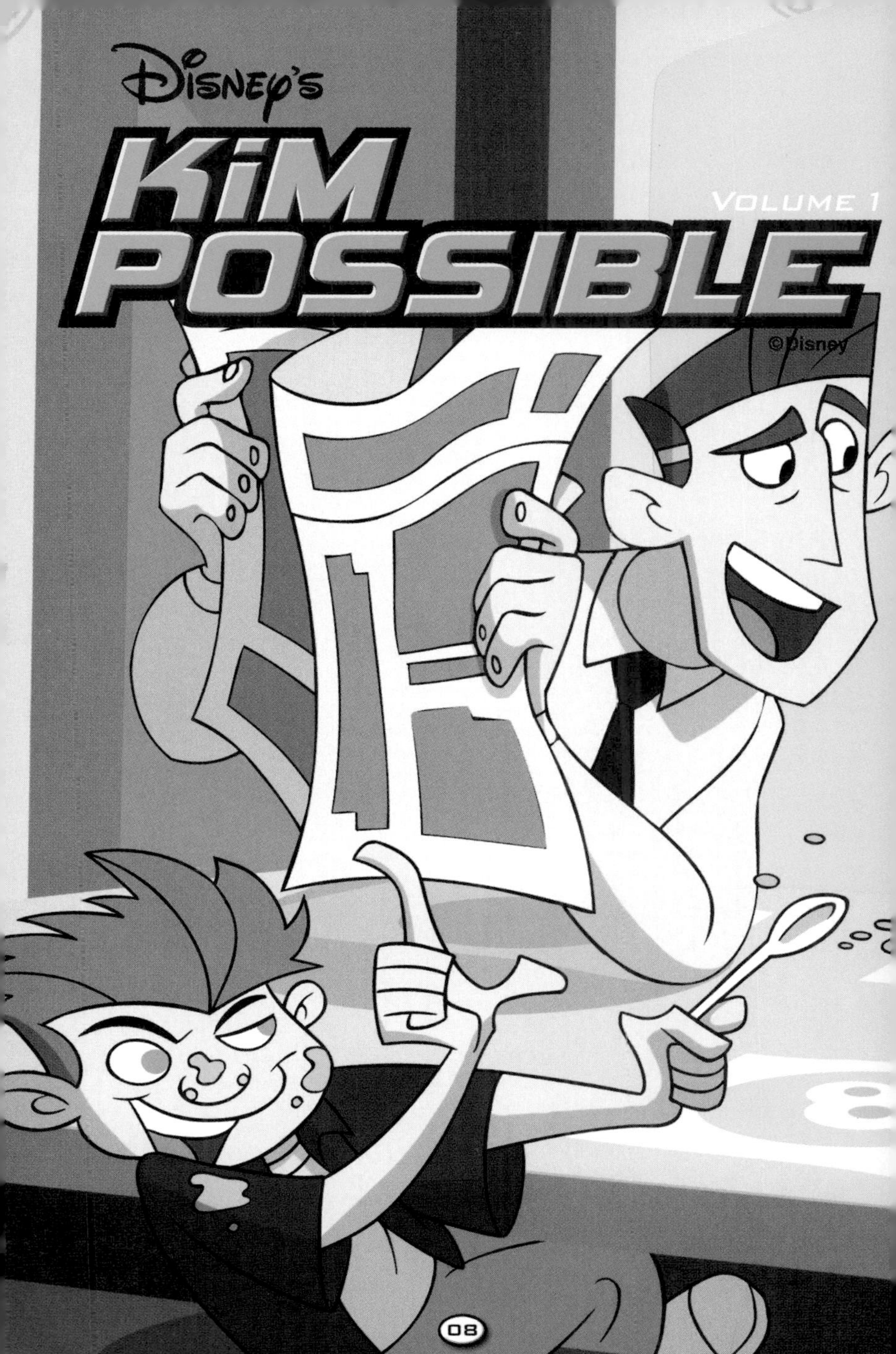
Disney's
Kim
Possible
Volume 1
©Disney

EPISODE 1: BUENO NACHO

KIM AND RON'S NEW FAST FOOD JOB –AND THEIR FRIENDSHIP– IS PUT TO THE TEST BY DRAKKEN'S SCHEME TO COVER THE MIDWEST IN MAGMA.

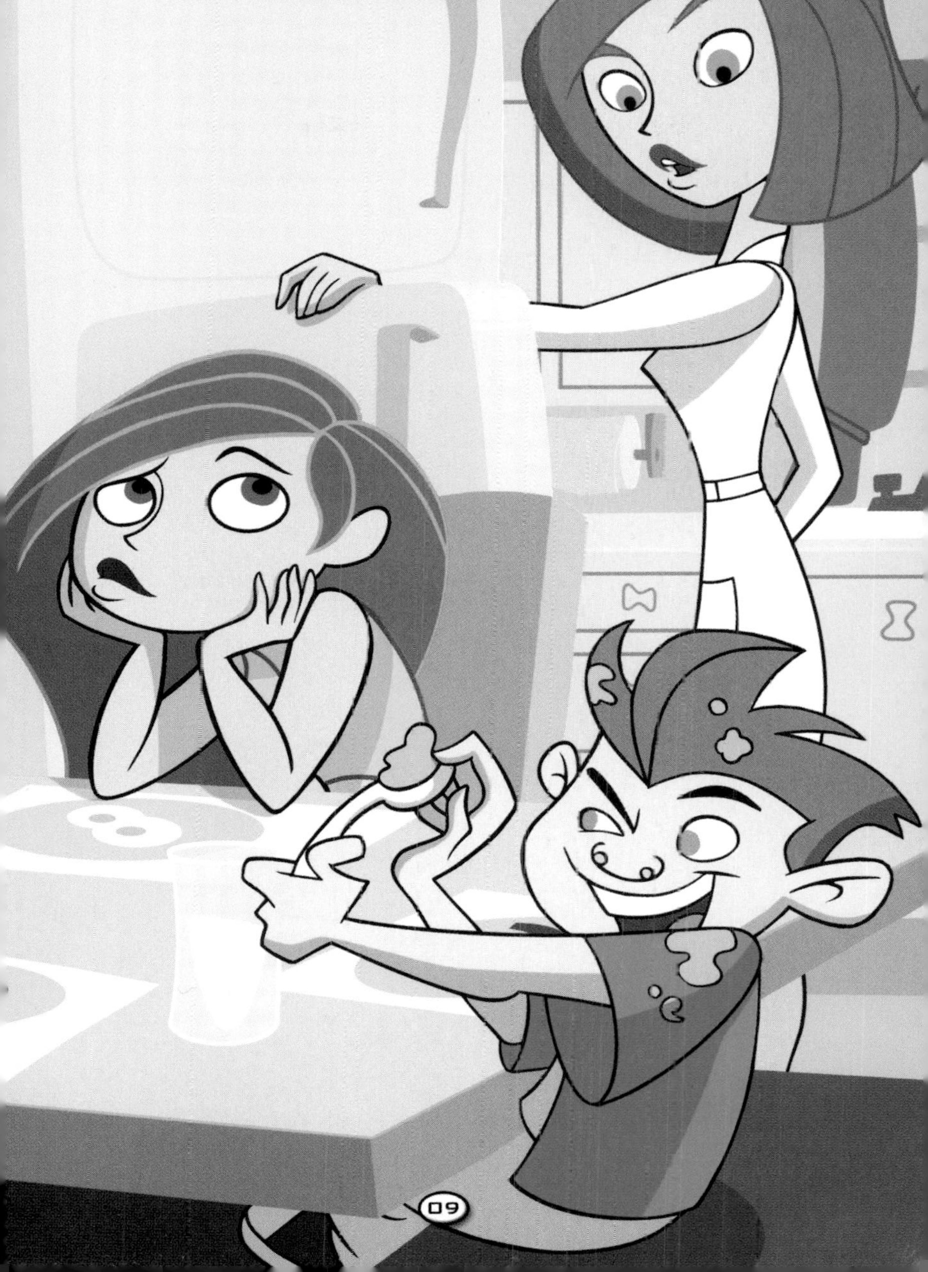

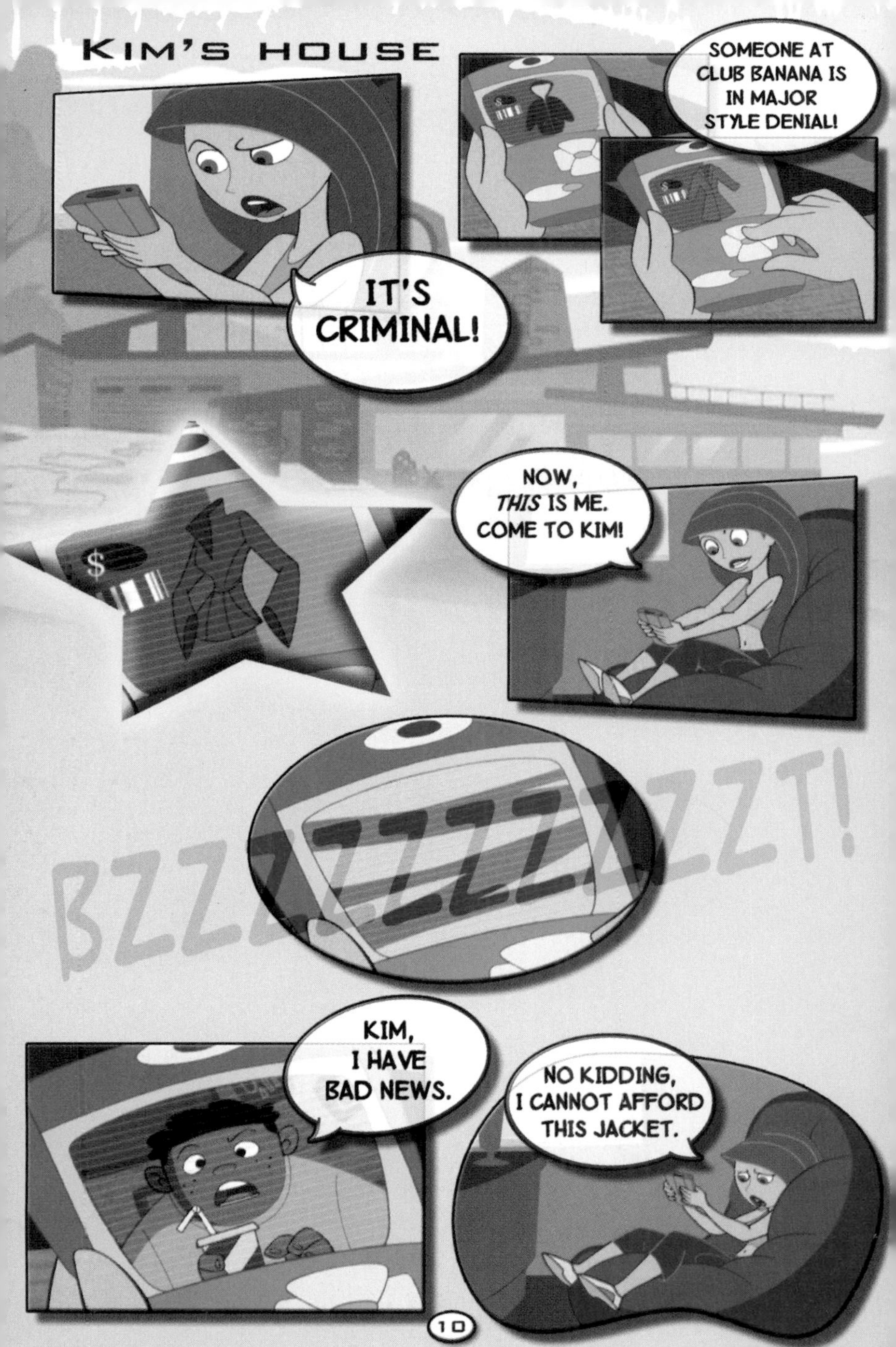
KIM'S HOUSE
IT'S CRIMINAL!
SOMEONE AT CLUB BANANA IS IN MAJOR STYLE DENIAL!
NOW, *THIS* IS ME. COME TO KIM!
BZZZZZZZZZT!
KIM, I HAVE BAD NEWS.
NO KIDDING, I CANNOT AFFORD THIS JACKET.

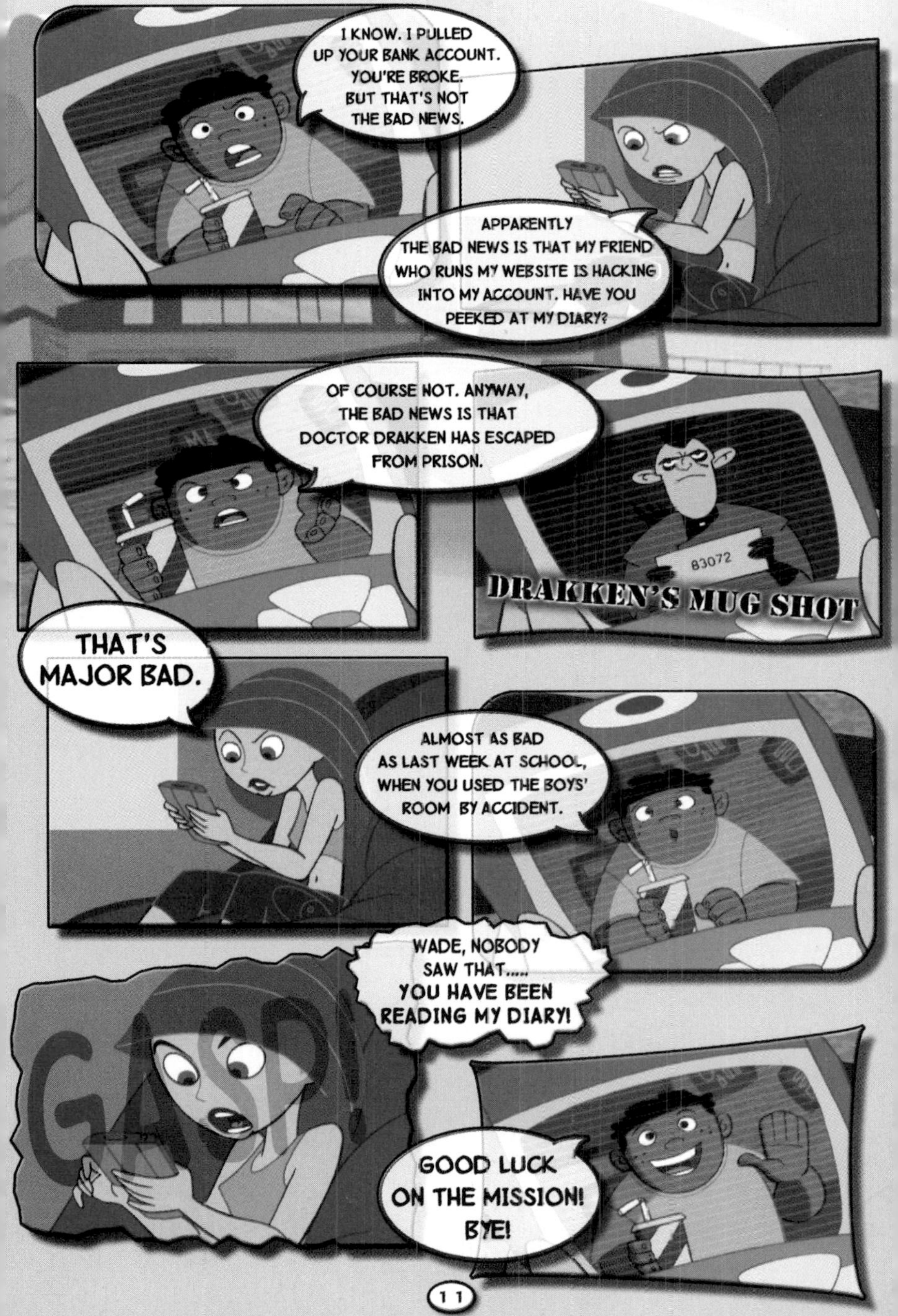
I KNOW. I PULLED UP YOUR BANK ACCOUNT. YOU'RE BROKE. BUT THAT'S NOT THE BAD NEWS.
APPARENTLY THE BAD NEWS IS THAT MY FRIEND WHO RUNS MY WEBSITE IS HACKING INTO MY ACCOUNT. HAVE YOU PEEKED AT MY DIARY?
OF COURSE NOT. ANYWAY, THE BAD NEWS IS THAT DOCTOR DRAKKEN HAS ESCAPED FROM PRISON.
83072
DRAKKEN'S MUG SHOT
THAT'S MAJOR BAD.
ALMOST AS BAD AS LAST WEEK AT SCHOOL, WHEN YOU USED THE BOYS' ROOM BY ACCIDENT.
WADE, NOBODY SAW THAT..... YOU HAVE BEEN READING MY DIARY!
GASP!
GOOD LUCK ON THE MISSION! BYE!

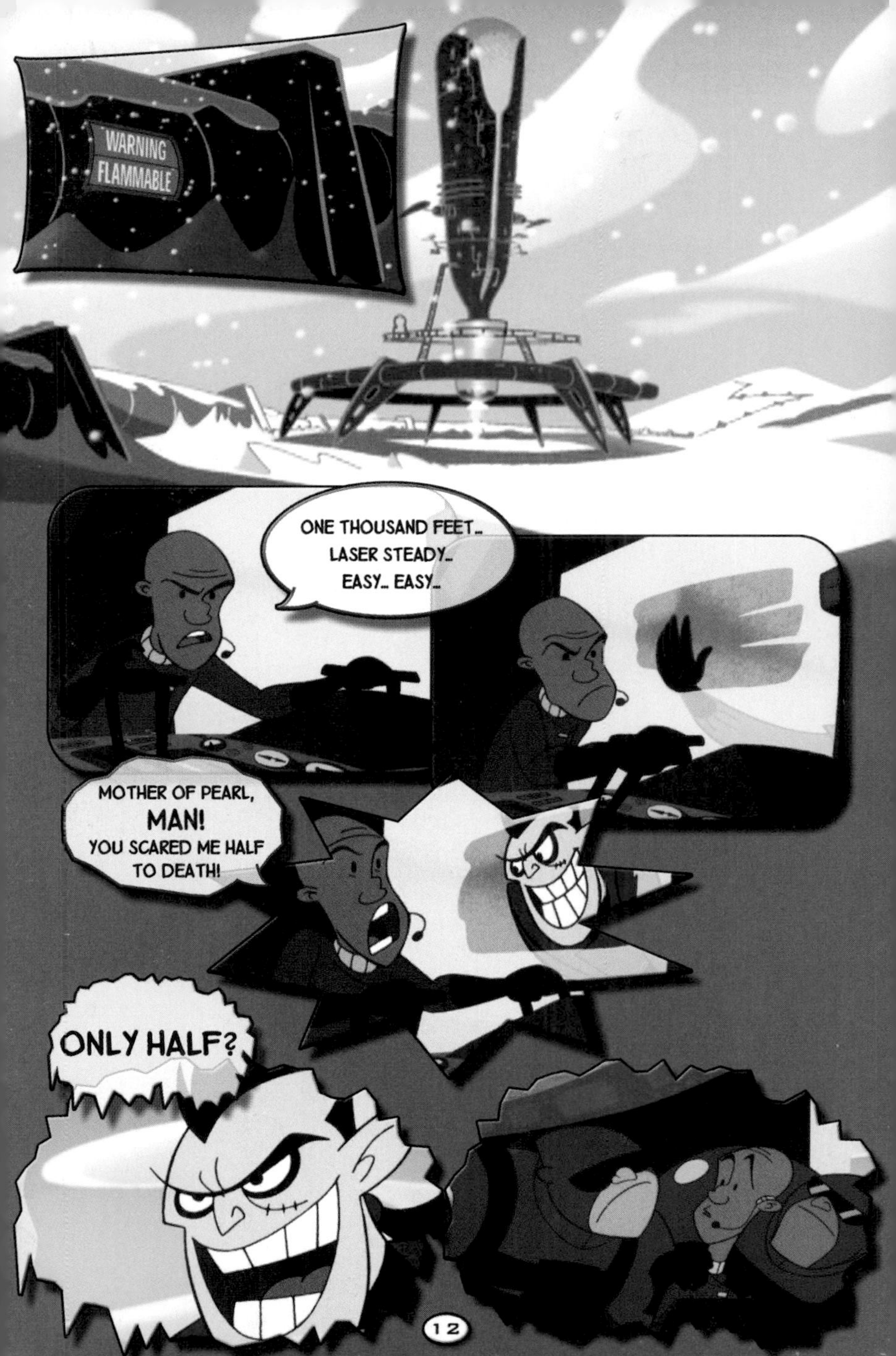
WARNING FLAMMABLE
ONE THOUSAND FEET... LASER STEADY... EASY... EASY...
MOTHER OF PEARL, MAN! YOU SCARED ME HALF TO DEATH!
ONLY HALF?

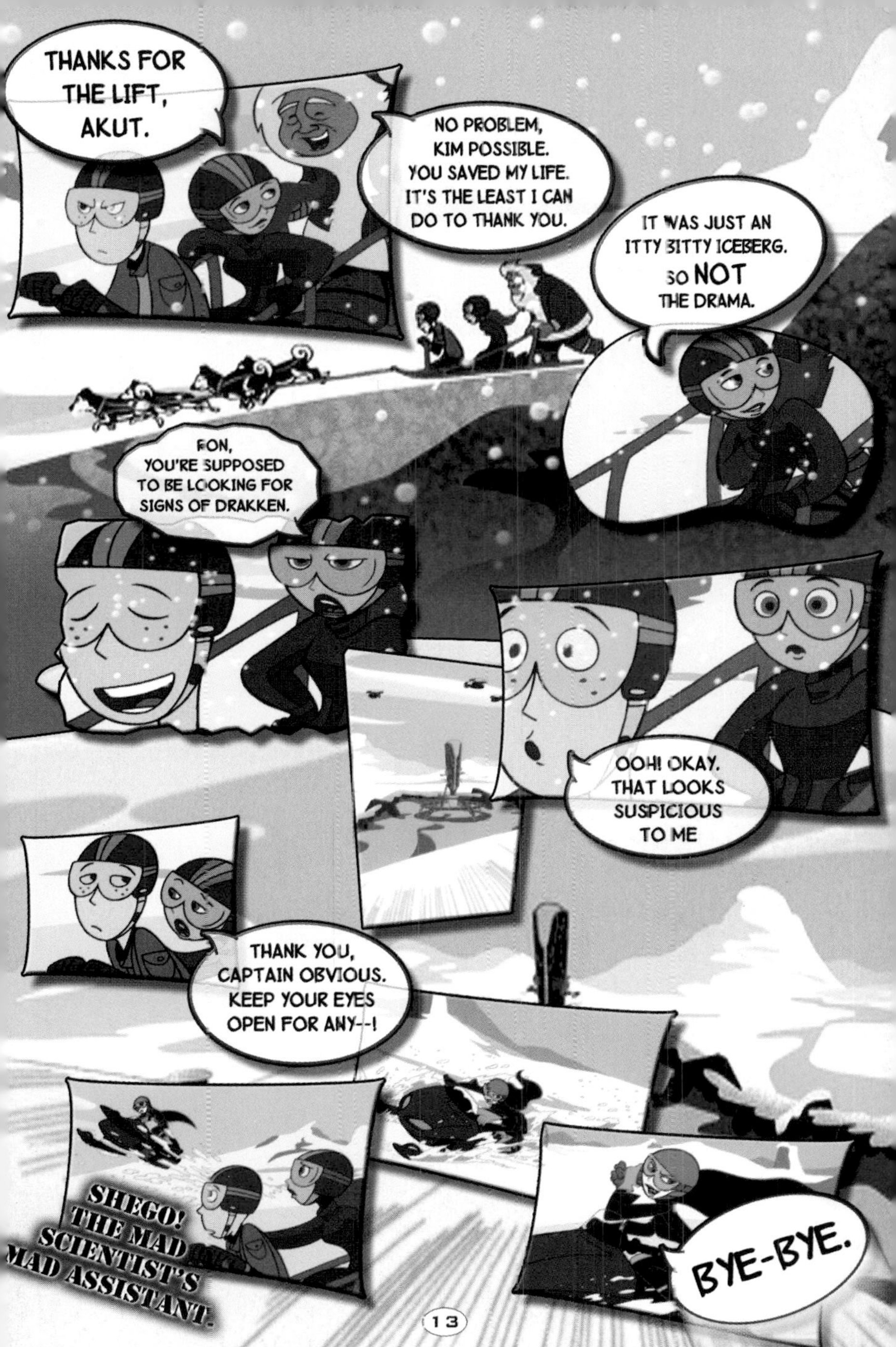
THANKS FOR THE LIFT, AKUT.
NO PROBLEM, KIM POSSIBLE. YOU SAVED MY LIFE. IT'S THE LEAST I CAN DO TO THANK YOU.
IT WAS JUST AN ITTY BITTY ICEBERG. SO NOT THE DRAMA.
RON, YOU'RE SUPPOSED TO BE LOOKING FOR SIGNS OF DRAKKEN.
OOH! OKAY. THAT LOOKS SUSPICIOUS TO ME
THANK YOU, CAPTAIN OBVIOUS. KEEP YOUR EYES OPEN FOR ANY--!
SHEGO! THE MAD SCIENTIST'S MAD ASSISTANT.
BYE-BYE.

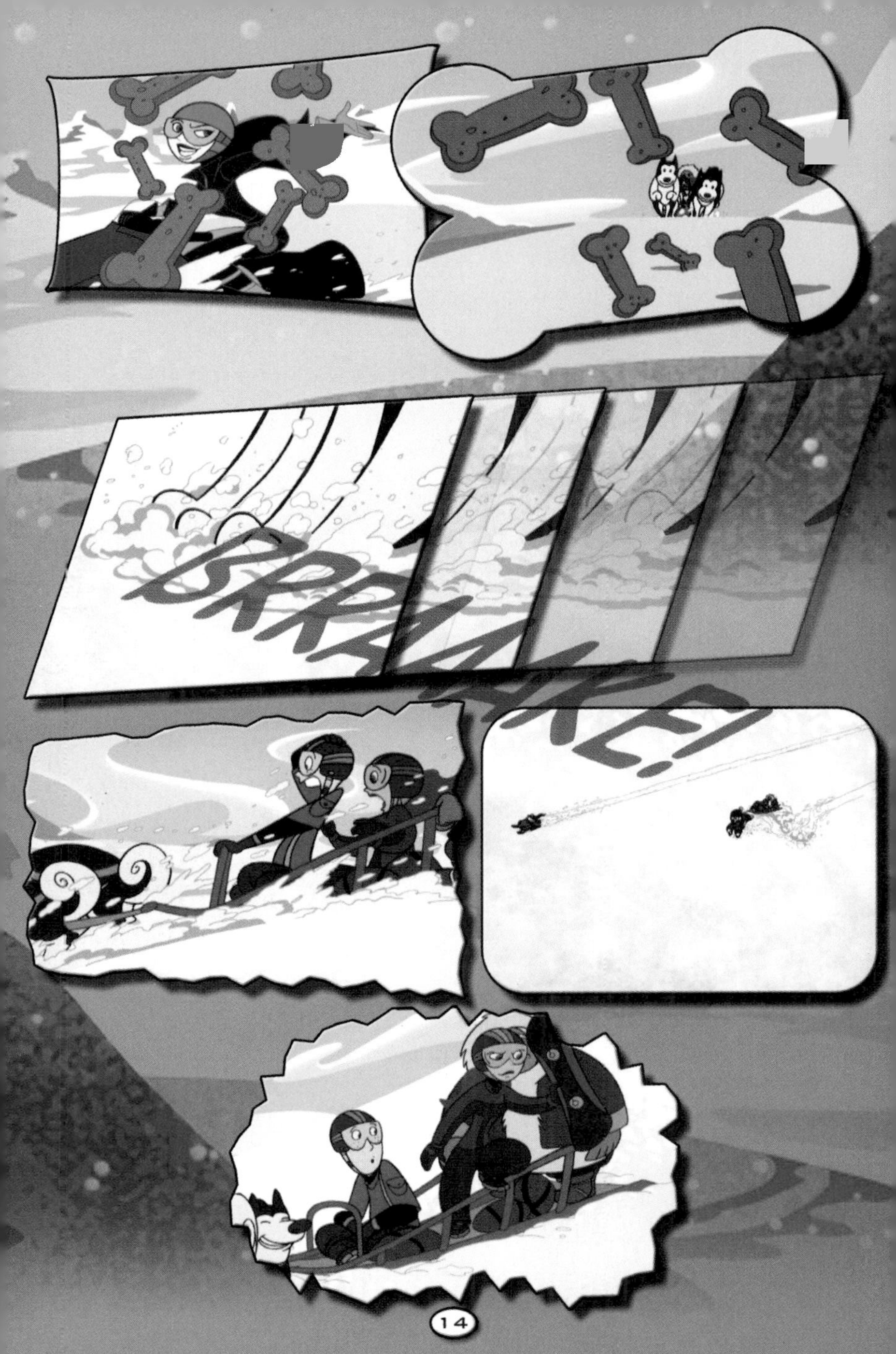
BRRAAKE!

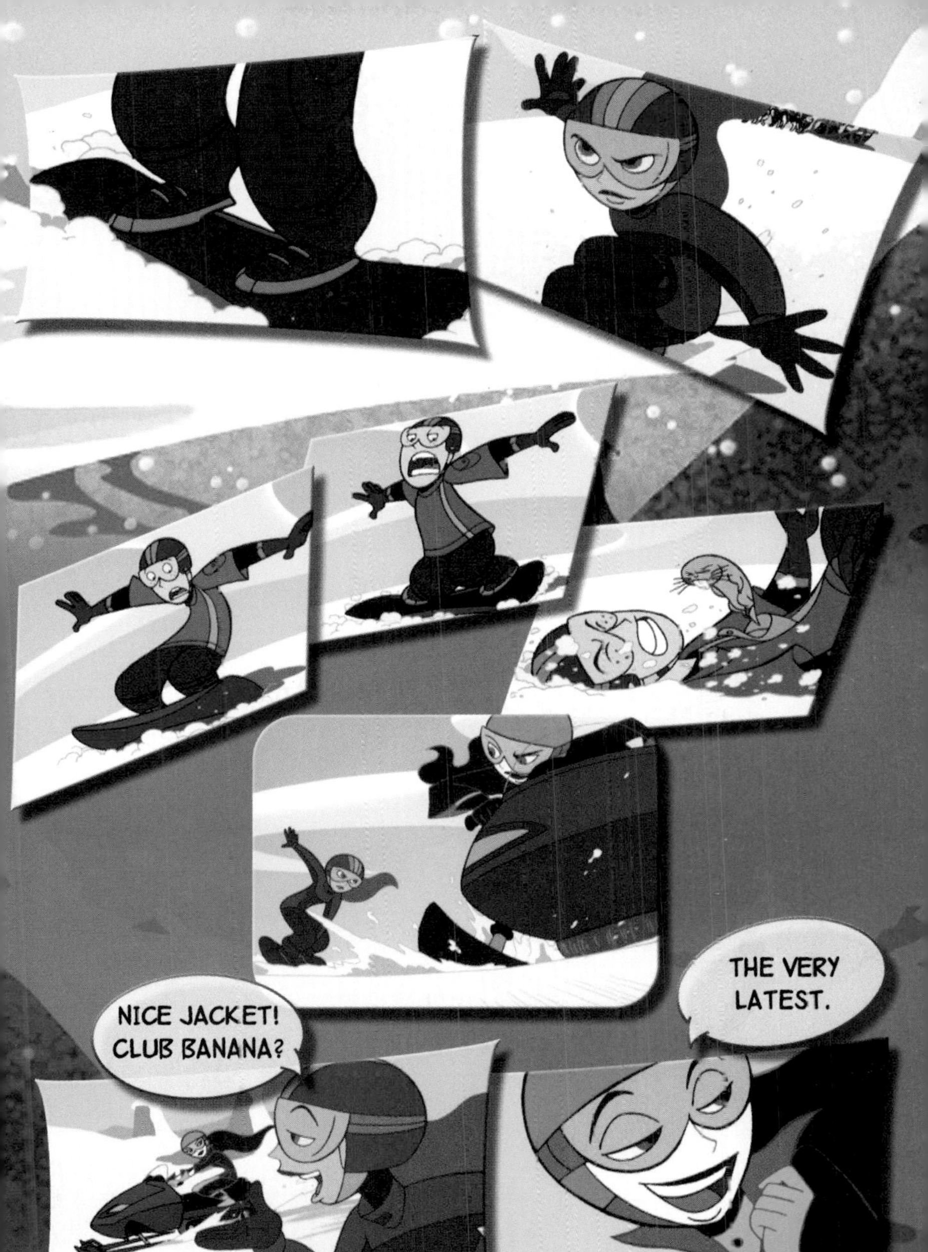
NICE JACKET! CLUB BANANA?
THE VERY LATEST.

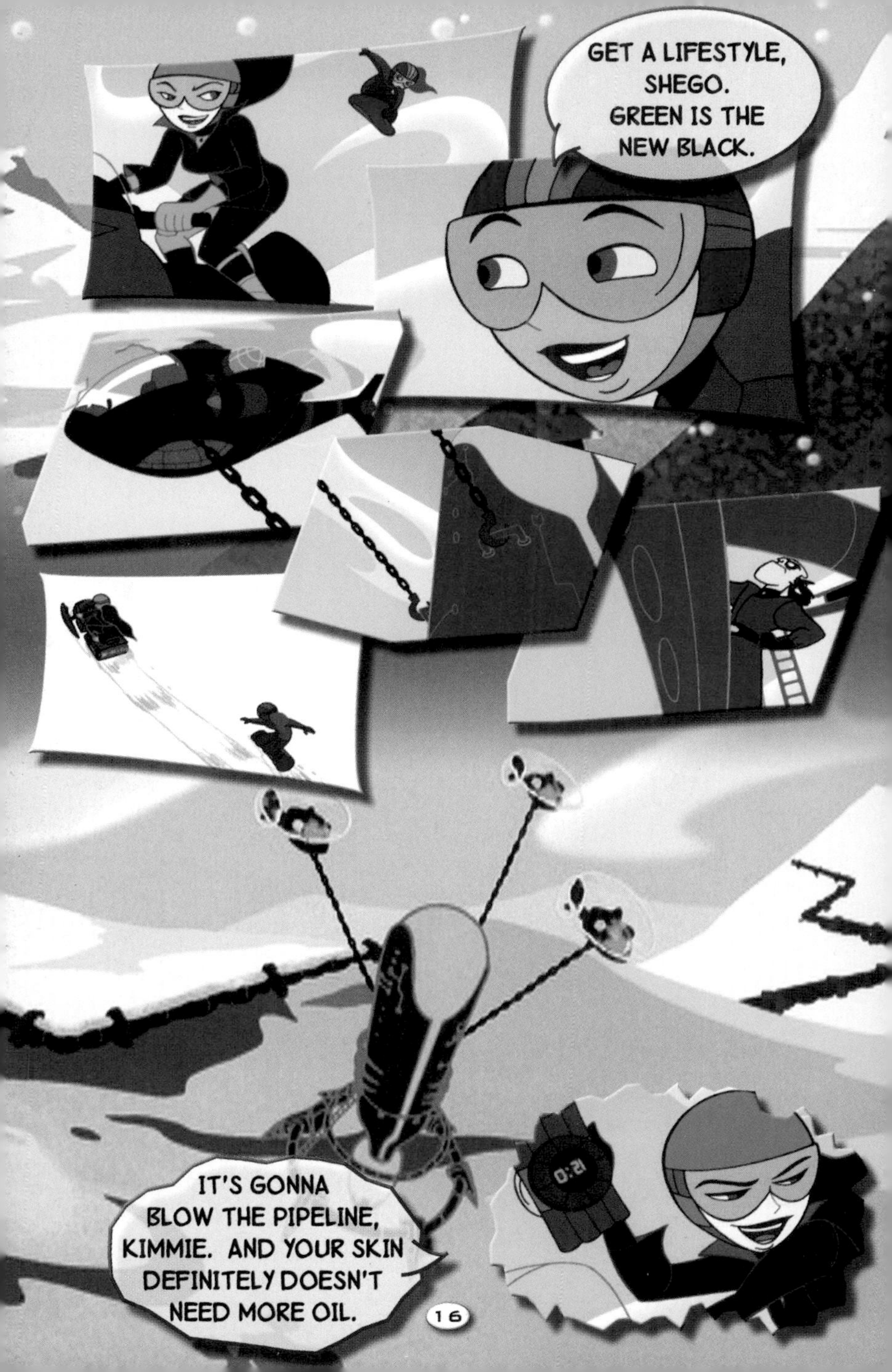
GET A LIFESTYLE, SHEGO. GREEN IS THE NEW BLACK.
IT'S GONNA BLOW THE PIPELINE, KIMMIE. AND YOUR SKIN DEFINITELY DOESN'T NEED MORE OIL.

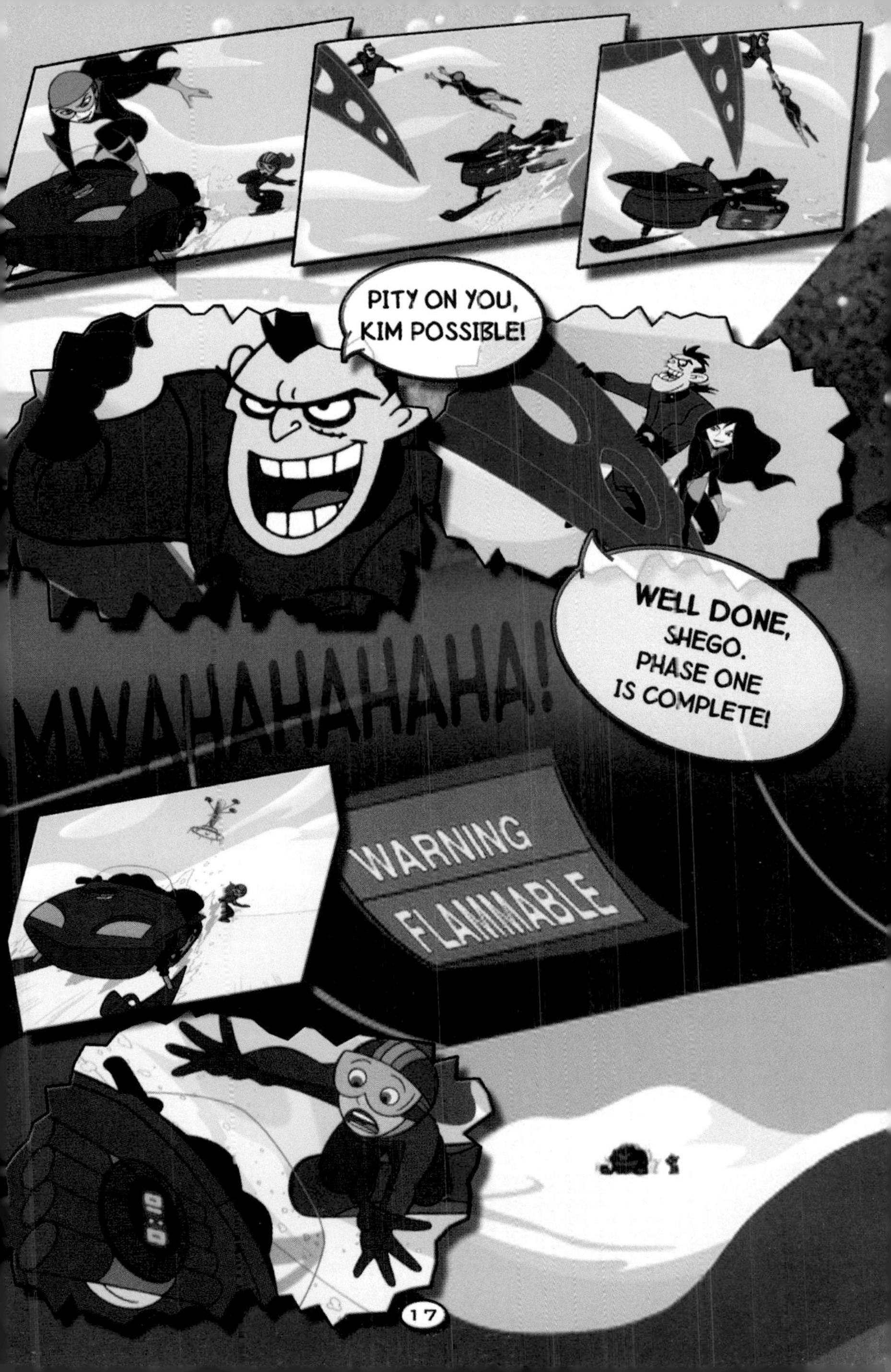

PITY ON YOU, KIM POSSIBLE!
MWAHAHAHAHA!
WELL DONE, SHEGO. PHASE ONE IS COMPLETE!
WARNING
FLAMMABLE

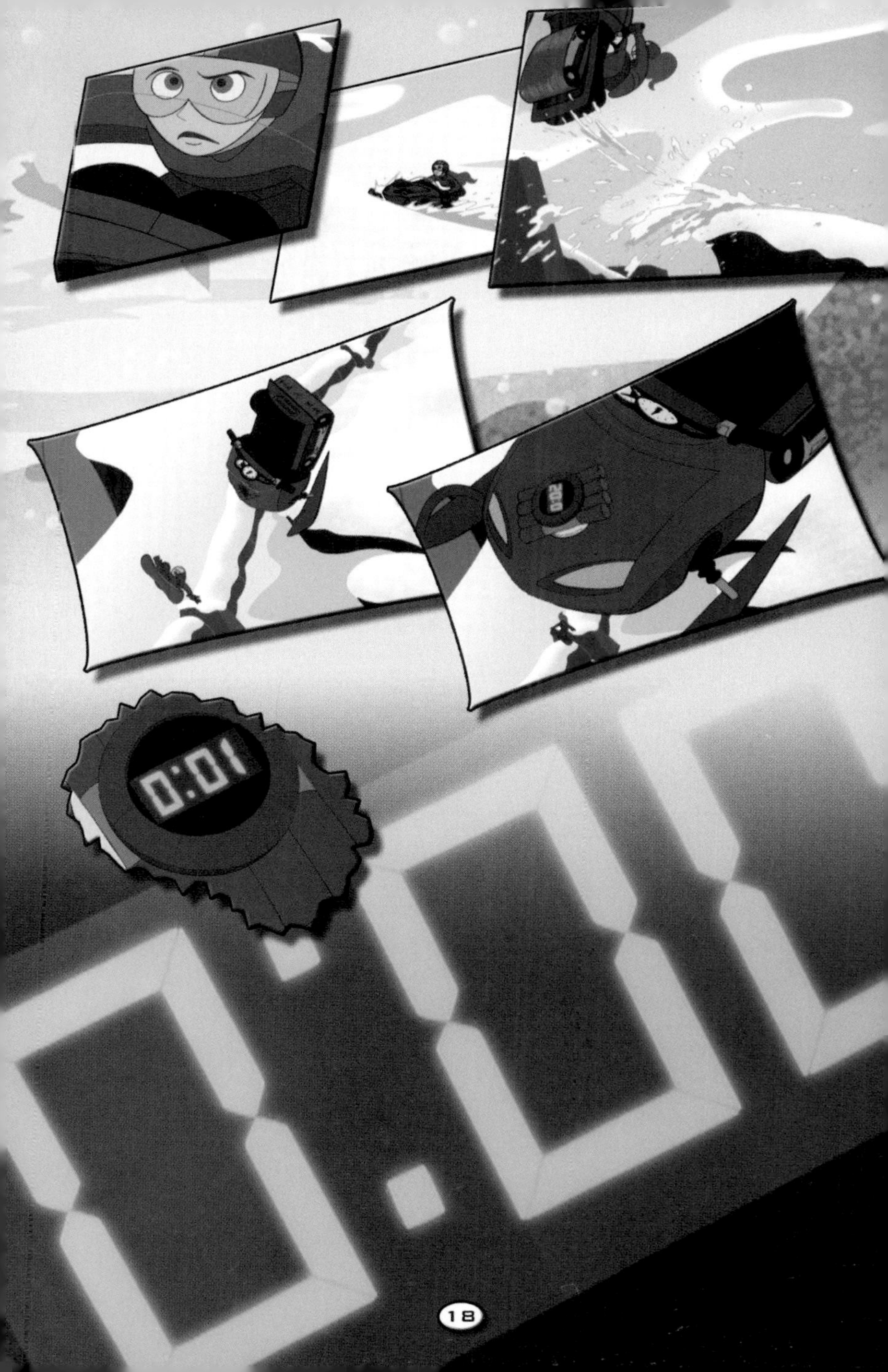
0:01

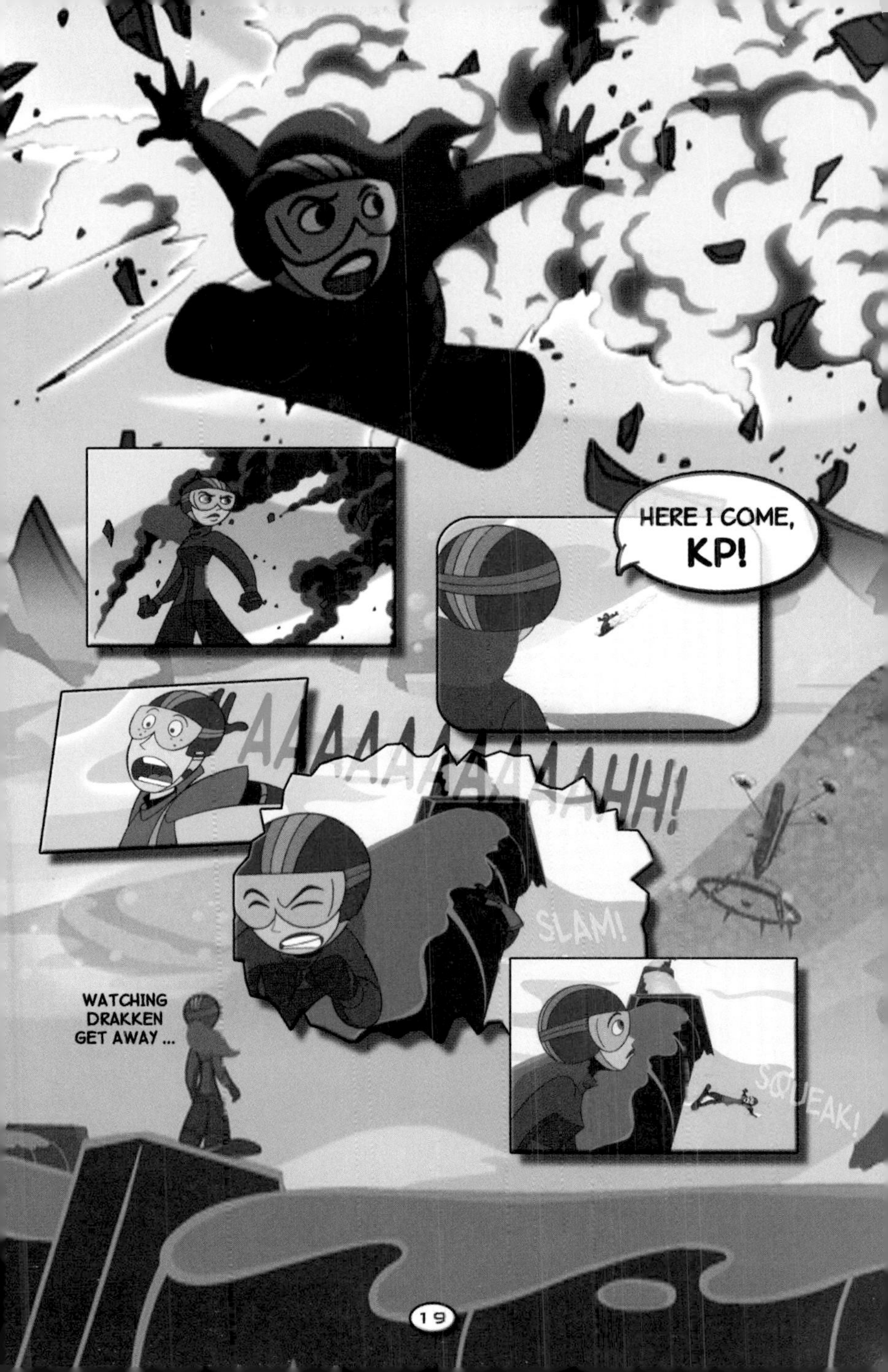
HERE I COME, KP!
AAAAAAAAAAAHH!
SLAM!
WATCHING DRAKKEN GET AWAY ...
SQUEAK!

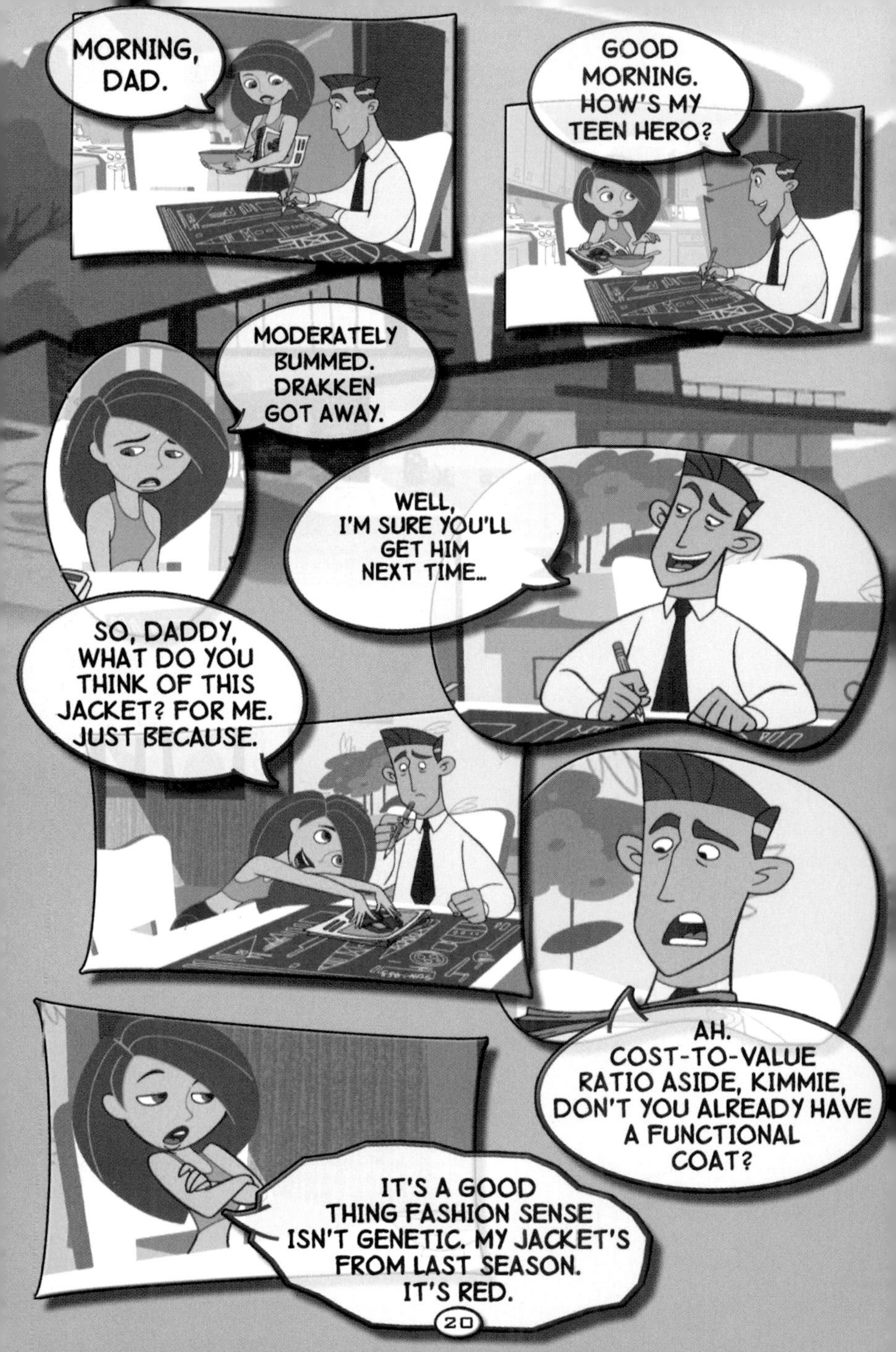
MORNING, DAD.
GOOD MORNING. HOW'S MY TEEN HERO?
MODERATELY BUMMED. DRAKKEN GOT AWAY.
WELL, I'M SURE YOU'LL GET HIM NEXT TIME...
SO, DADDY, WHAT DO YOU THINK OF THIS JACKET? FOR ME. JUST BECAUSE.
AH. COST-TO-VALUE RATIO ASIDE, KIMMIE, DON'T YOU ALREADY HAVE A FUNCTIONAL COAT?
IT'S A GOOD THING FASHION SENSE ISN'T GENETIC. MY JACKET'S FROM LAST SEASON. IT'S RED.

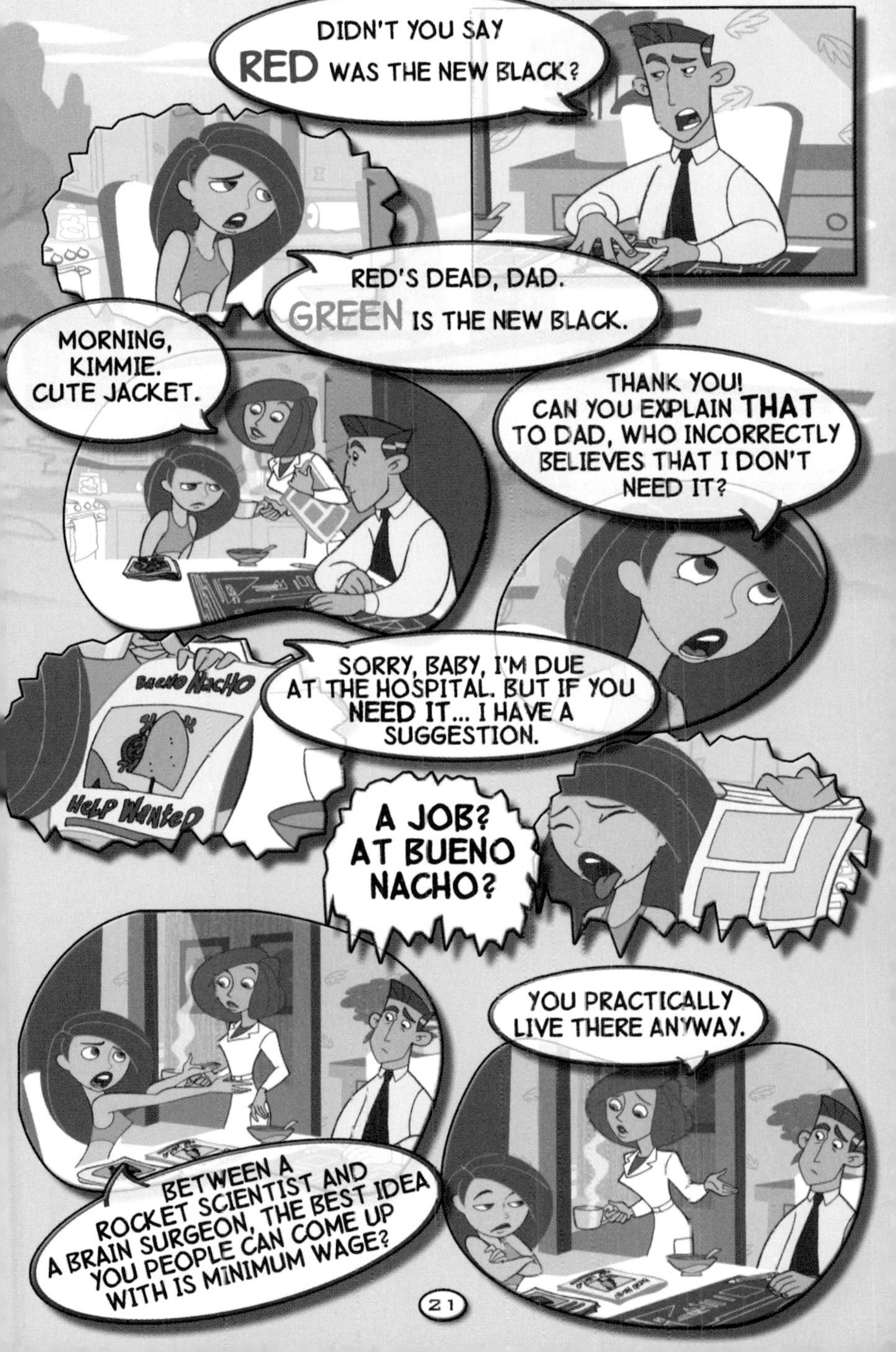
DIDN'T YOU SAY RED WAS THE NEW BLACK?
RED'S DEAD, DAD. GREEN IS THE NEW BLACK.
MORNING, KIMMIE. CUTE JACKET.
THANK YOU! CAN YOU EXPLAIN THAT TO DAD, WHO INCORRECTLY BELIEVES THAT I DON'T NEED IT?
BUENO NACHO
HELP WANTED
SORRY, BABY, I'M DUE AT THE HOSPITAL. BUT IF YOU NEED IT... I HAVE A SUGGESTION.
A JOB? AT BUENO NACHO?
BETWEEN A ROCKET SCIENTIST AND A BRAIN SURGEON, THE BEST IDEA YOU PEOPLE CAN COME UP WITH IS MINIMUM WAGE?
YOU PRACTICALLY LIVE THERE ANYWAY.

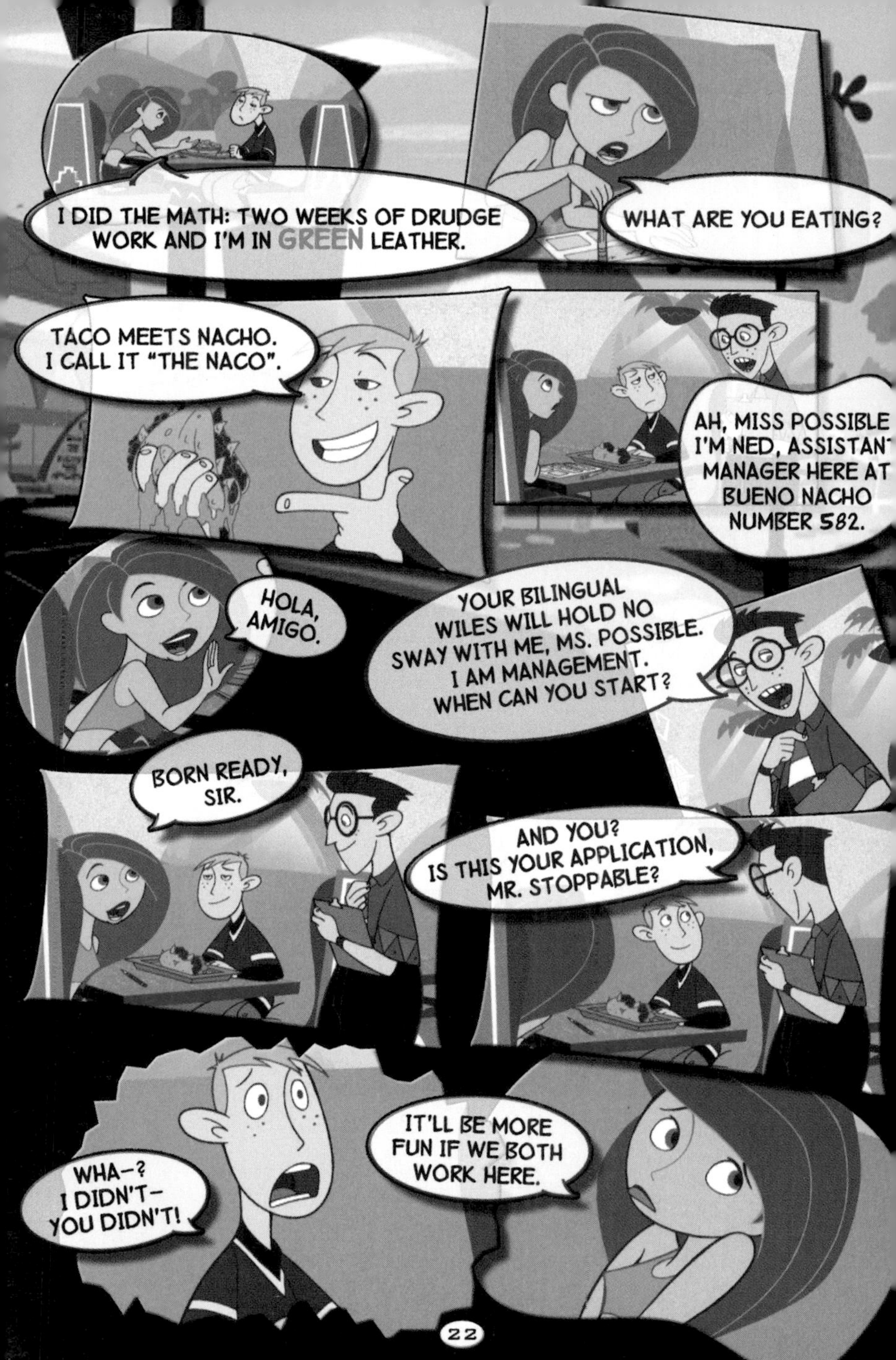
I DID THE MATH: TWO WEEKS OF DRUDGE WORK AND I'M IN GREEN LEATHER.
WHAT ARE YOU EATING?
TACO MEETS NACHO. I CALL IT "THE NACO".
AH, MISS POSSIBLE I'M NED, ASSISTANT MANAGER HERE AT BUENO NACHO NUMBER 582.
HOLA, AMIGO.
YOUR BILINGUAL WILES WILL HOLD NO SWAY WITH ME, MS. POSSIBLE. I AM MANAGEMENT. WHEN CAN YOU START?
BORN READY, SIR.
AND YOU? IS THIS YOUR APPLICATION, MR. STOPPABLE?
WHA-? I DIDN'T- YOU DIDN'T!
IT'LL BE MORE FUN IF WE BOTH WORK HERE.

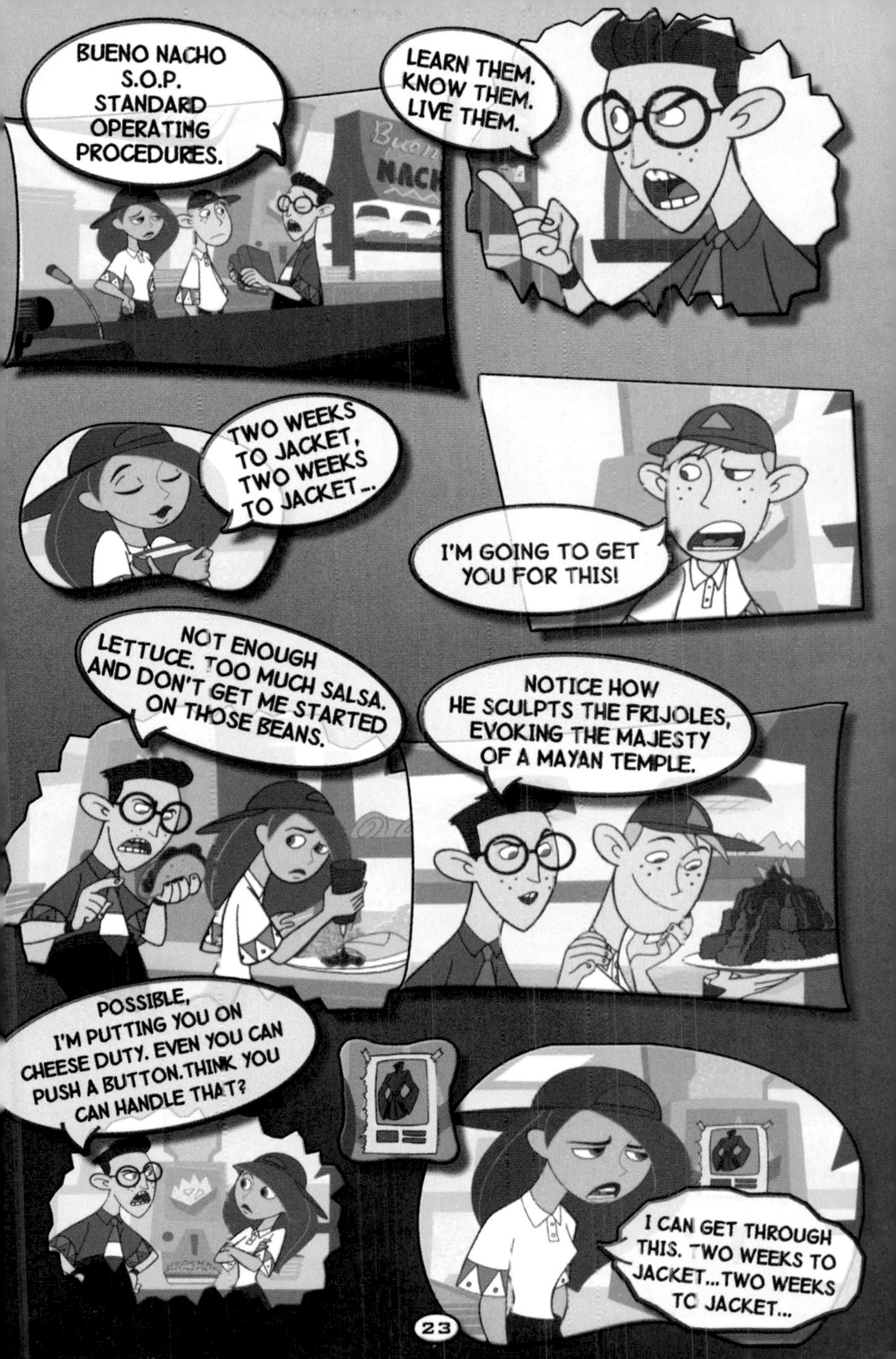
BUENO NACHO S.O.P. STANDARD OPERATING PROCEDURES.
LEARN THEM. KNOW THEM. LIVE THEM.
TWO WEEKS TO JACKET, TWO WEEKS TO JACKET...
I'M GOING TO GET YOU FOR THIS!
NOT ENOUGH LETTUCE. TOO MUCH SALSA. AND DON'T GET ME STARTED ON THOSE BEANS.
NOTICE HOW HE SCULPTS THE FRIJOLES, EVOKING THE MAJESTY OF A MAYAN TEMPLE.
POSSIBLE, I'M PUTTING YOU ON CHEESE DUTY. EVEN YOU CAN PUSH A BUTTON.THINK YOU CAN HANDLE THAT?
I CAN GET THROUGH THIS. TWO WEEKS TO JACKET...TWO WEEKS TO JACKET...

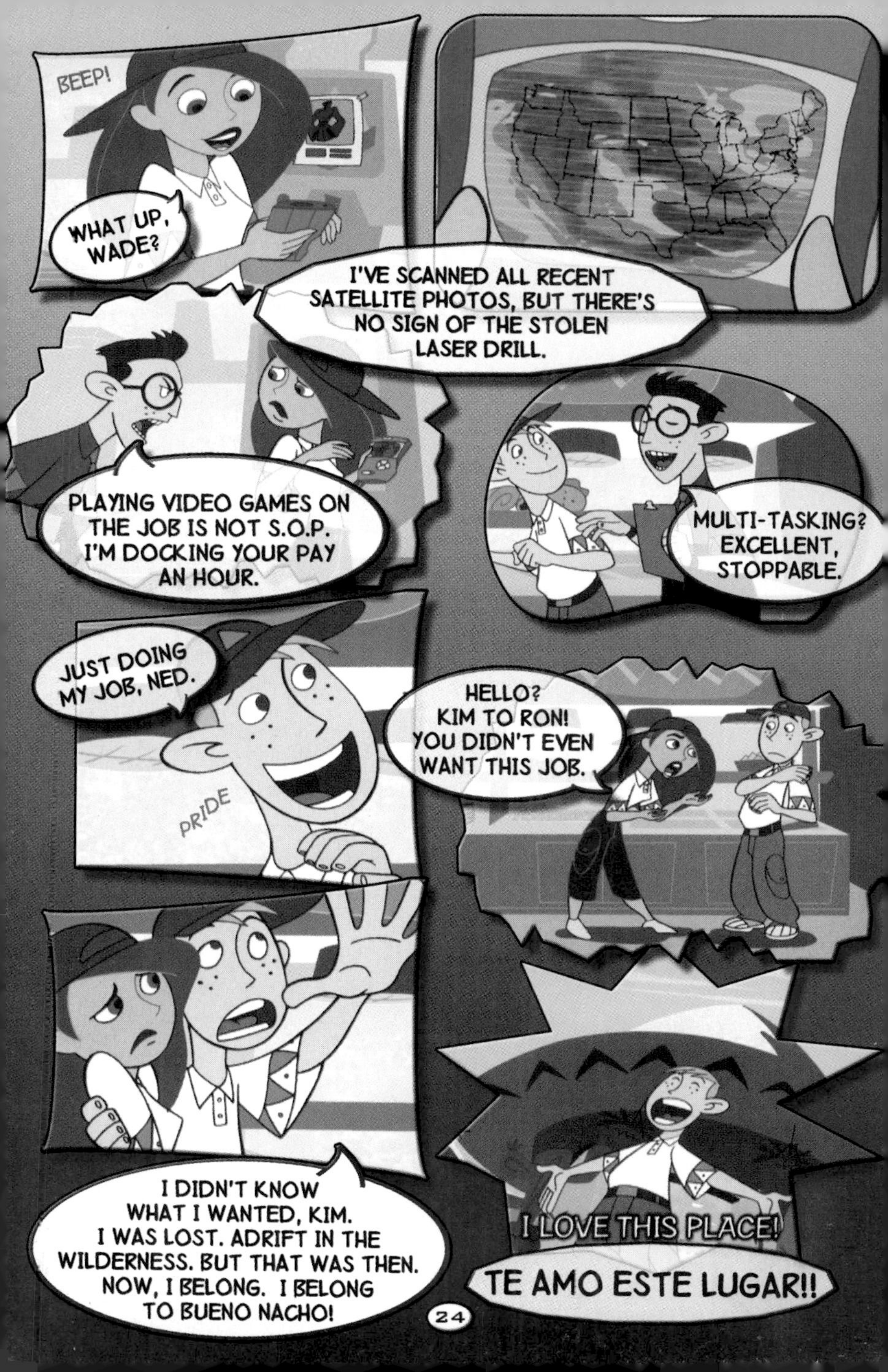
BEEP!
WHAT UP, WADE?
I'VE SCANNED ALL RECENT SATELLITE PHOTOS, BUT THERE'S NO SIGN OF THE STOLEN LASER DRILL.
PLAYING VIDEO GAMES ON THE JOB IS NOT S.O.P. I'M DOCKING YOUR PAY AN HOUR.
MULTI-TASKING? EXCELLENT, STOPPABLE.
JUST DOING MY JOB, NED.
PRIDE
HELLO? KIM TO RON! YOU DIDN'T EVEN WANT THIS JOB.
I DIDN'T KNOW WHAT I WANTED, KIM. I WAS LOST. ADRIFT IN THE WILDERNESS. BUT THAT WAS THEN. NOW, I BELONG. I BELONG TO BUENO NACHO!
I LOVE THIS PLACE!
TE AMO ESTE LUGAR!!

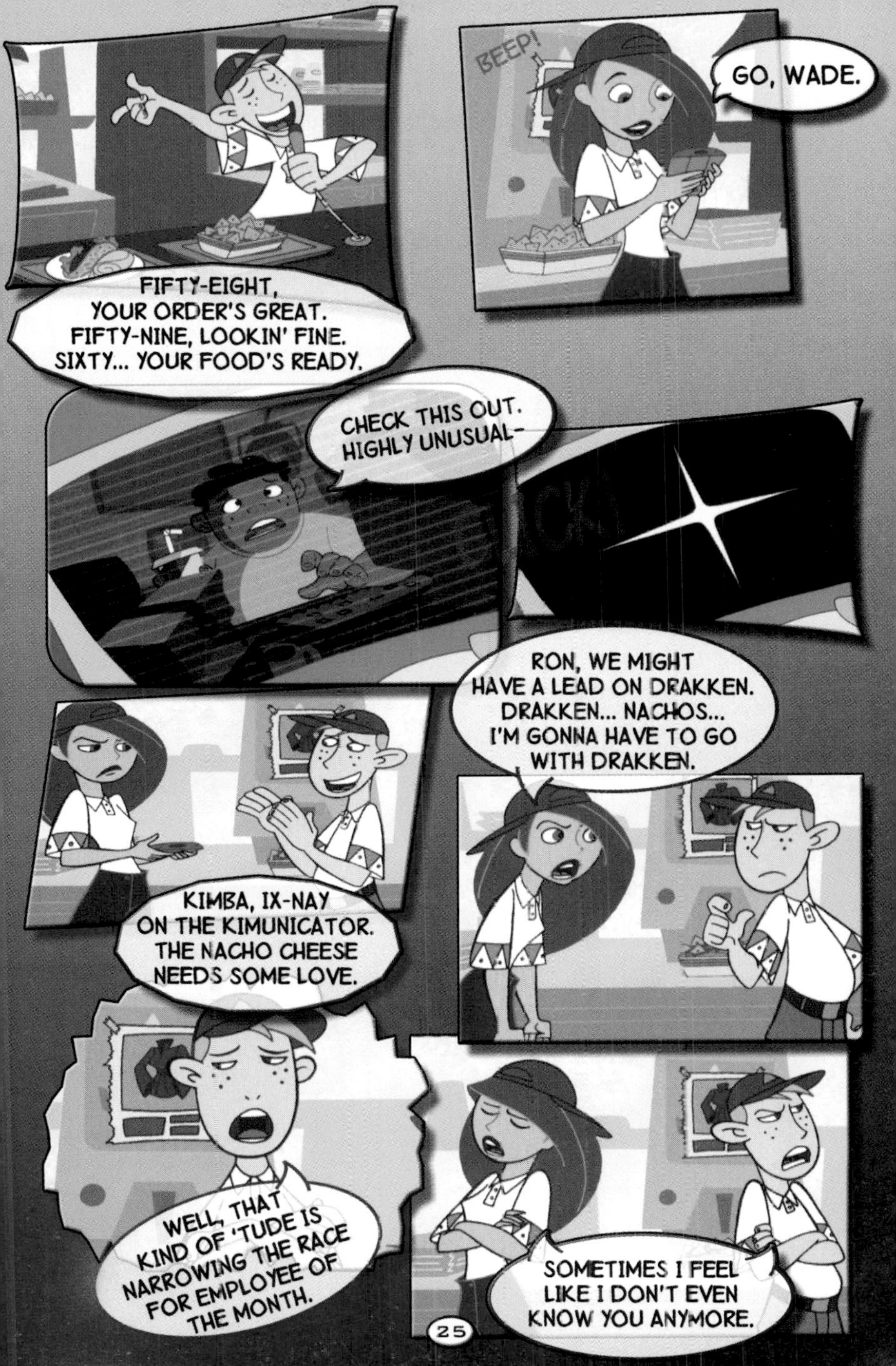
FIFTY-EIGHT, YOUR ORDER'S GREAT. FIFTY-NINE, LOOKIN' FINE. SIXTY... YOUR FOOD'S READY.
BEEP!
GO, WADE.
CHECK THIS OUT. HIGHLY UNUSUAL-
KIMBA, IX-NAY ON THE KIMUNICATOR. THE NACHO CHEESE NEEDS SOME LOVE.
RON, WE MIGHT HAVE A LEAD ON DRAKKEN.
DRAKKEN... NACHOS... I'M GONNA HAVE TO GO WITH DRAKKEN.
WELL, THAT KIND OF 'TUDE IS NARROWING THE RACE FOR EMPLOYEE OF THE MONTH.
SOMETIMES I FEEL LIKE I DON'T EVEN KNOW YOU ANYMORE.

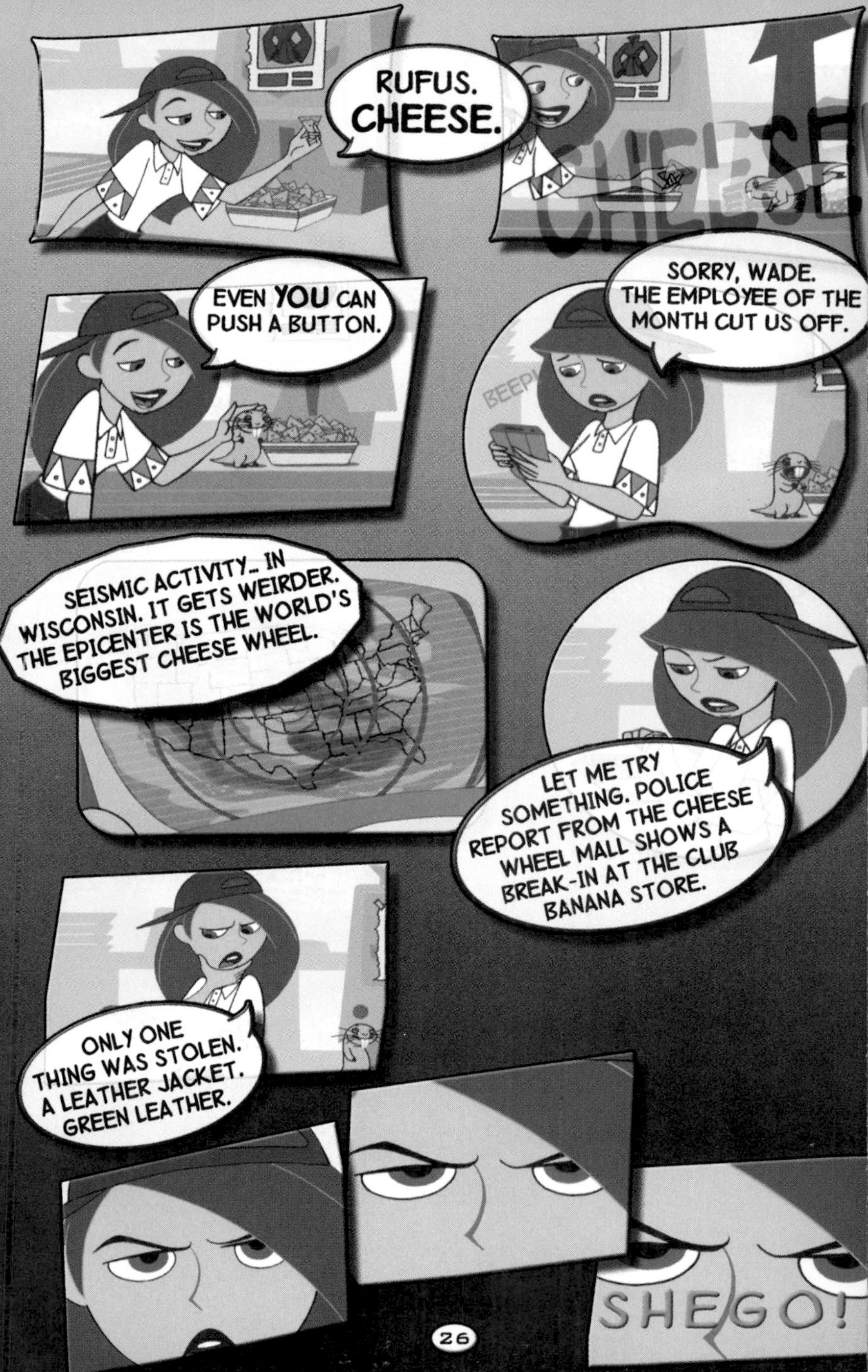

RUFUS. CHEESE.
CHEESE!
EVEN YOU CAN PUSH A BUTTON.
SORRY, WADE. THE EMPLOYEE OF THE MONTH CUT US OFF.
BEEP!
SEISMIC ACTIVITY... IN WISCONSIN. IT GETS WEIRDER. THE EPICENTER IS THE WORLD'S BIGGEST CHEESE WHEEL.
LET ME TRY SOMETHING. POLICE REPORT FROM THE CHEESE WHEEL MALL SHOWS A BREAK-IN AT THE CLUB BANANA STORE.
ONLY ONE THING WAS STOLEN. A LEATHER JACKET. GREEN LEATHER.
SHEGO!

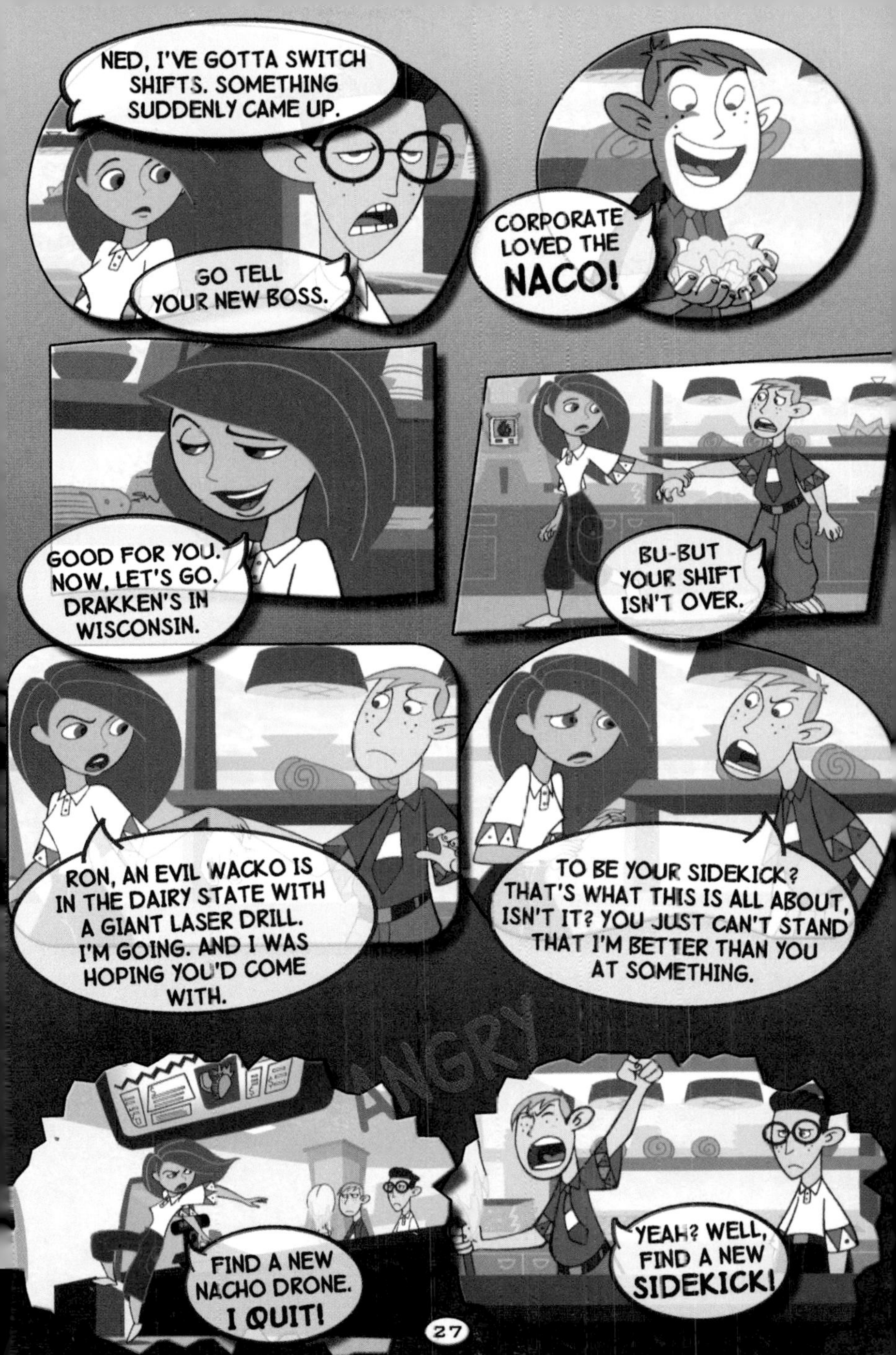
NED, I'VE GOTTA SWITCH SHIFTS. SOMETHING SUDDENLY CAME UP.
GO TELL YOUR NEW BOSS.
CORPORATE LOVED THE NACO!
GOOD FOR YOU. NOW, LET'S GO. DRAKKEN'S IN WISCONSIN.
BU-BUT YOUR SHIFT ISN'T OVER.
RON, AN EVIL WACKO IS IN THE DAIRY STATE WITH A GIANT LASER DRILL. I'M GOING. AND I WAS HOPING YOU'D COME WITH.
TO BE YOUR SIDEKICK? THAT'S WHAT THIS IS ALL ABOUT, ISN'T IT? YOU JUST CAN'T STAND THAT I'M BETTER THAN YOU AT SOMETHING.
ANGRY
FIND A NEW NACHO DRONE. I QUIT!
YEAH? WELL, FIND A NEW SIDEKICK!

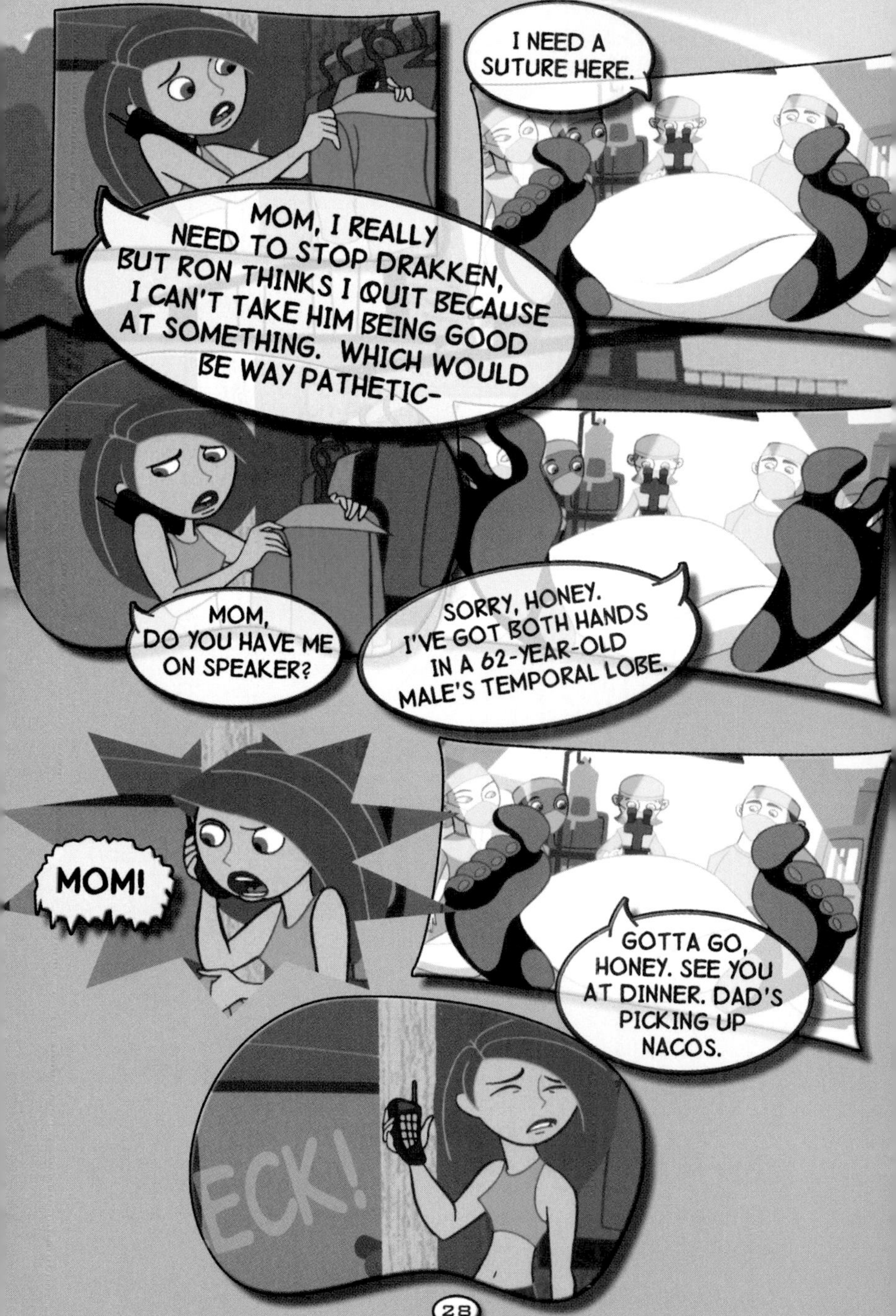
I NEED A SUTURE HERE.
MOM, I REALLY NEED TO STOP DRAKKEN, BUT RON THINKS I QUIT BECAUSE I CAN'T TAKE HIM BEING GOOD AT SOMETHING. WHICH WOULD BE WAY PATHETIC-
MOM, DO YOU HAVE ME ON SPEAKER?
SORRY, HONEY. I'VE GOT BOTH HANDS IN A 62-YEAR-OLD MALE'S TEMPORAL LOBE.
MOM!
GOTTA GO, HONEY. SEE YOU AT DINNER. DAD'S PICKING UP NACOS.
ECK!

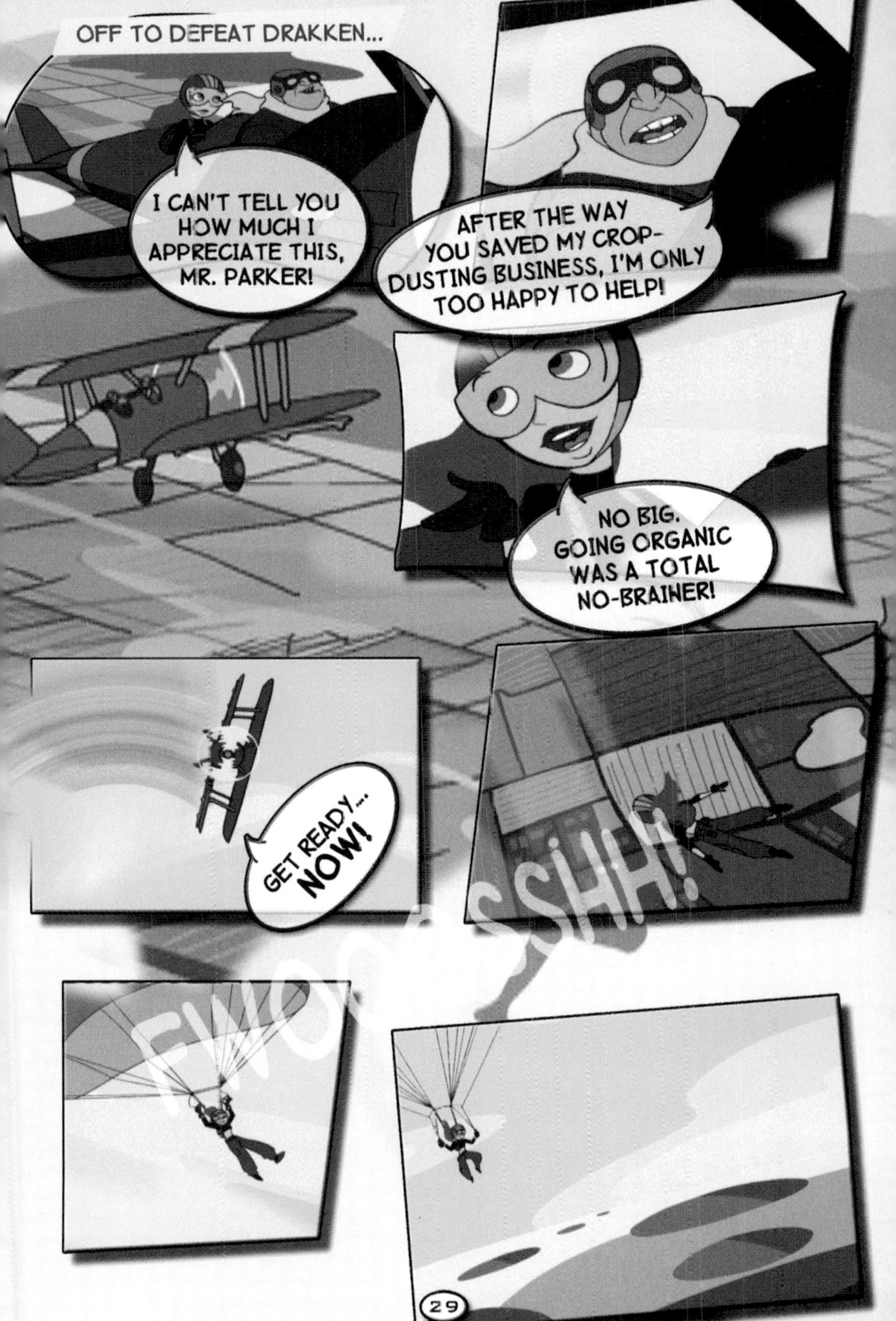
OFF TO DEFEAT DRAKKEN...
I CAN'T TELL YOU HOW MUCH I APPRECIATE THIS, MR. PARKER!
AFTER THE WAY YOU SAVED MY CROP-DUSTING BUSINESS, I'M ONLY TOO HAPPY TO HELP!
NO BIG. GOING ORGANIC WAS A TOTAL NO-BRAINER!
GET READY... NOW!
FWOOSSHH!

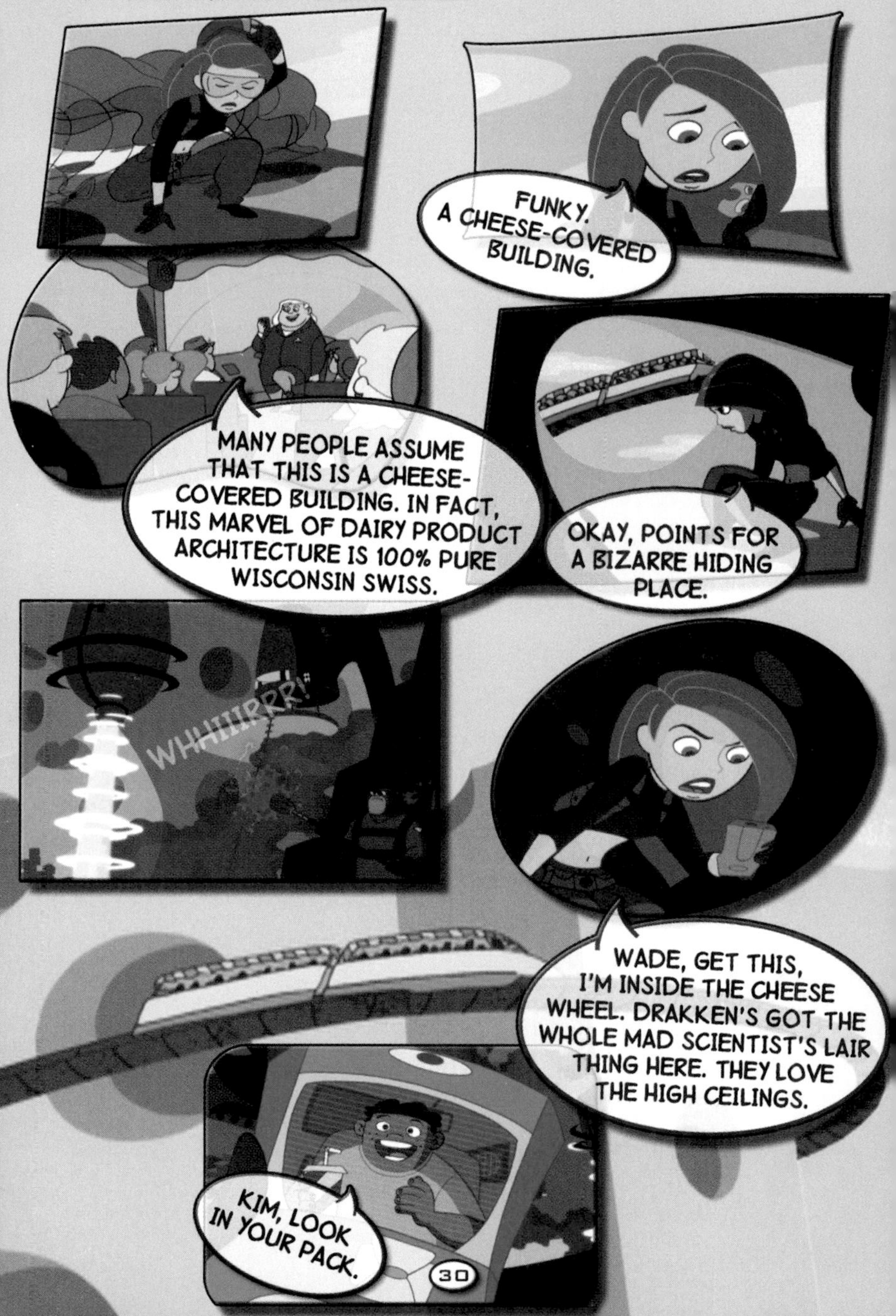
FUNKY. A CHEESE-COVERED BUILDING.
MANY PEOPLE ASSUME THAT THIS IS A CHEESE-COVERED BUILDING. IN FACT, THIS MARVEL OF DAIRY PRODUCT ARCHITECTURE IS 100% PURE WISCONSIN SWISS.
OKAY, POINTS FOR A BIZARRE HIDING PLACE.
WHHIIIRRR!
WADE, GET THIS, I'M INSIDE THE CHEESE WHEEL. DRAKKEN'S GOT THE WHOLE MAD SCIENTIST'S LAIR THING HERE. THEY LOVE THE HIGH CEILINGS.
KIM, LOOK IN YOUR PACK.

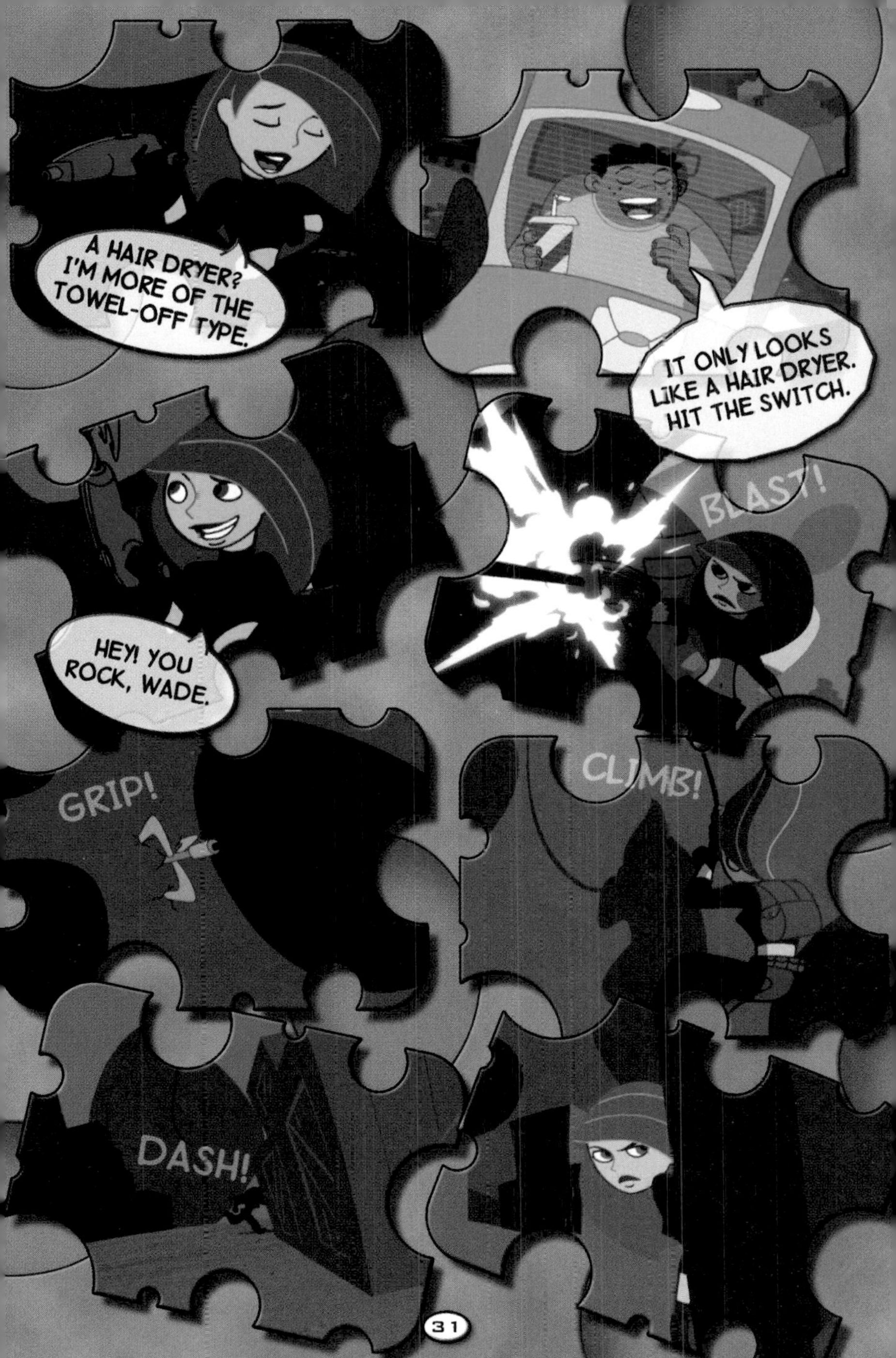
A HAIR DRYER? I'M MORE OF THE TOWEL-OFF TYPE.
IT ONLY LOOKS LIKE A HAIR DRYER. HIT THE SWITCH.
HEY! YOU ROCK, WADE.
BLAST!
GRIP!
CLIMB!
DASH!

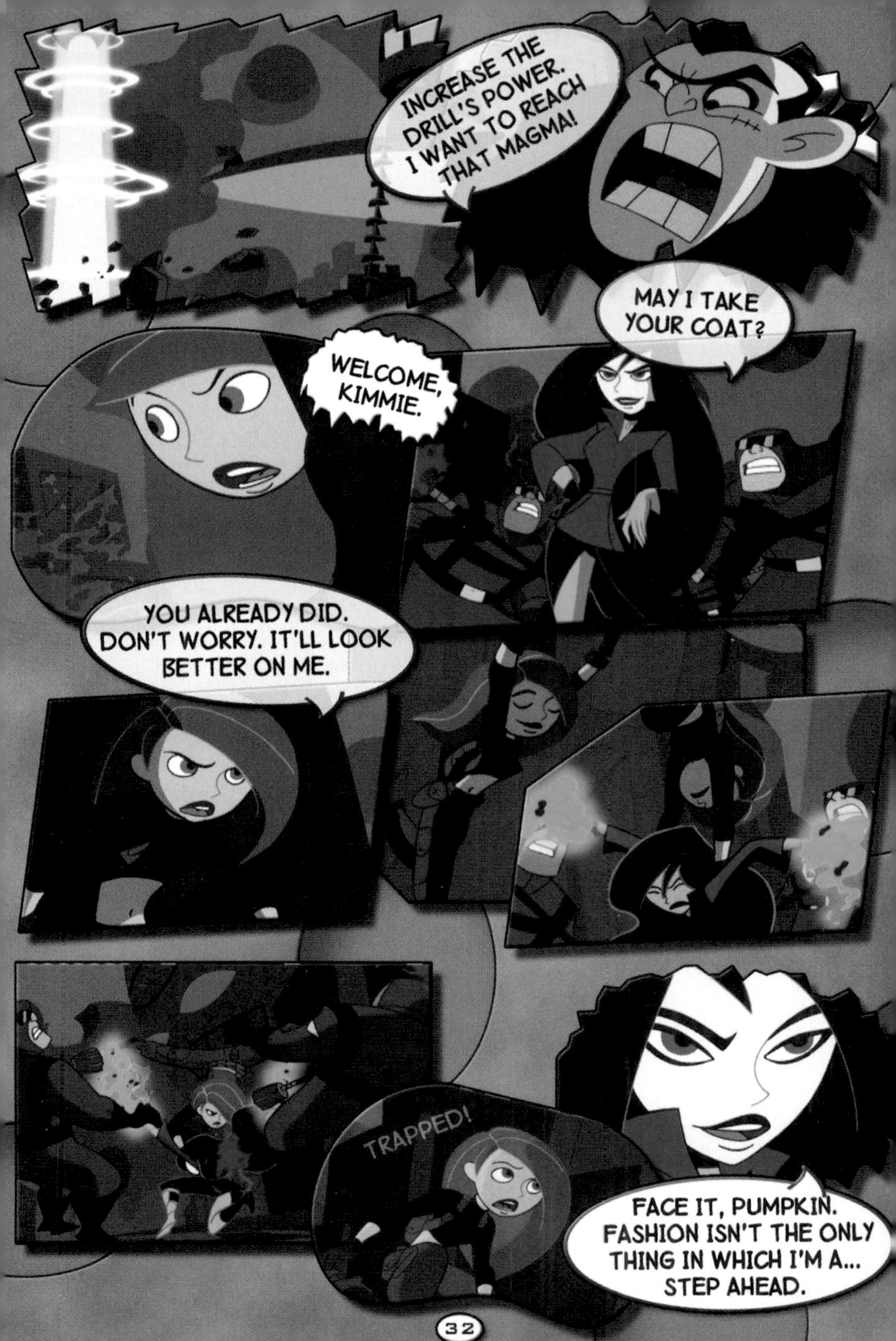
INCREASE THE DRILL'S POWER. I WANT TO REACH THAT MAGMA!
WELCOME, KIMMIE.
MAY I TAKE YOUR COAT?
YOU ALREADY DID. DON'T WORRY. IT'LL LOOK BETTER ON ME.
TRAPPED!
FACE IT, PUMPKIN. FASHION ISN'T THE ONLY THING IN WHICH I'M A... STEP AHEAD.

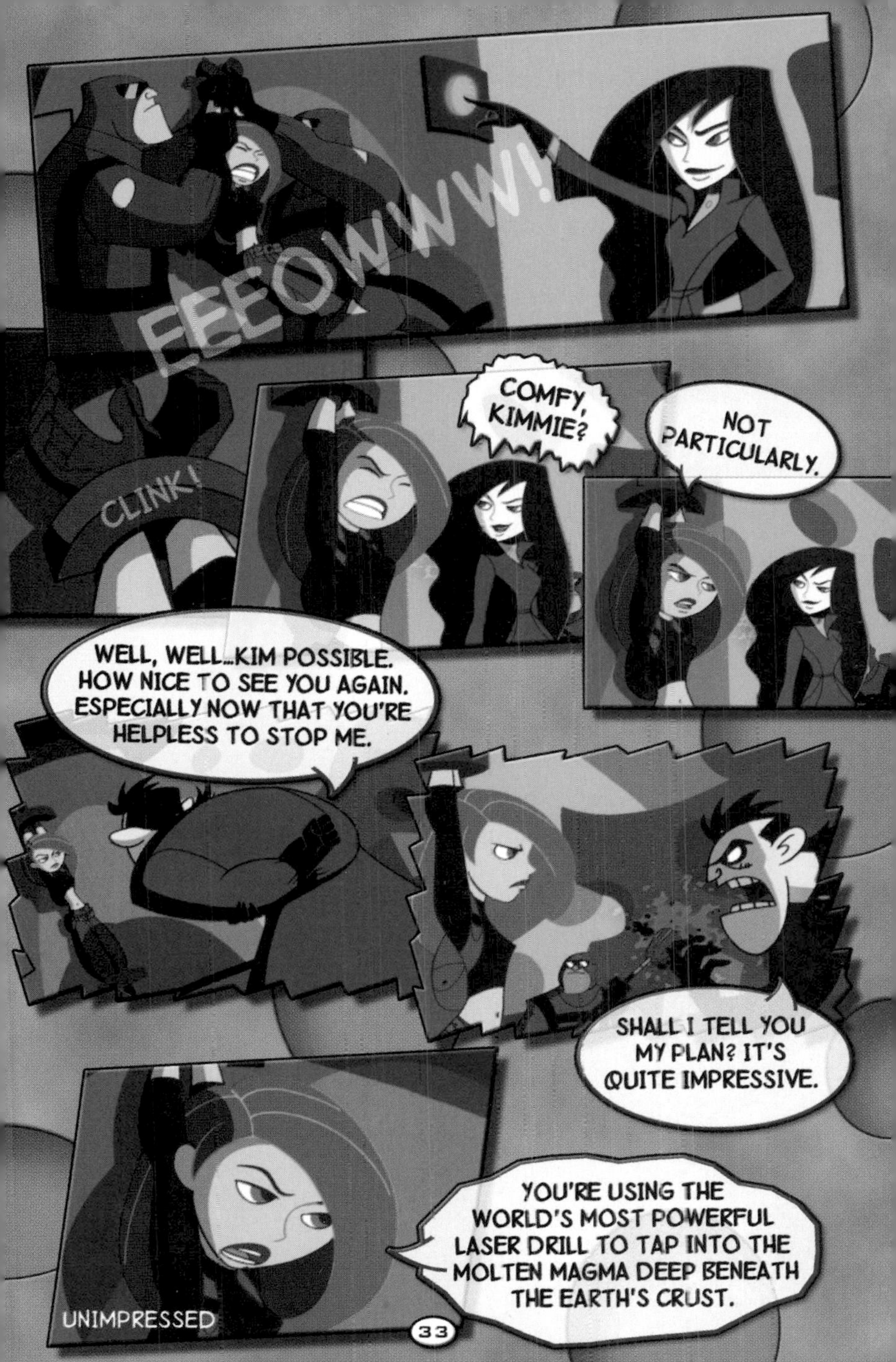
EEEOWWW!
CLINK!
COMFY, KIMMIE?
NOT PARTICULARLY.
WELL, WELL...KIM POSSIBLE. HOW NICE TO SEE YOU AGAIN. ESPECIALLY NOW THAT YOU'RE HELPLESS TO STOP ME.
SHALL I TELL YOU MY PLAN? IT'S QUITE IMPRESSIVE.
YOU'RE USING THE WORLD'S MOST POWERFUL LASER DRILL TO TAP INTO THE MOLTEN MAGMA DEEP BENEATH THE EARTH'S CRUST.
UNIMPRESSED

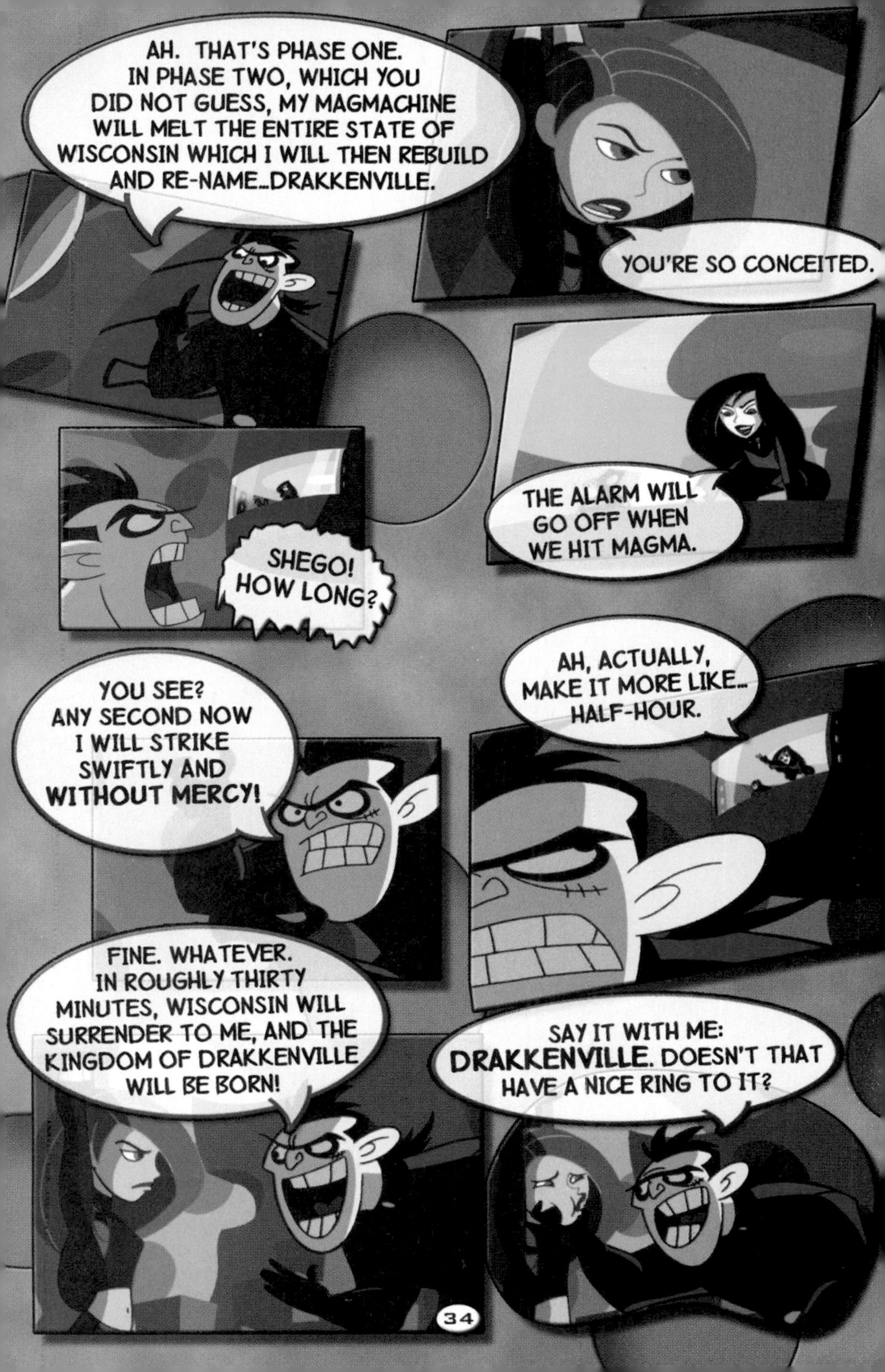
AH. THAT'S PHASE ONE. IN PHASE TWO, WHICH YOU DID NOT GUESS, MY MAGMACHINE WILL MELT THE ENTIRE STATE OF WISCONSIN WHICH I WILL THEN REBUILD AND RE-NAME...DRAKKENVILLE.
YOU'RE SO CONCEITED.
SHEGO! HOW LONG?
THE ALARM WILL GO OFF WHEN WE HIT MAGMA.
YOU SEE? ANY SECOND NOW I WILL STRIKE SWIFTLY AND WITHOUT MERCY!
AH, ACTUALLY, MAKE IT MORE LIKE... HALF-HOUR.
FINE. WHATEVER. IN ROUGHLY THIRTY MINUTES, WISCONSIN WILL SURRENDER TO ME, AND THE KINGDOM OF DRAKKENVILLE WILL BE BORN!
SAY IT WITH ME: DRAKKENVILLE. DOESN'T THAT HAVE A NICE RING TO IT?

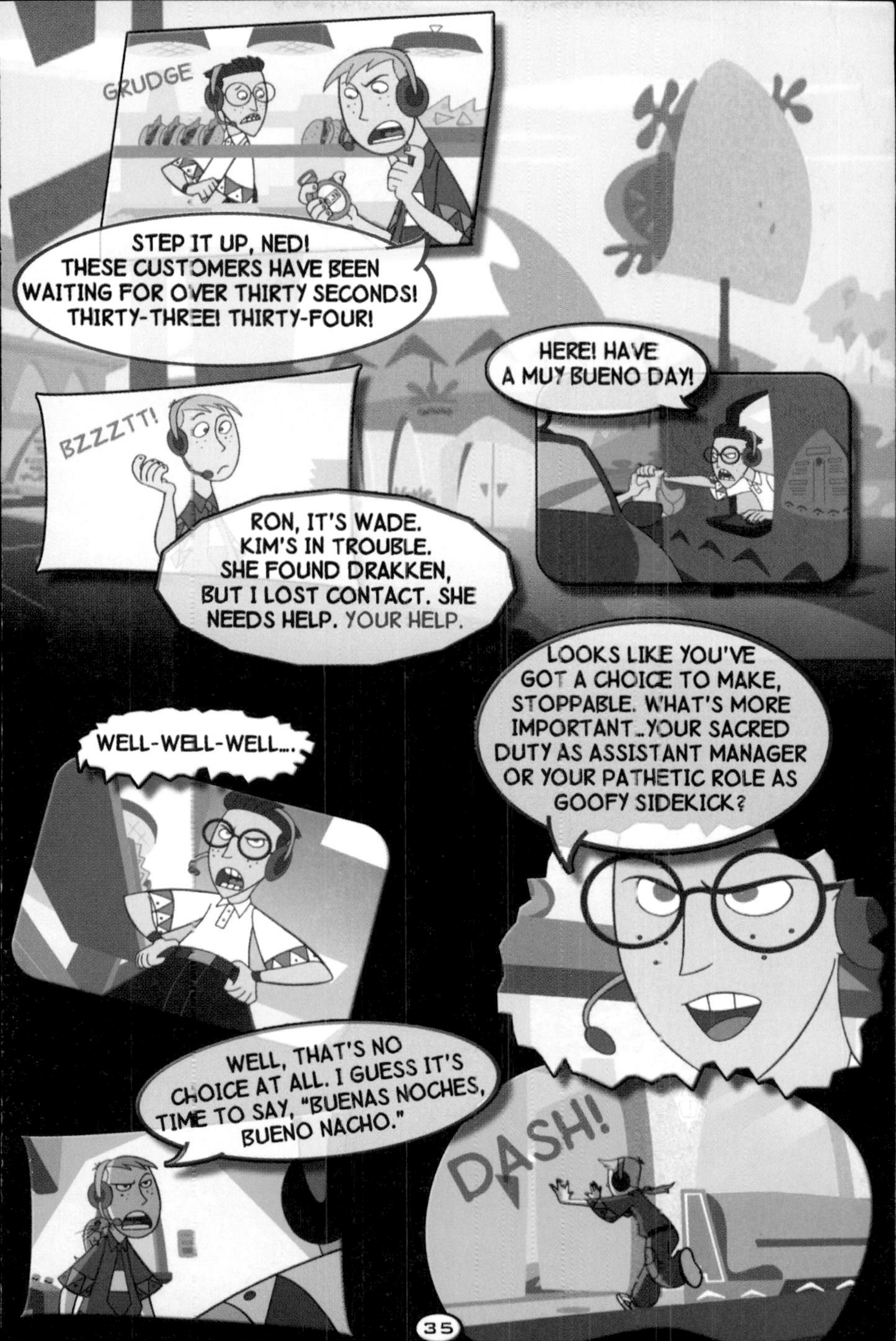
GRUDGE
STEP IT UP, NED! THESE CUSTOMERS HAVE BEEN WAITING FOR OVER THIRTY SECONDS! THIRTY-THREE! THIRTY-FOUR!
BZZZTT!
RON, IT'S WADE. KIM'S IN TROUBLE. SHE FOUND DRAKKEN, BUT I LOST CONTACT. SHE NEEDS HELP. YOUR HELP.
HERE! HAVE A MUY BUENO DAY!
WELL-WELL-WELL....
LOOKS LIKE YOU'VE GOT A CHOICE TO MAKE, STOPPABLE. WHAT'S MORE IMPORTANT...YOUR SACRED DUTY AS ASSISTANT MANAGER OR YOUR PATHETIC ROLE AS GOOFY SIDEKICK?
WELL, THAT'S NO CHOICE AT ALL. I GUESS IT'S TIME TO SAY, "BUENAS NOCHES, BUENO NACHO."
DASH!

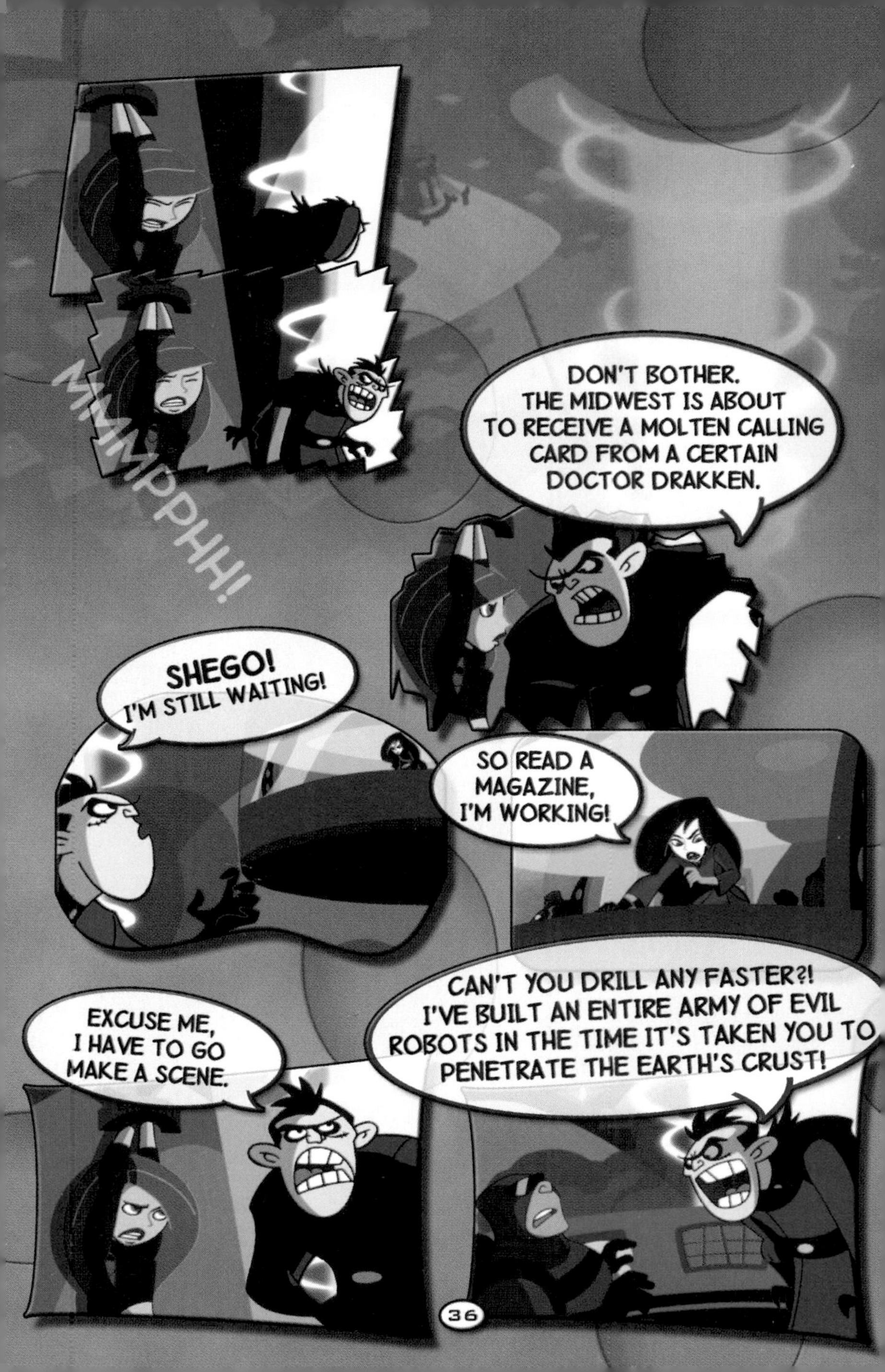
MMMMPPHH!
DON'T BOTHER. THE MIDWEST IS ABOUT TO RECEIVE A MOLTEN CALLING CARD FROM A CERTAIN DOCTOR DRAKKEN.
SHEGO! I'M STILL WAITING!
SO READ A MAGAZINE, I'M WORKING!
EXCUSE ME, I HAVE TO GO MAKE A SCENE.
CAN'T YOU DRILL ANY FASTER?! I'VE BUILT AN ENTIRE ARMY OF EVIL ROBOTS IN THE TIME IT'S TAKEN YOU TO PENETRATE THE EARTH'S CRUST!

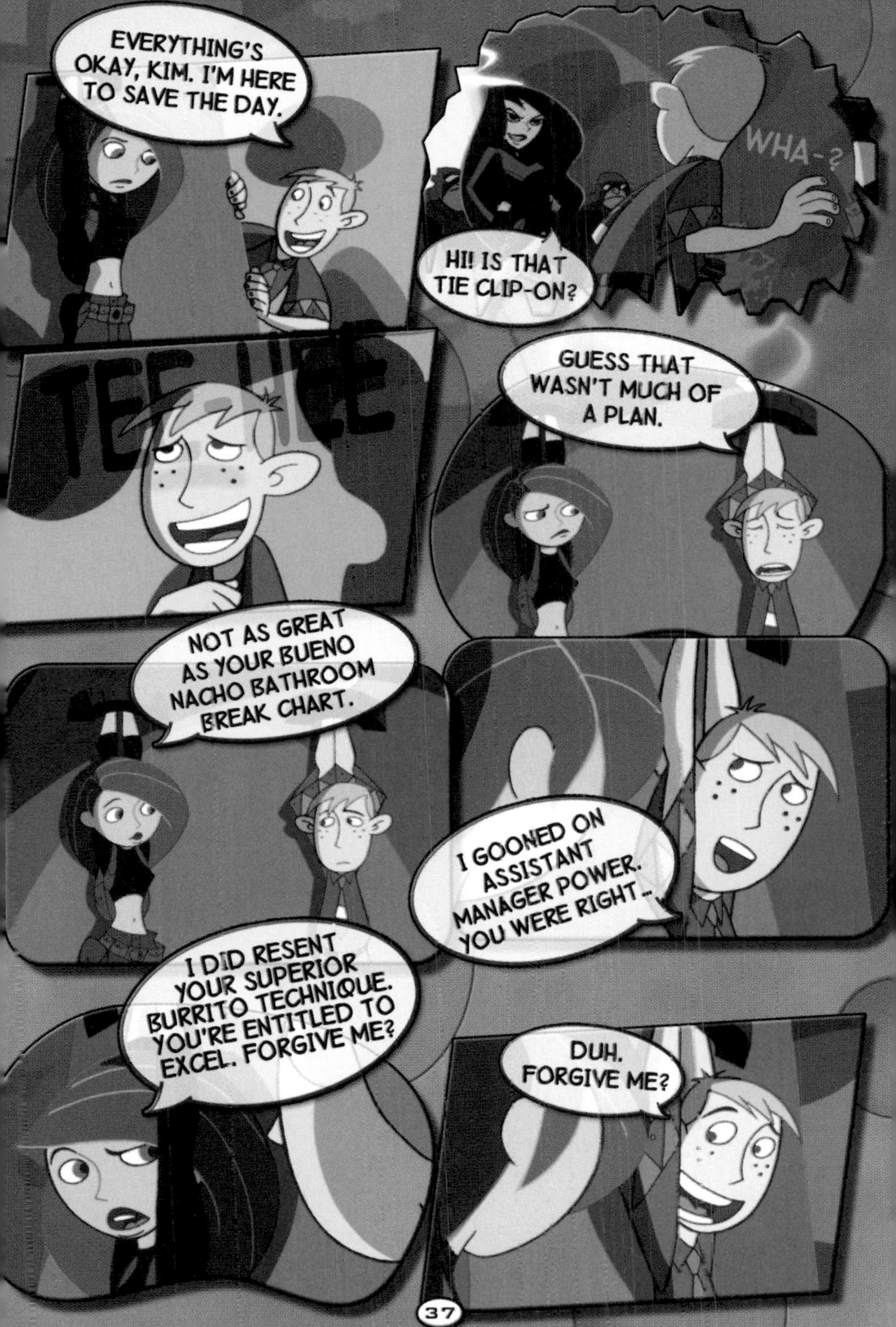
EVERYTHING'S OKAY, KIM. I'M HERE TO SAVE THE DAY.
WHA-?
HI! IS THAT TIE CLIP-ON?
TEE HEE
GUESS THAT WASN'T MUCH OF A PLAN.
NOT AS GREAT AS YOUR BUENO NACHO BATHROOM BREAK CHART.
I GOONED ON ASSISTANT MANAGER POWER. YOU WERE RIGHT...
I DID RESENT YOUR SUPERIOR BURRITO TECHNIQUE. YOU'RE ENTITLED TO EXCEL. FORGIVE ME?
DUH. FORGIVE ME?

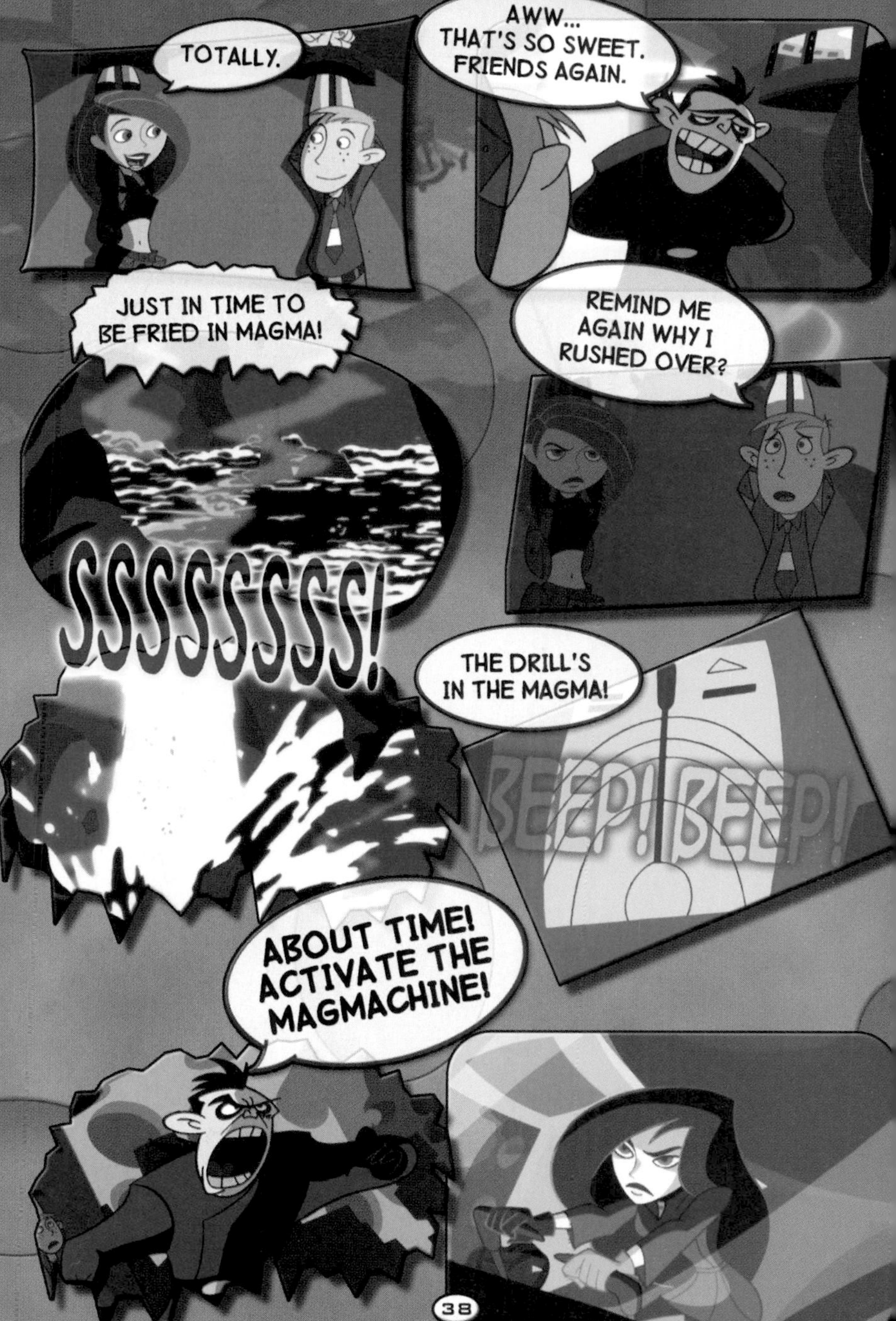
TOTALLY.
AWW... THAT'S SO SWEET. FRIENDS AGAIN.
JUST IN TIME TO BE FRIED IN MAGMA!
SSSSSSSS!
REMIND ME AGAIN WHY I RUSHED OVER?
THE DRILL'S IN THE MAGMA!
BEEP! BEEP!
ABOUT TIME! ACTIVATE THE MAGMACHINE!

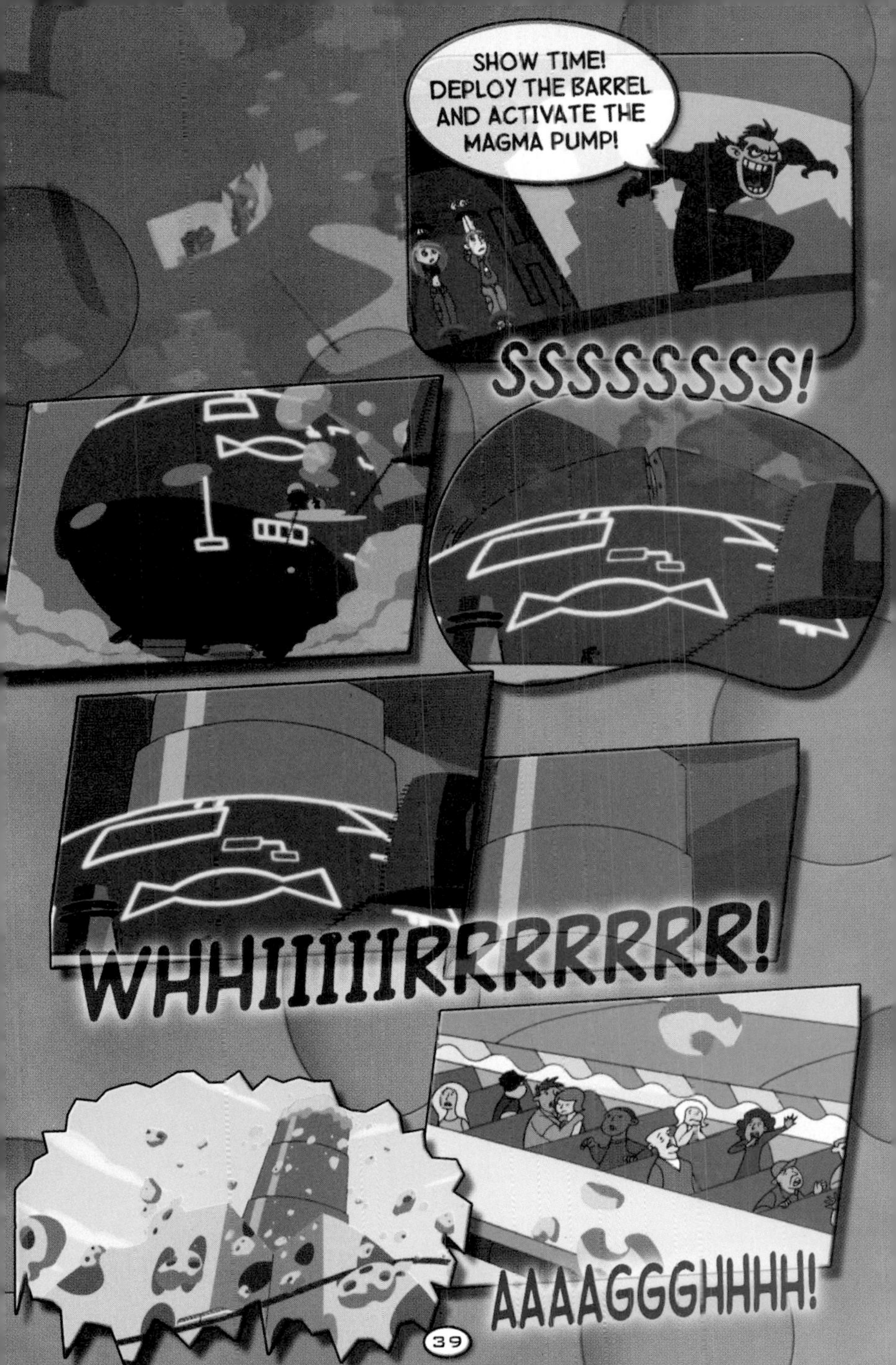
SHOW TIME! DEPLOY THE BARREL AND ACTIVATE THE MAGMA PUMP!
SSSSSSSS!
WHHIIIIIRRRRRRR!
AAAAGGGHHHH!

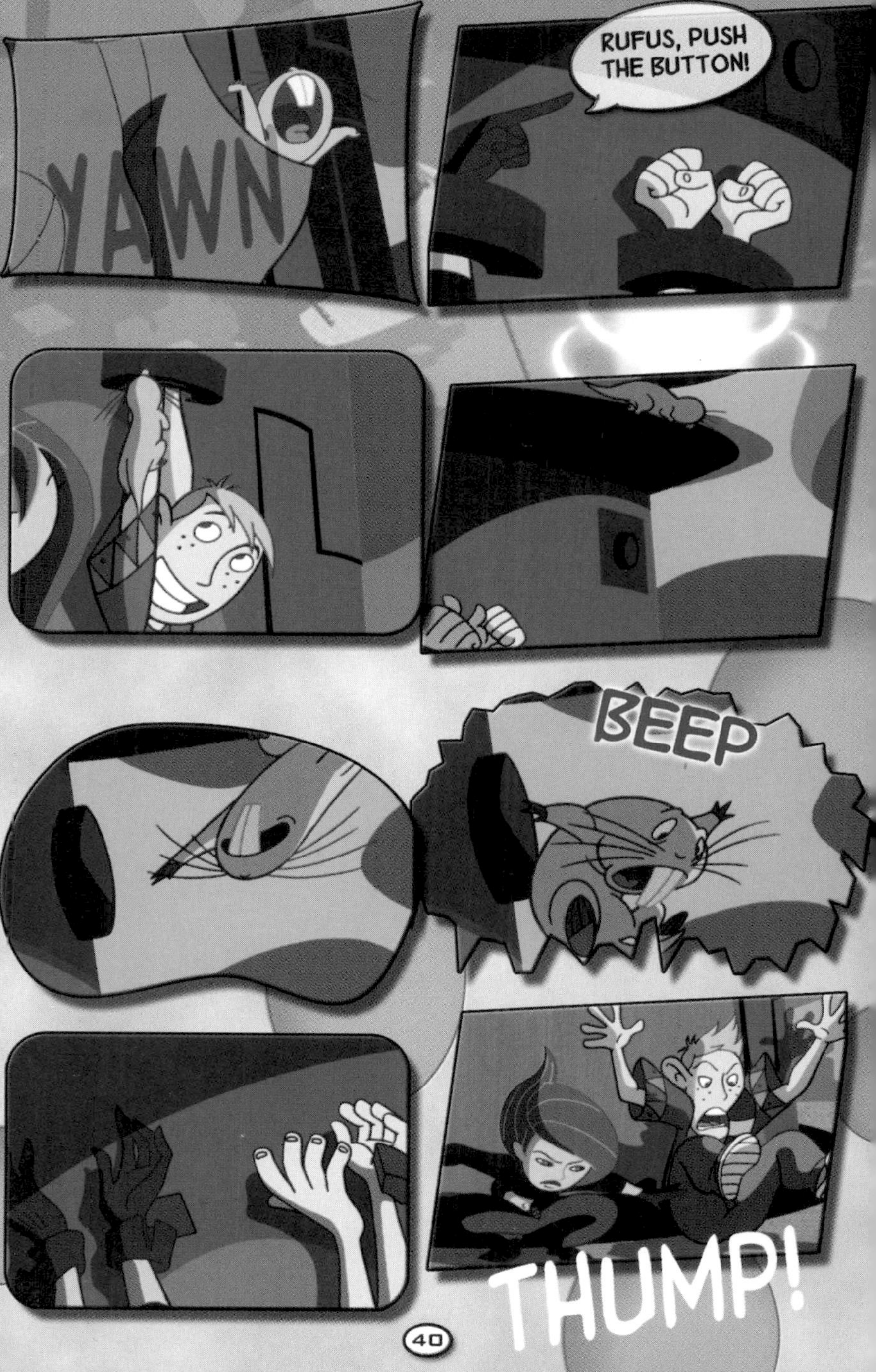
YAWN
RUFUS, PUSH THE BUTTON!
BEEP
THUMP!

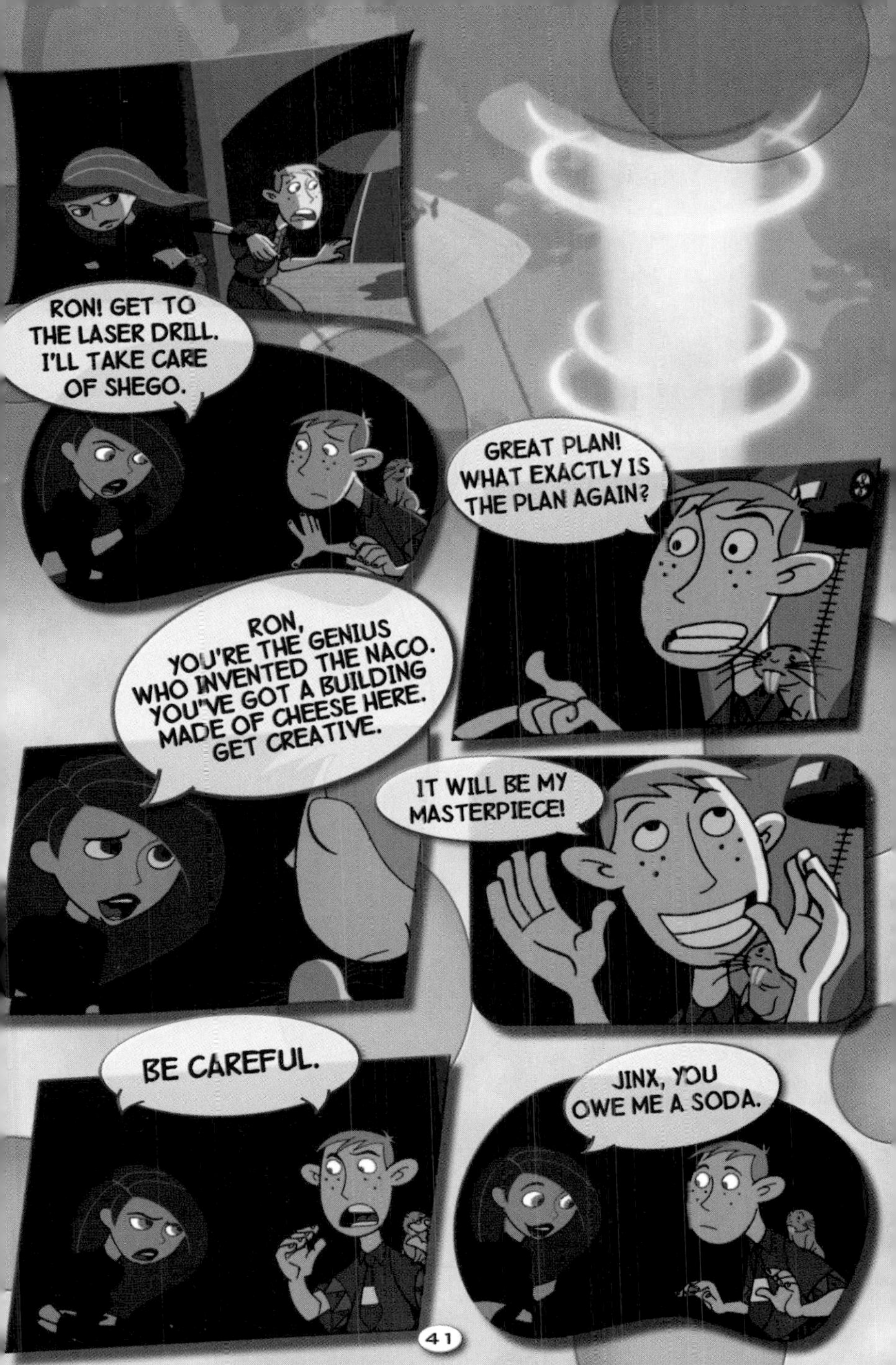
RON! GET TO THE LASER DRILL. I'LL TAKE CARE OF SHEGO.
GREAT PLAN! WHAT EXACTLY IS THE PLAN AGAIN?
RON, YOU'RE THE GENIUS WHO INVENTED THE NACO. YOU'VE GOT A BUILDING MADE OF CHEESE HERE. GET CREATIVE.
IT WILL BE MY MASTERPIECE!
BE CAREFUL.
JINX, YOU OWE ME A SODA.

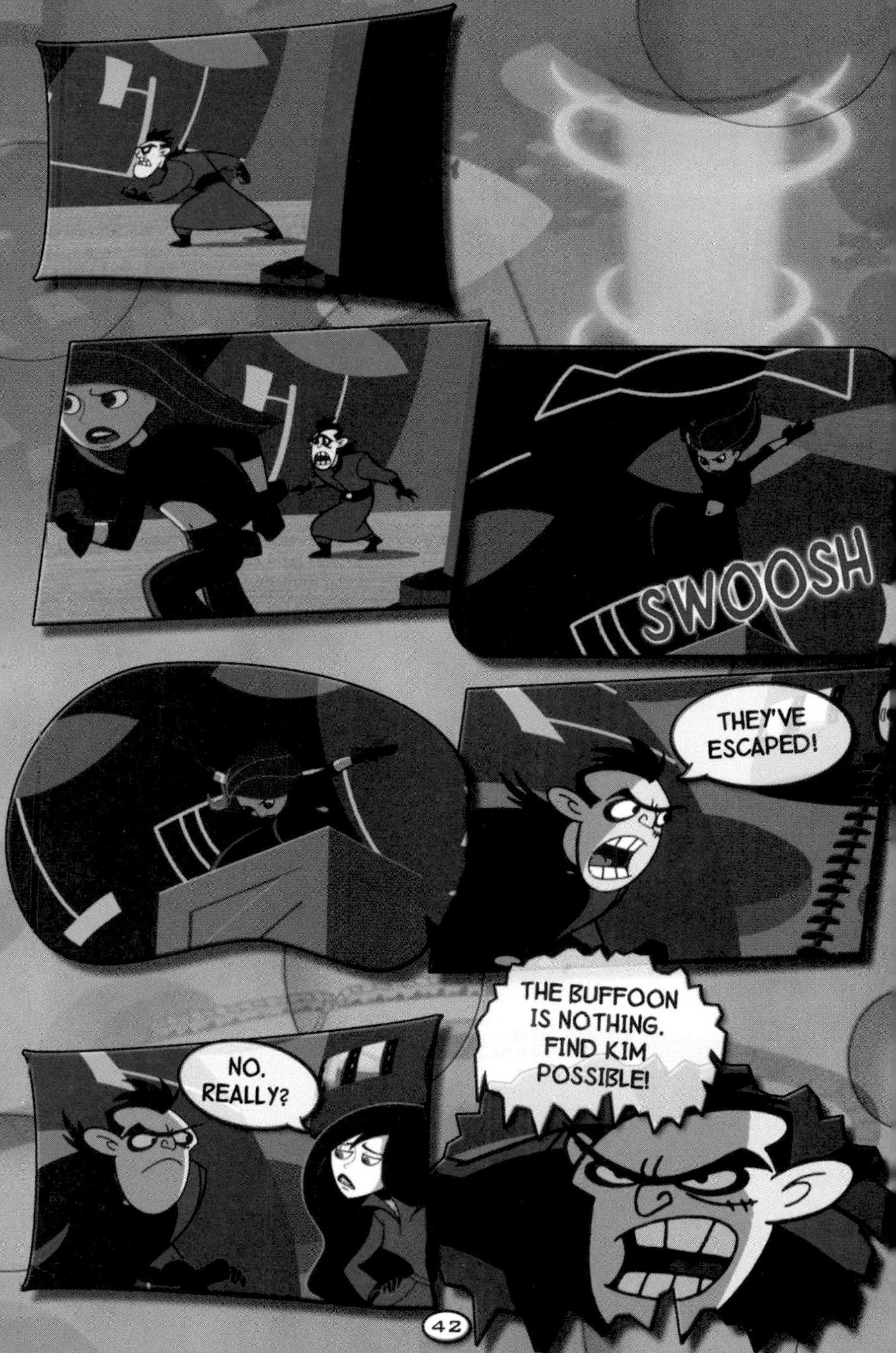
SWOOSH
THEY'VE ESCAPED!
NO. REALLY?
THE BUFFOON IS NOTHING. FIND KIM POSSIBLE!

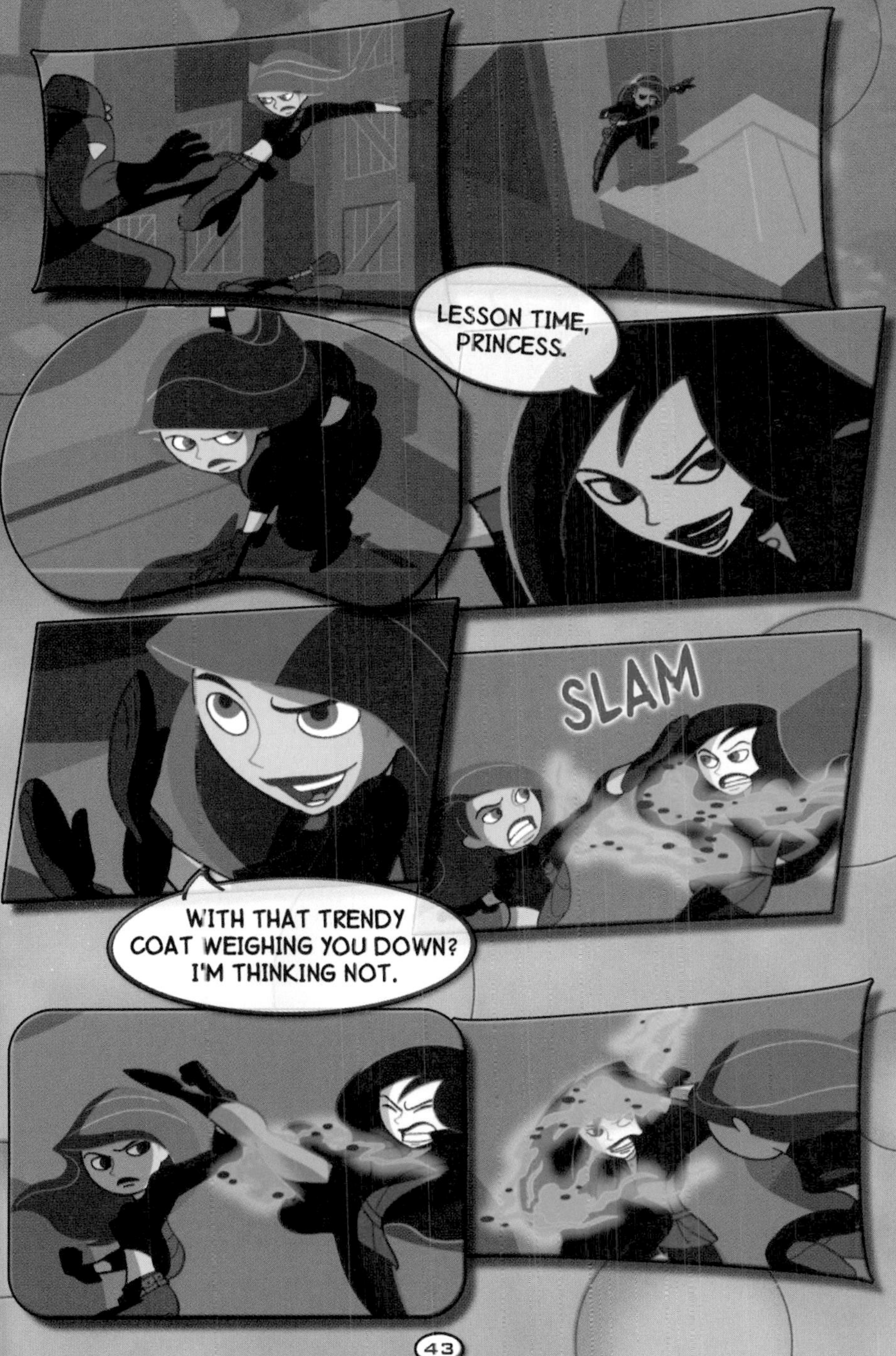
LESSON TIME, PRINCESS.
SLAM
WITH THAT TRENDY COAT WEIGHING YOU DOWN? I'M THINKING NOT.

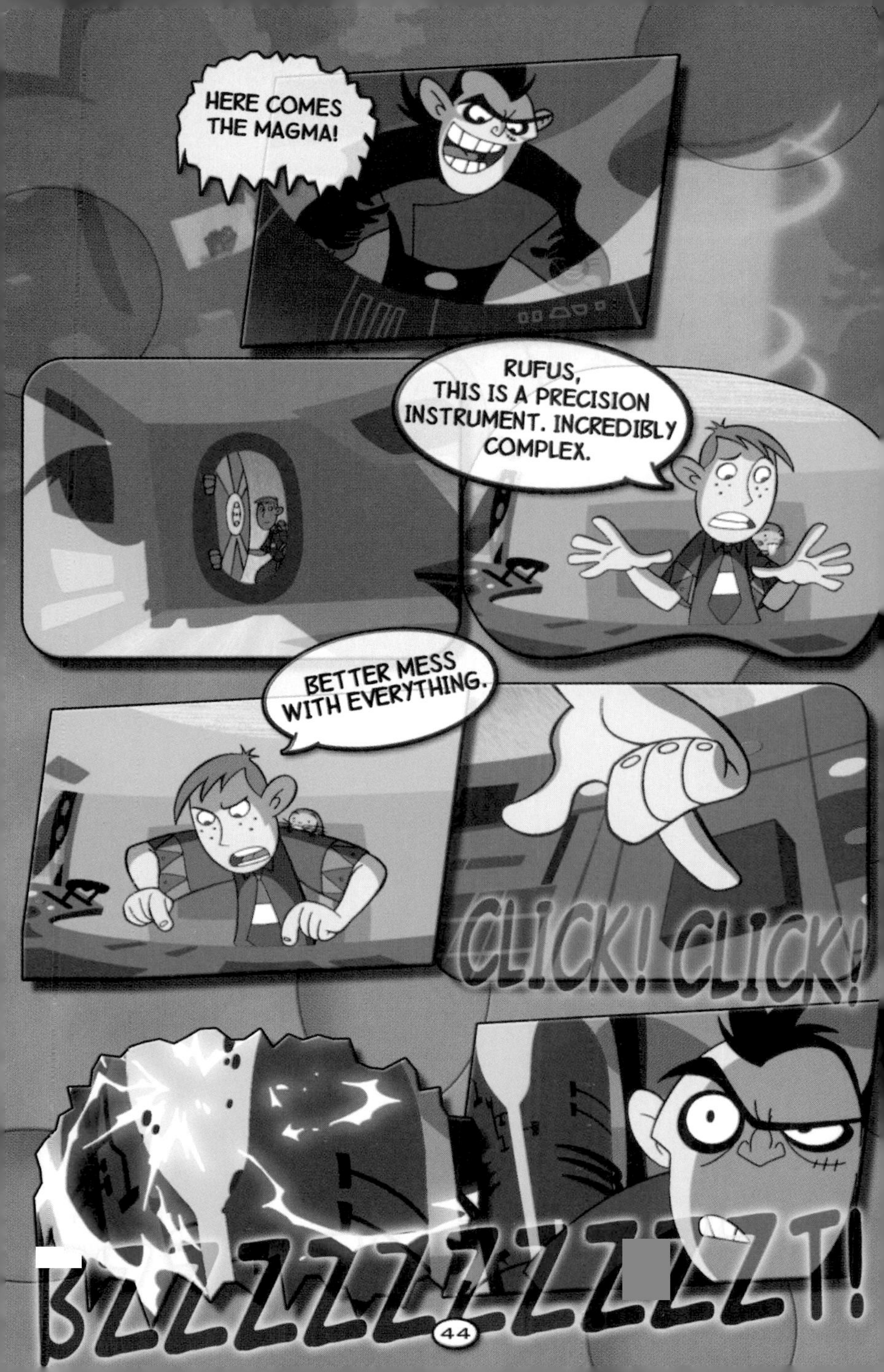
HERE COMES THE MAGMA!
RUFUS, THIS IS A PRECISION INSTRUMENT. INCREDIBLY COMPLEX.
BETTER MESS WITH EVERYTHING.
CLICK! CLICK!
BZZZZZZZZZZZZT!

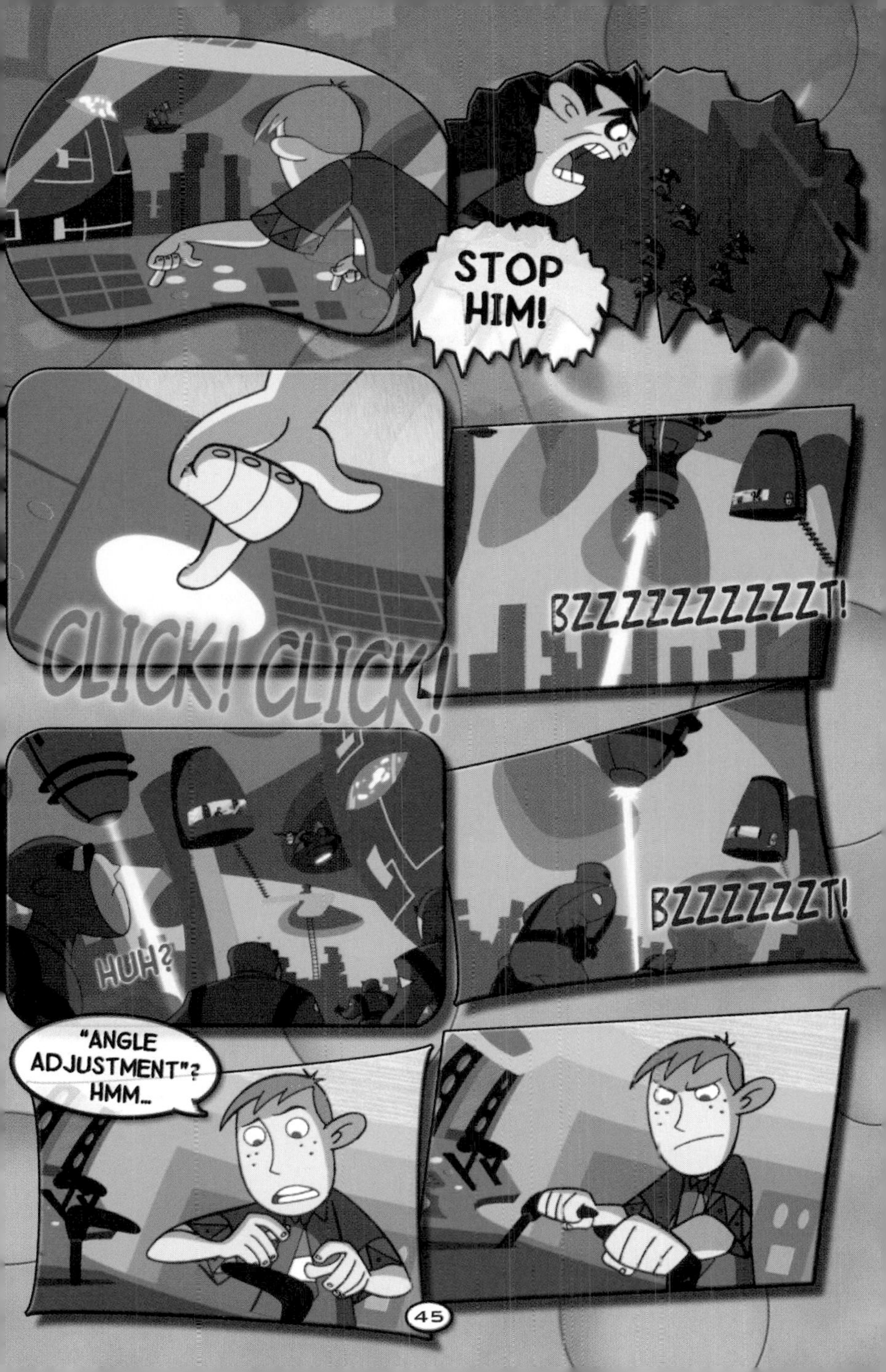
STOP HIM!
CLICK! CLICK!
BZZZZZZZZZZZT!
HUH?
BZZZZZZT!
"ANGLE ADJUSTMENT"? HMM...

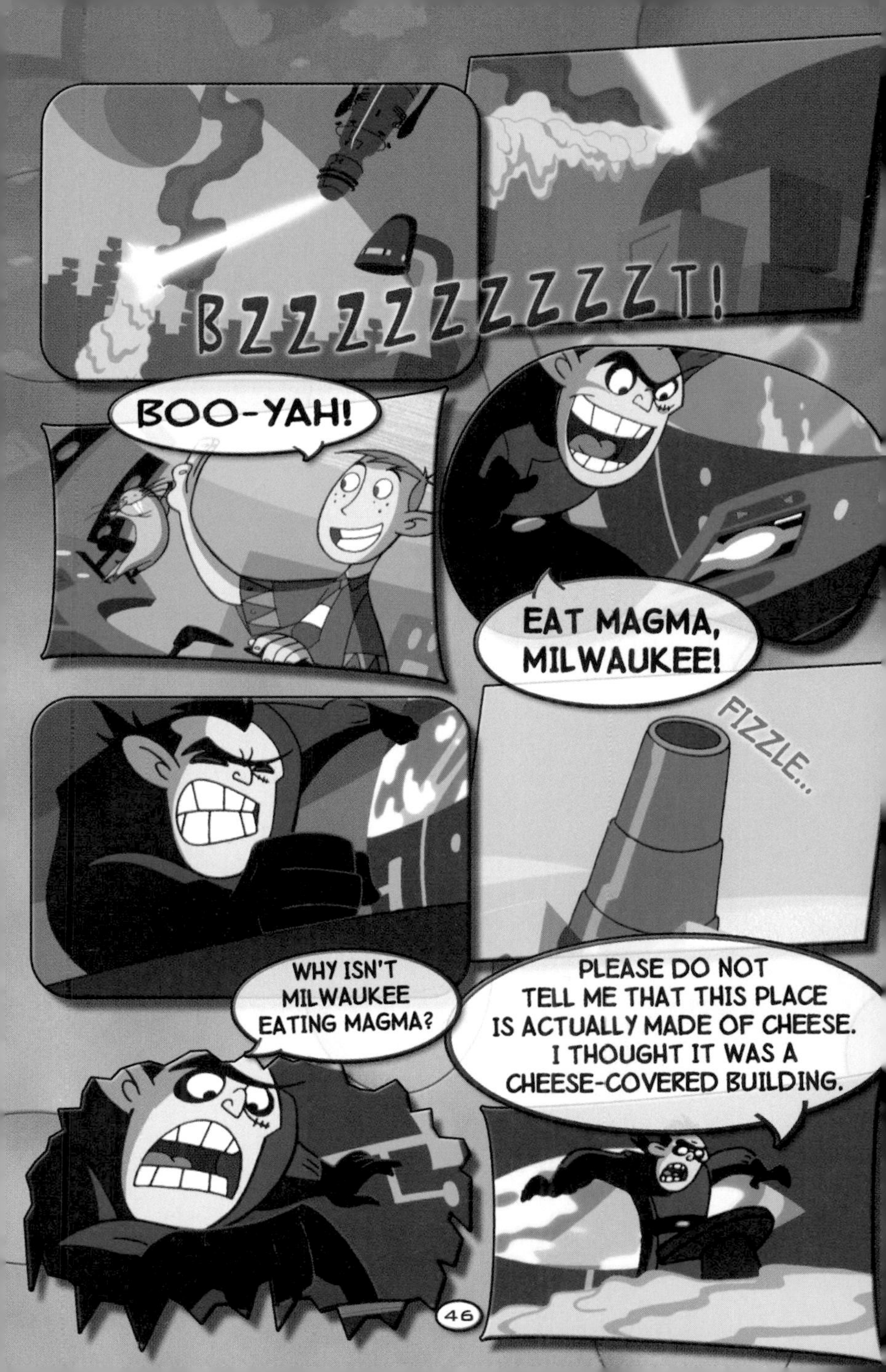
BZZZZZZZZZZT!
BOO-YAH!
EAT MAGMA, MILWAUKEE!
FIZZLE...
WHY ISN'T MILWAUKEE EATING MAGMA?
PLEASE DO NOT TELL ME THAT THIS PLACE IS ACTUALLY MADE OF CHEESE. I THOUGHT IT WAS A CHEESE-COVERED BUILDING.

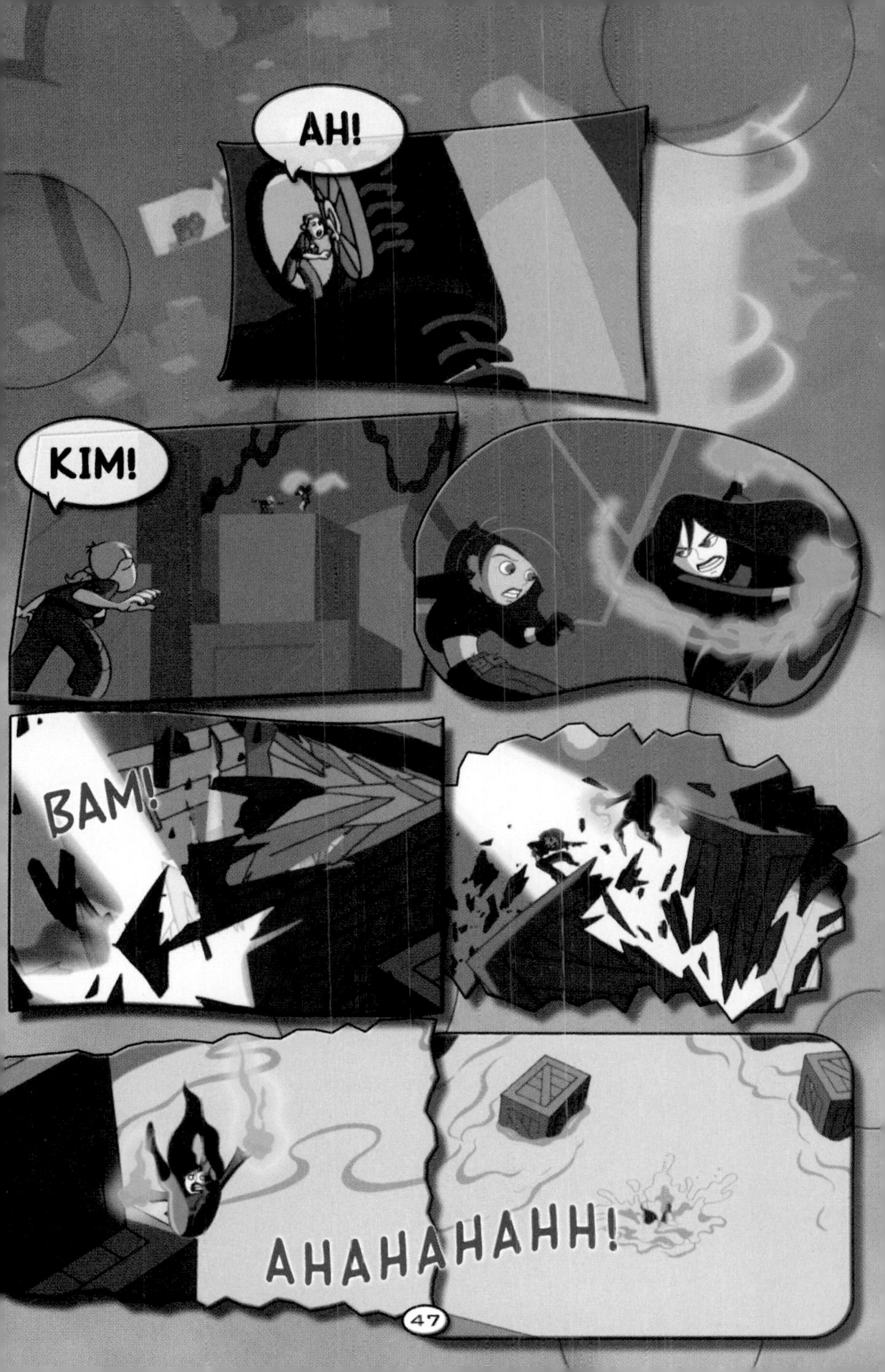
AH!
KIM!
BAM!
AHAHAHAHH!

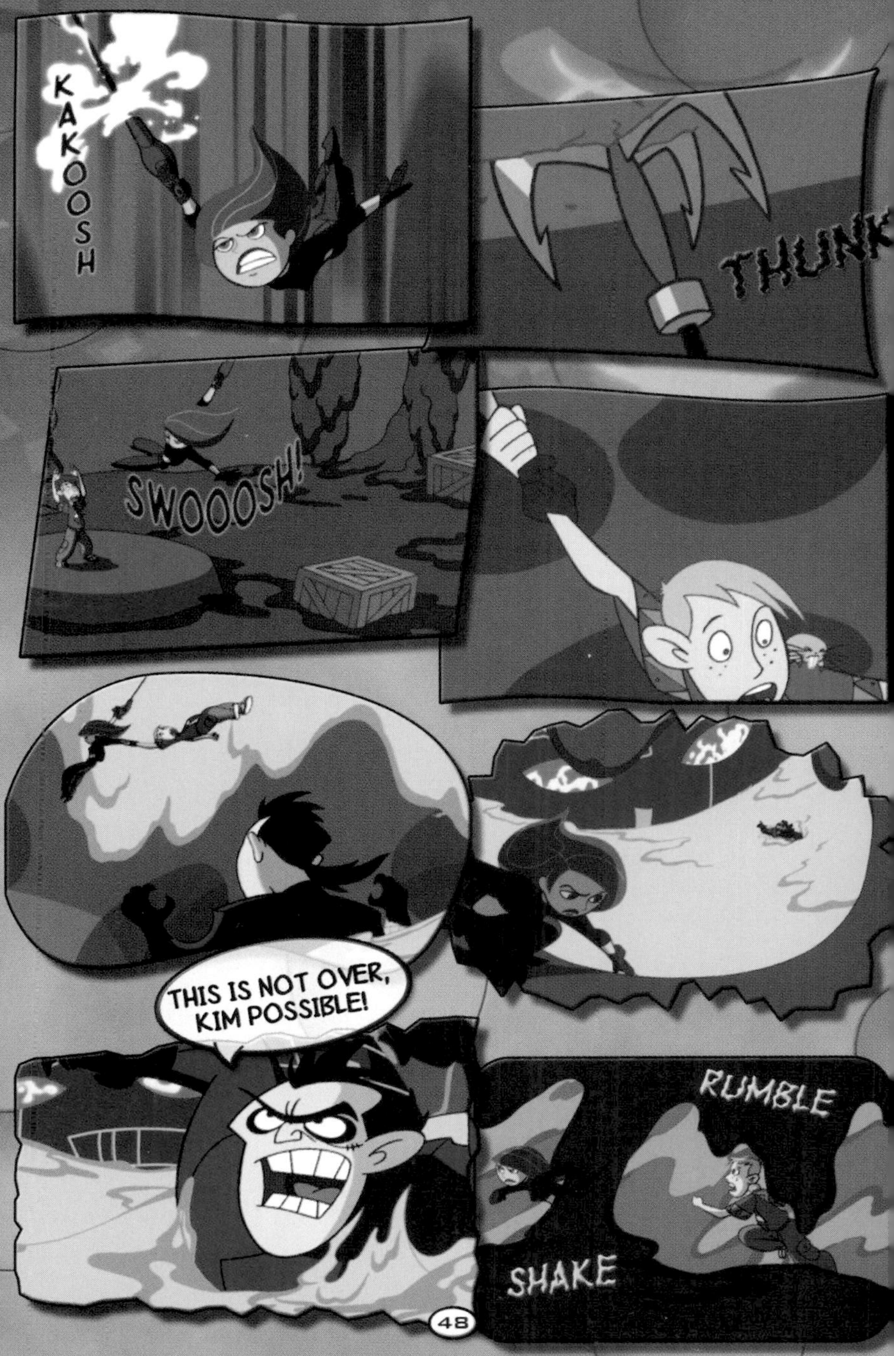
KAKOOSH
THUNK
SWOOOSH!
THIS IS NOT OVER, KIM POSSIBLE!
RUMBLE
SHAKE

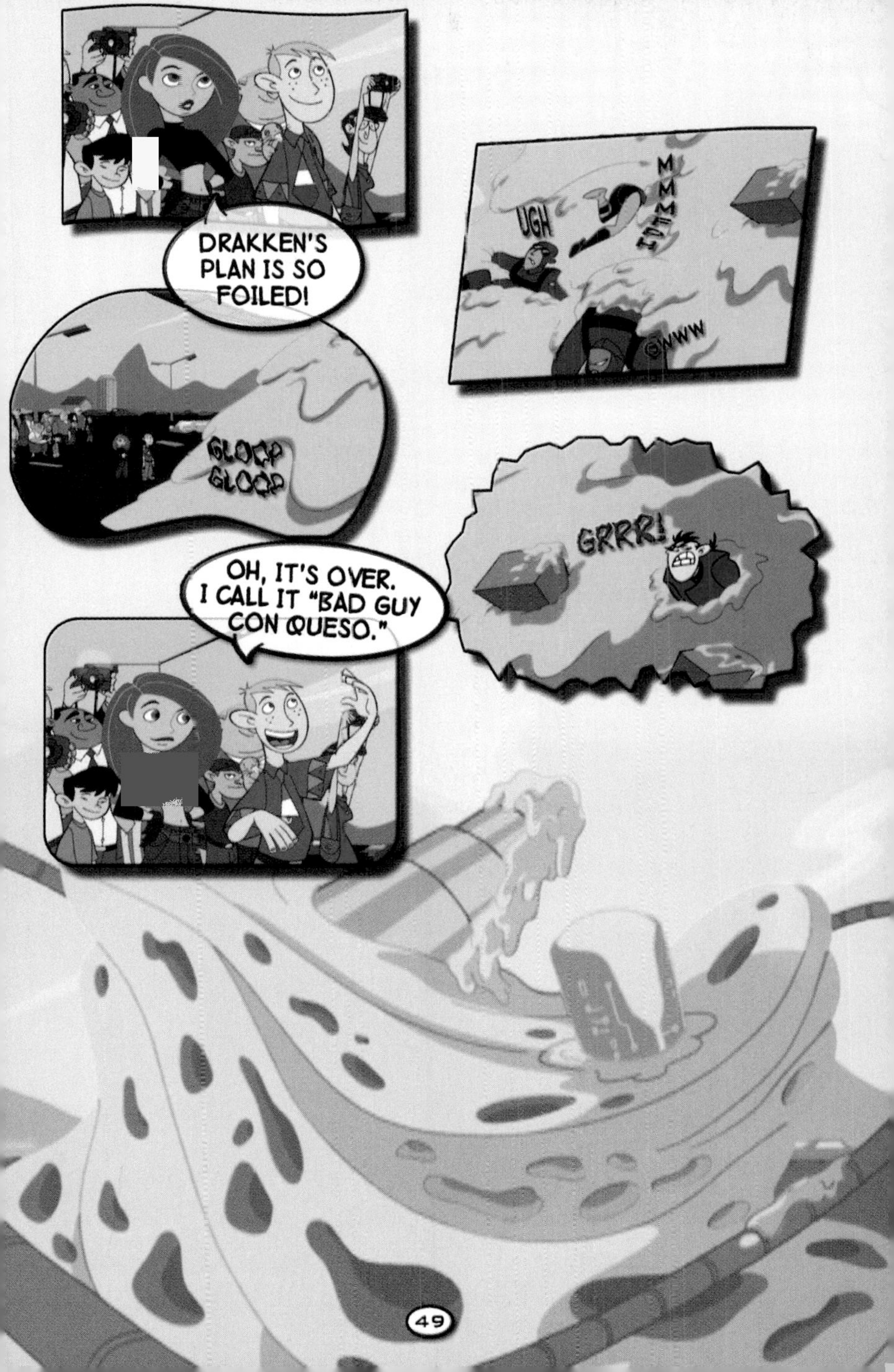
DRAKKEN'S PLAN IS SO FOILED!
UGH
MMMFPH
OWWW
GLOOP GLOOP
GRRR!
OH, IT'S OVER. I CALL IT "BAD GUY CON QUESO."

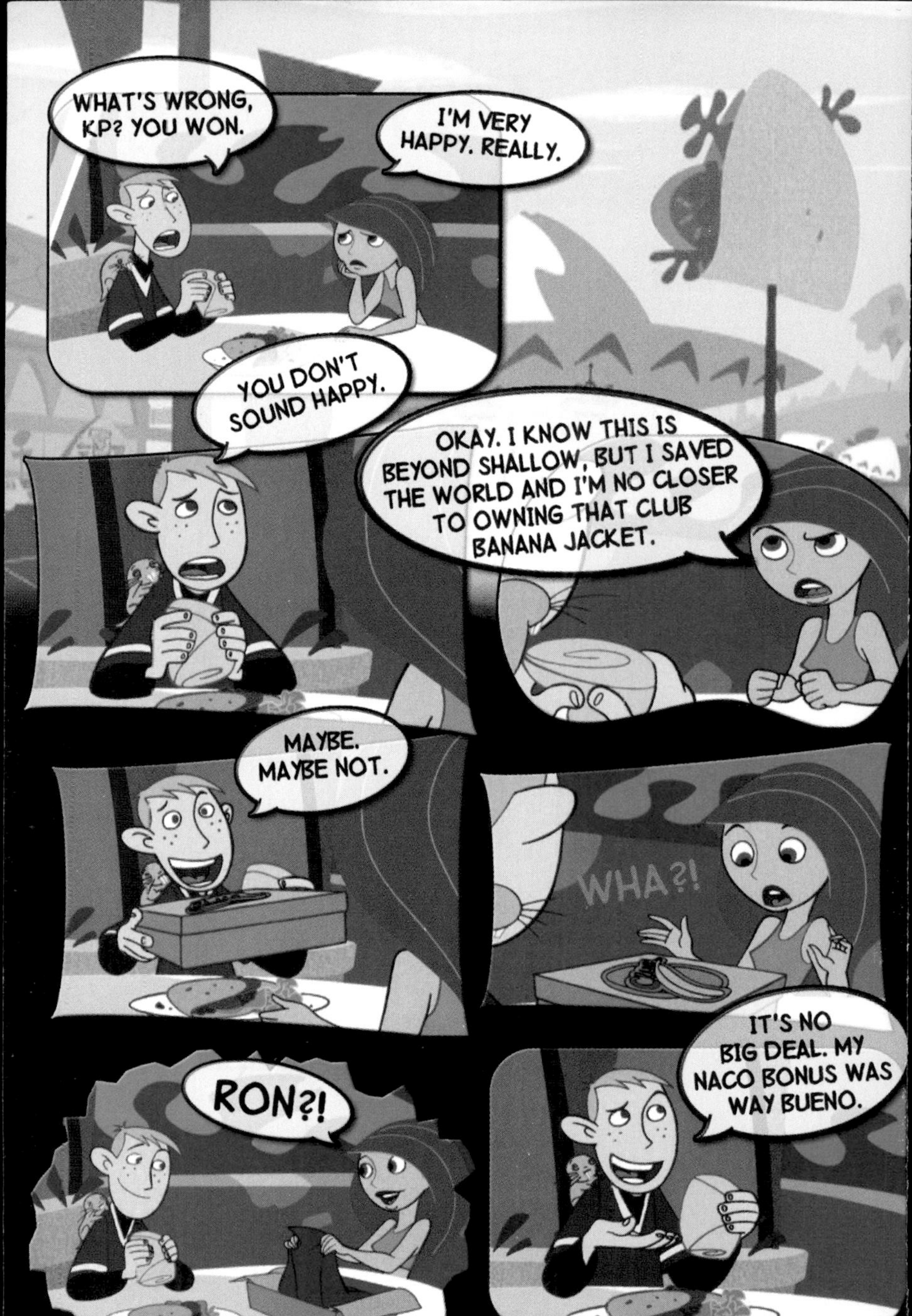
WHAT'S WRONG, KP? YOU WON.
I'M VERY HAPPY. REALLY.
YOU DON'T SOUND HAPPY.
OKAY. I KNOW THIS IS BEYOND SHALLOW, BUT I SAVED THE WORLD AND I'M NO CLOSER TO OWNING THAT CLUB BANANA JACKET.
MAYBE. MAYBE NOT.
WHA?!
RON?!
IT'S NO BIG DEAL. MY NACO BONUS WAS WAY BUENO.

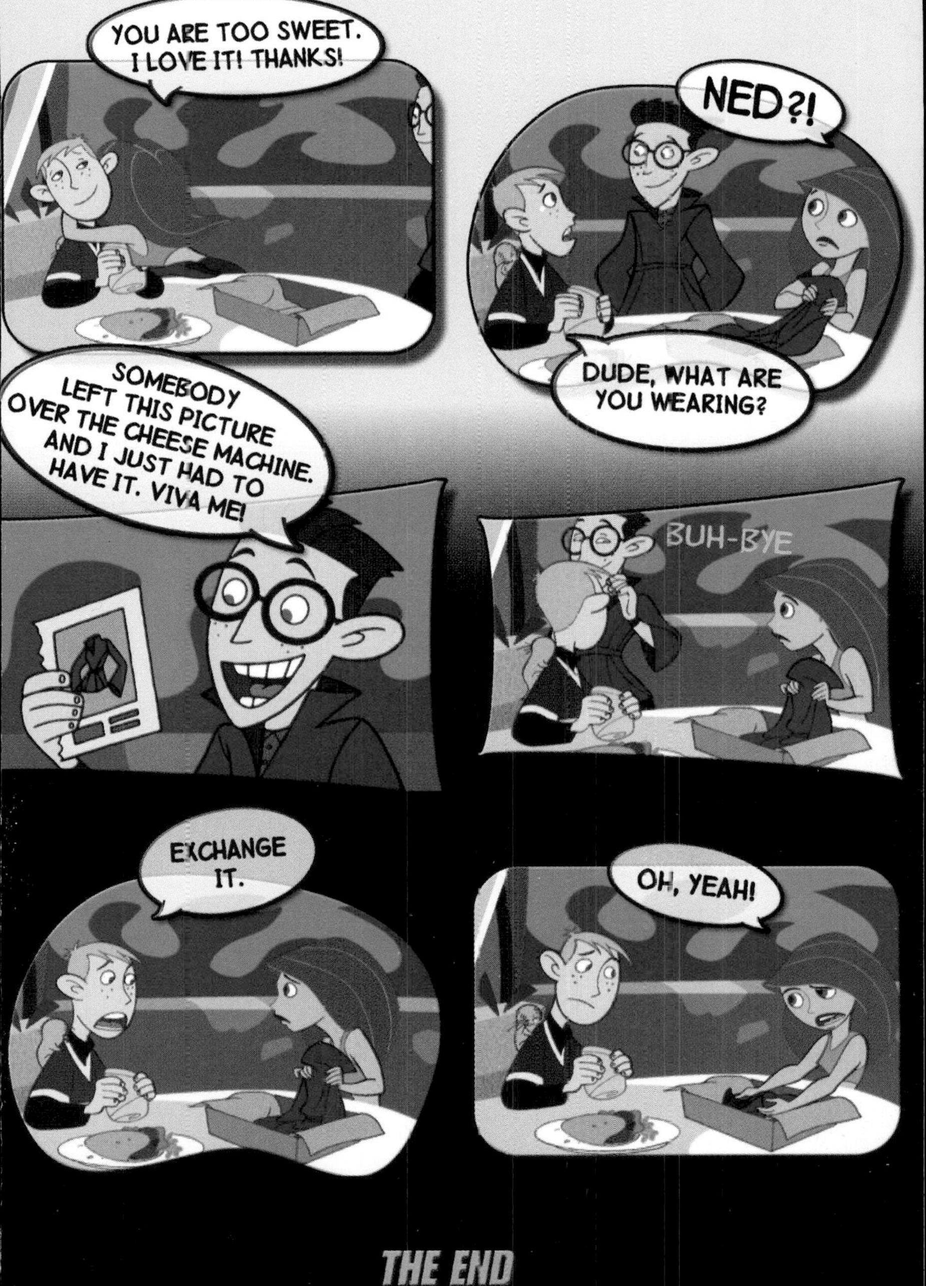
YOU ARE TOO SWEET. I LOVE IT! THANKS!
NED?!
DUDE, WHAT ARE YOU WEARING?
SOMEBODY LEFT THIS PICTURE OVER THE CHEESE MACHINE. AND I JUST HAD TO HAVE IT. VIVA ME!
BUH-BYE
EXCHANGE IT.
OH, YEAH!
THE END

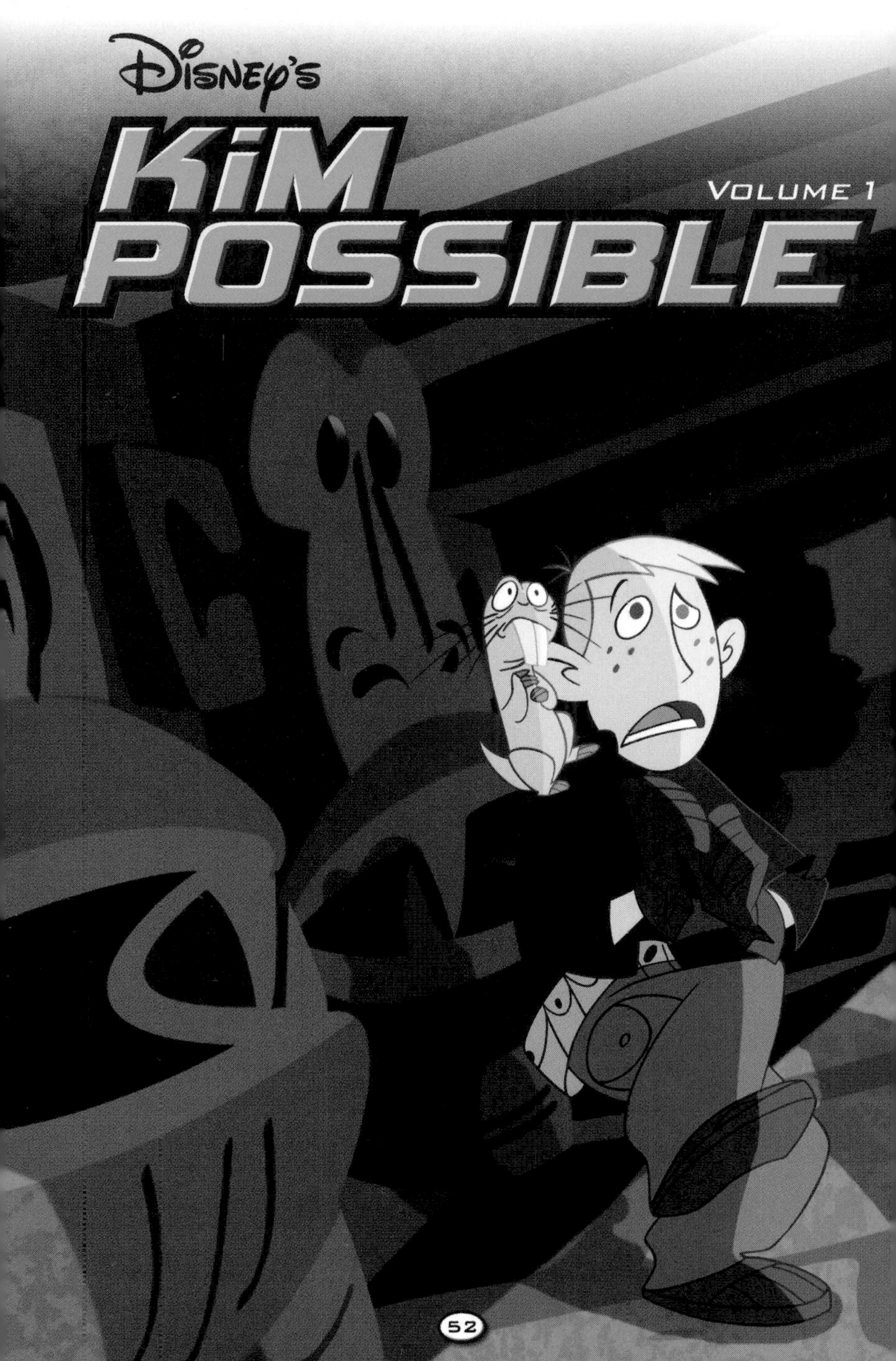
Disney's
Kim Possible
Volume 1

EPISODE 2: TICK-TICK-TICK

NOT ONLY DOES KIM FACE THE INDIGNITY OF DETENTION, BUT HUMILIATION NEARLY BECOMES ANNIHILATION WHEN DRAKKEN'S NEW NANO-EXPLOSIVE GETS STUCK ON HER NOSE.

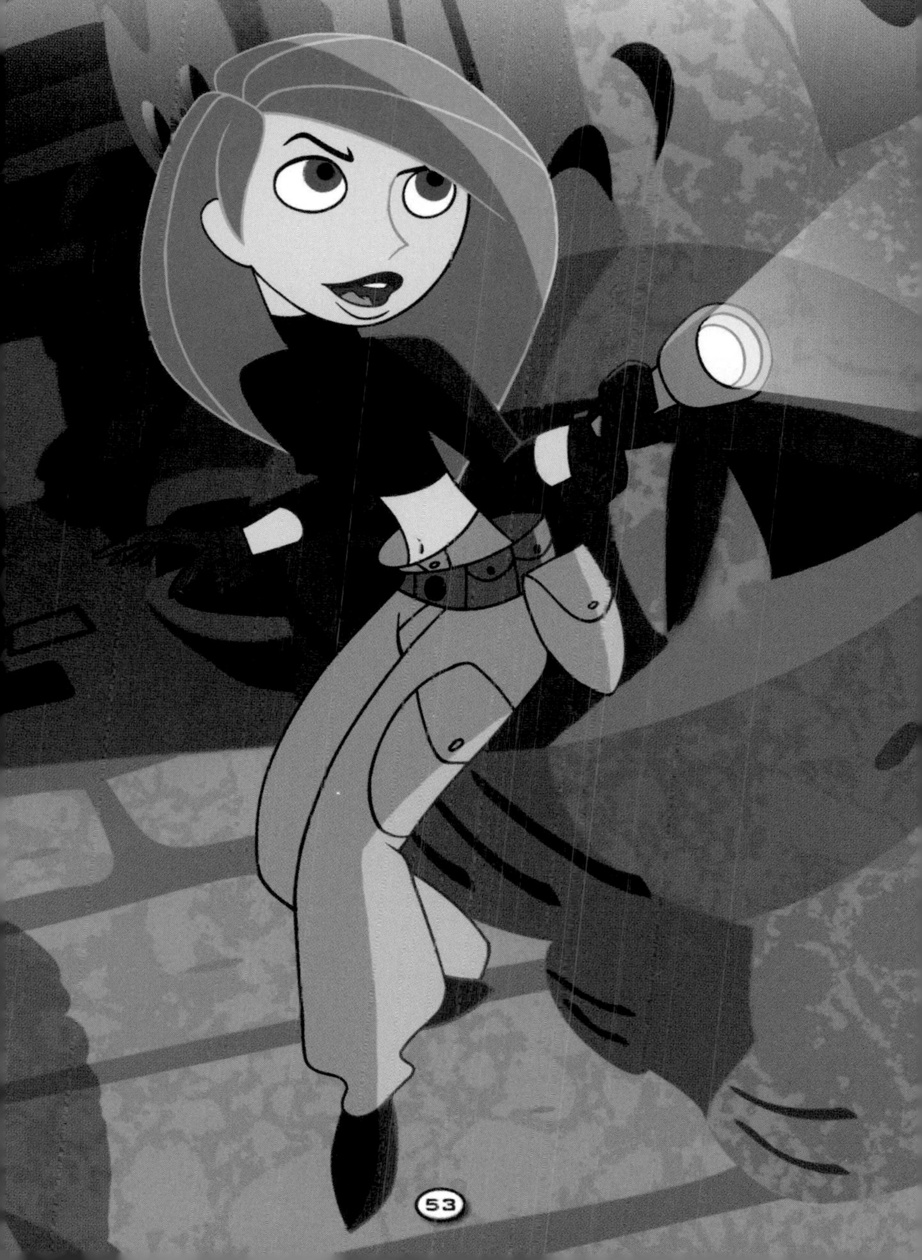

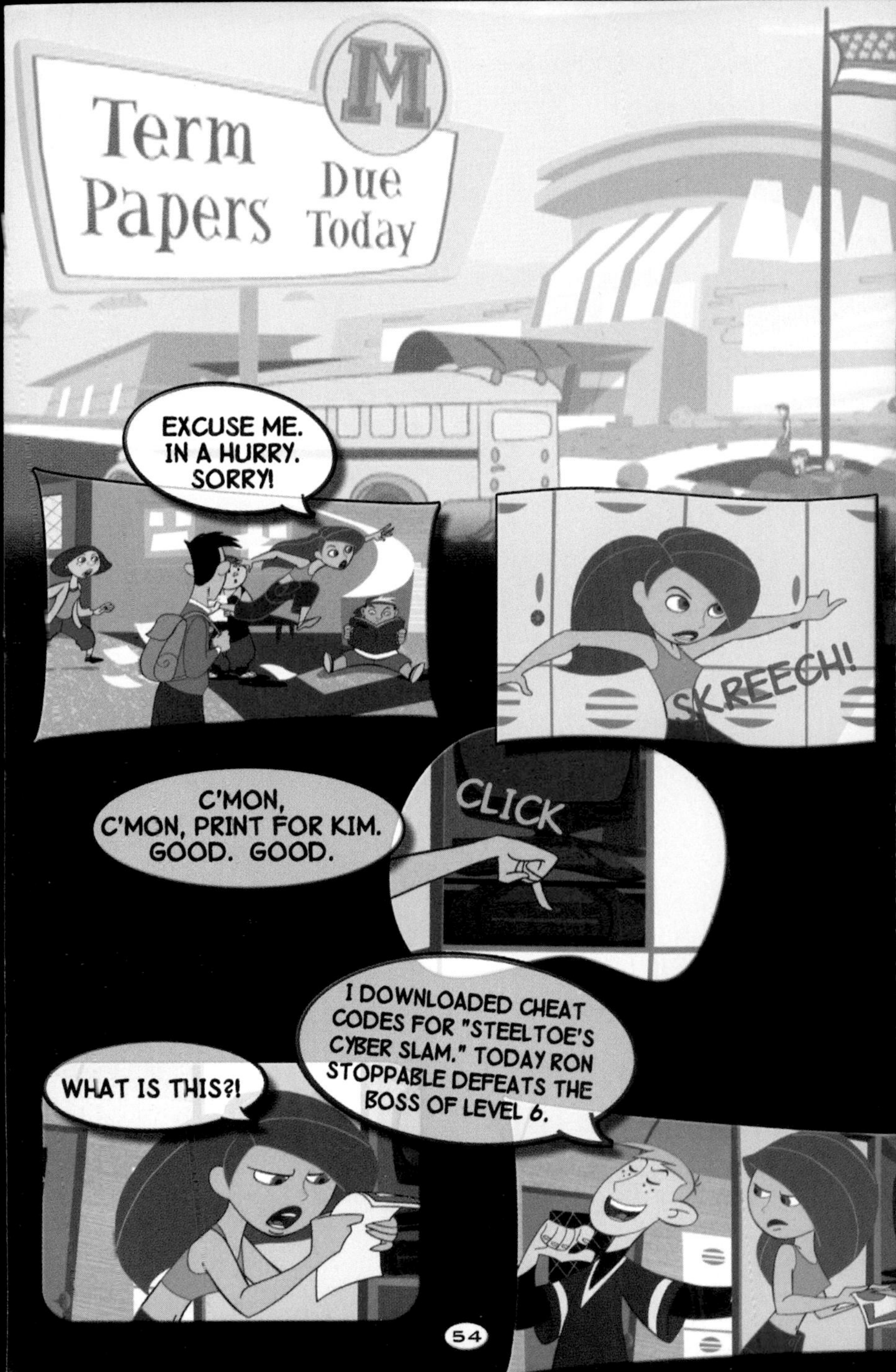
Term Papers Due Today
M
EXCUSE ME. IN A HURRY. SORRY!
SKREECH!
C'MON, C'MON, PRINT FOR KIM. GOOD. GOOD.
CLICK
WHAT IS THIS?!
I DOWNLOADED CHEAT CODES FOR "STEELTOE'S CYBER SLAM." TODAY RON STOPPABLE DEFEATS THE BOSS OF LEVEL 6.

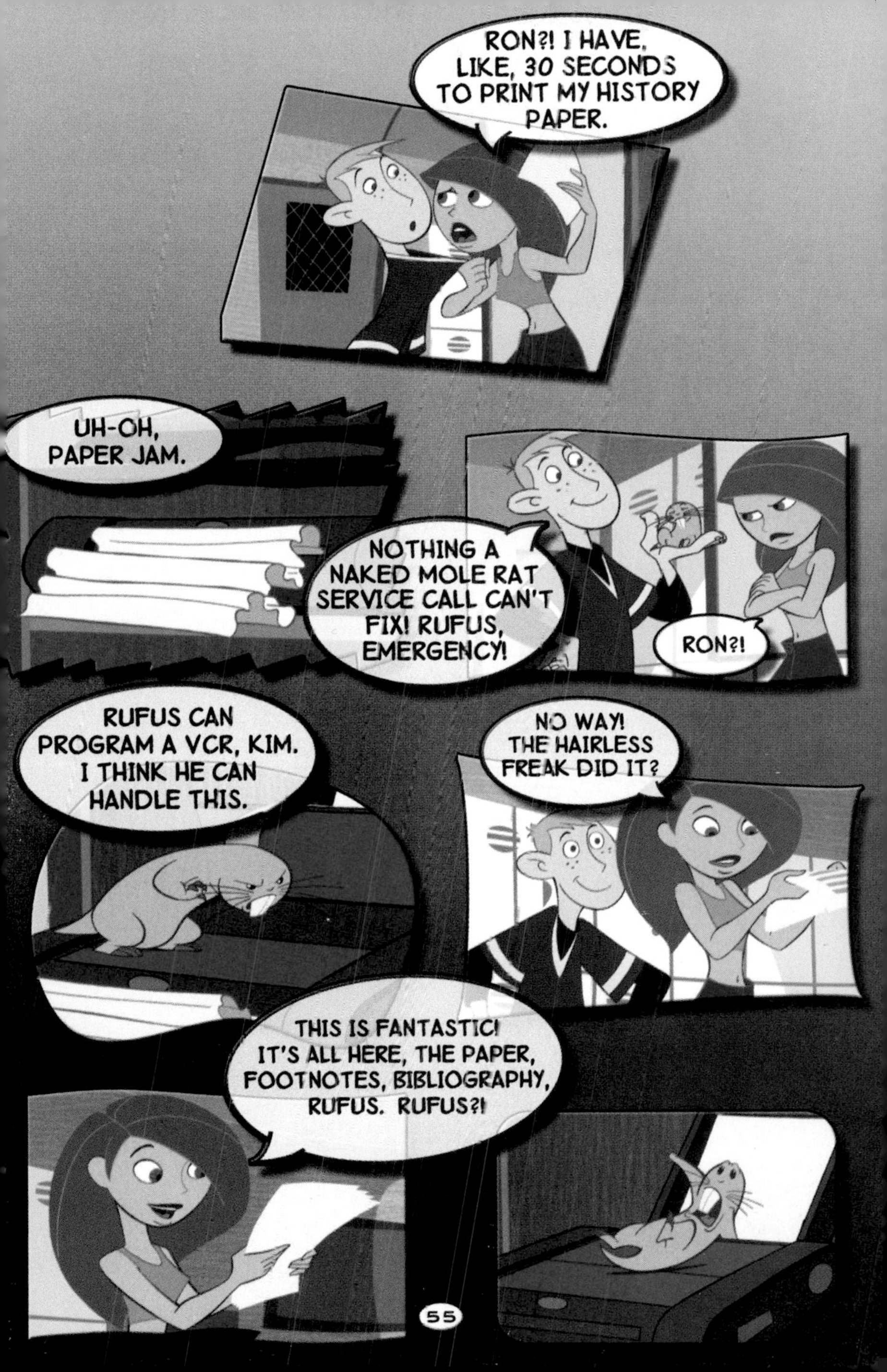
RON?! I HAVE, LIKE, 30 SECONDS TO PRINT MY HISTORY PAPER.
UH-OH, PAPER JAM.
NOTHING A NAKED MOLE RAT SERVICE CALL CAN'T FIX! RUFUS, EMERGENCY!
RON?!
RUFUS CAN PROGRAM A VCR, KIM. I THINK HE CAN HANDLE THIS.
NO WAY! THE HAIRLESS FREAK DID IT?
THIS IS FANTASTIC! IT'S ALL HERE, THE PAPER, FOOTNOTES, BIBLIOGRAPHY, RUFUS. RUFUS?!

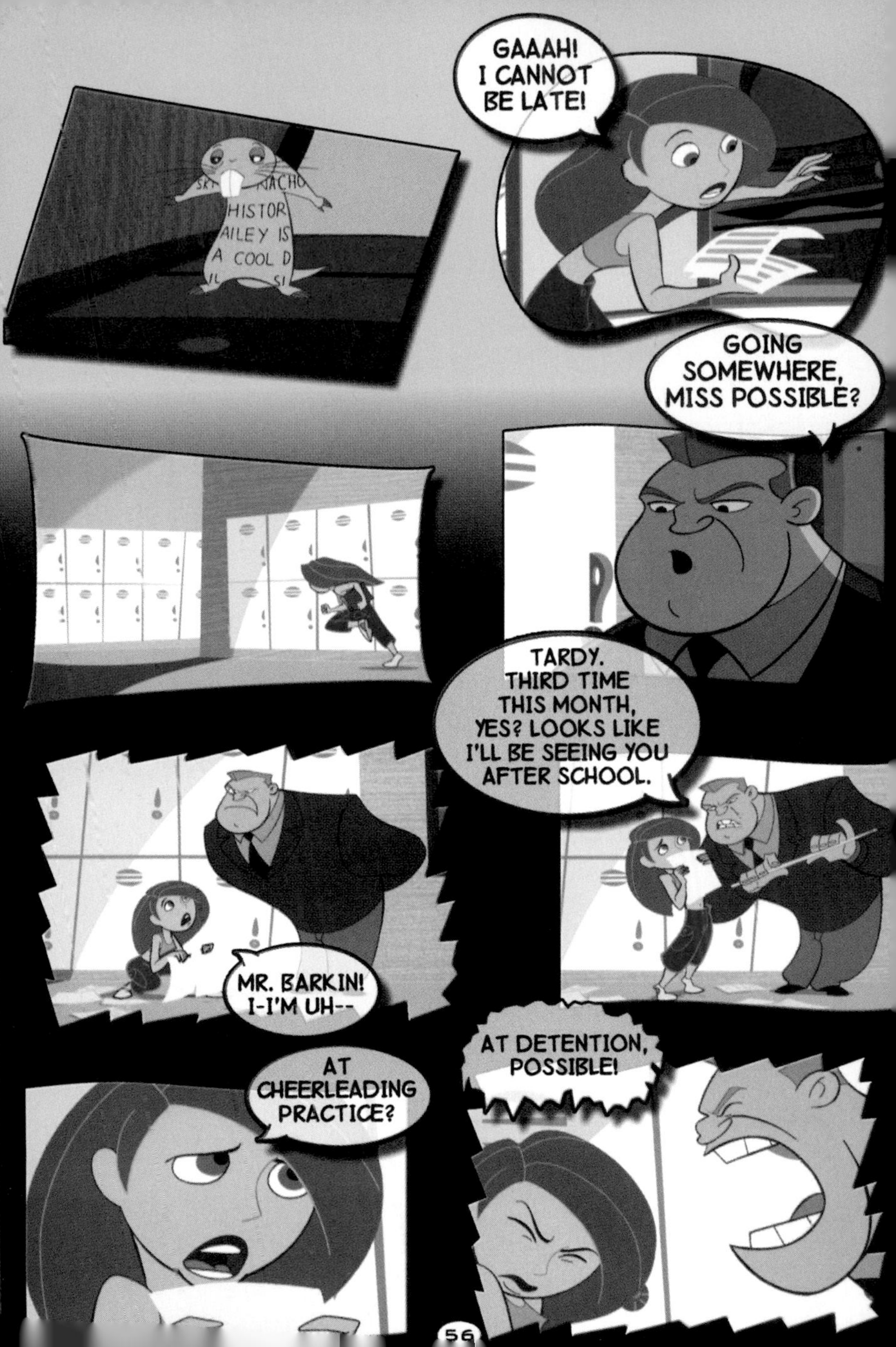
GAAAH! I CANNOT BE LATE!
GOING SOMEWHERE, MISS POSSIBLE?
MR. BARKIN! I-I'M UH--
TARDY. THIRD TIME THIS MONTH, YES? LOOKS LIKE I'LL BE SEEING YOU AFTER SCHOOL.
AT CHEERLEADING PRACTICE?
AT DETENTION, POSSIBLE!

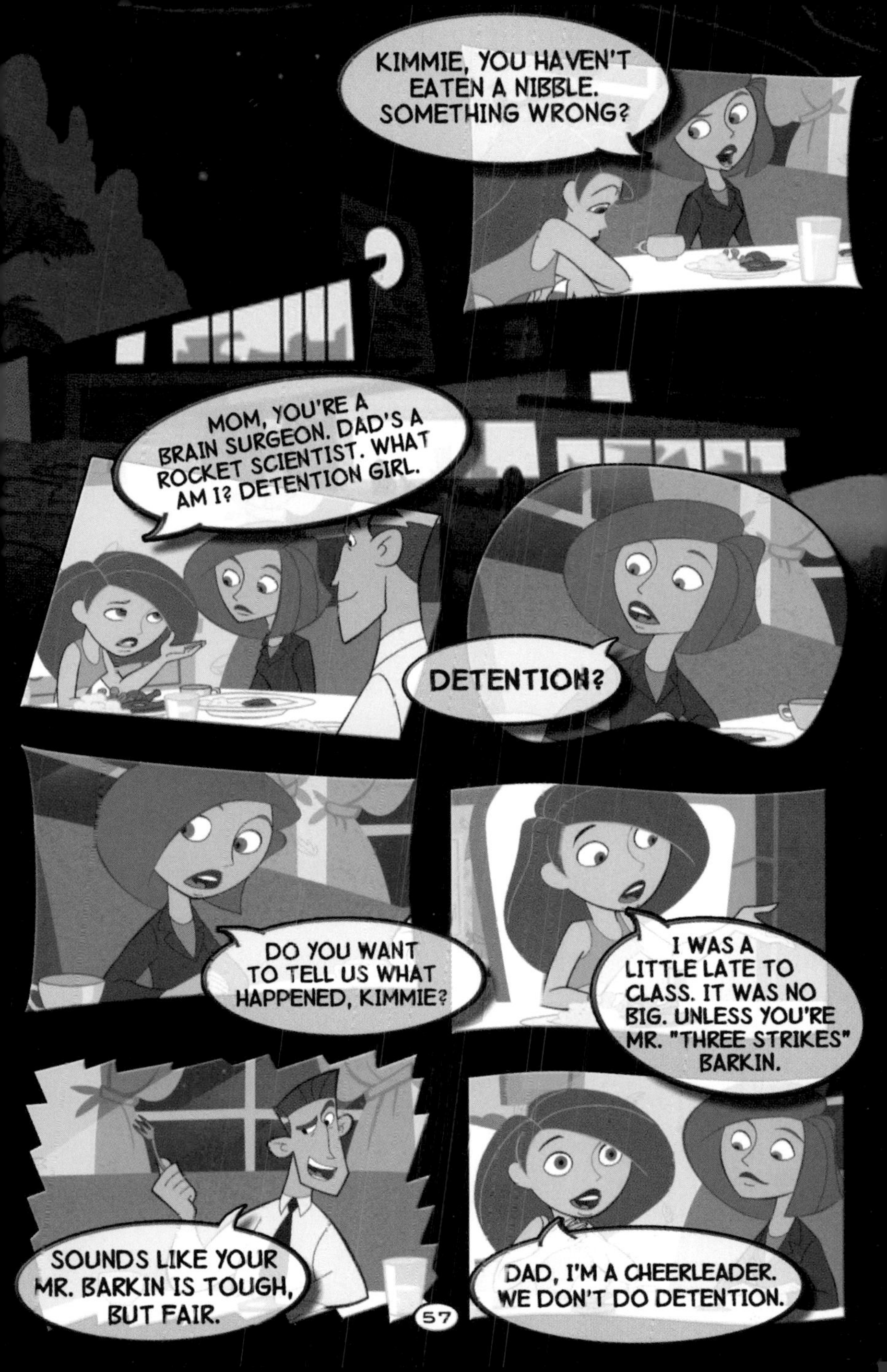
KIMMIE, YOU HAVEN'T EATEN A NIBBLE. SOMETHING WRONG?
MOM, YOU'RE A BRAIN SURGEON. DAD'S A ROCKET SCIENTIST. WHAT AM I? DETENTION GIRL.
DETENTION?
DO YOU WANT TO TELL US WHAT HAPPENED, KIMMIE?
I WAS A LITTLE LATE TO CLASS. IT WAS NO BIG. UNLESS YOU'RE MR. "THREE STRIKES" BARKIN.
SOUNDS LIKE YOUR MR. BARKIN IS TOUGH, BUT FAIR.
DAD, I'M A CHEERLEADER. WE DON'T DO DETENTION.

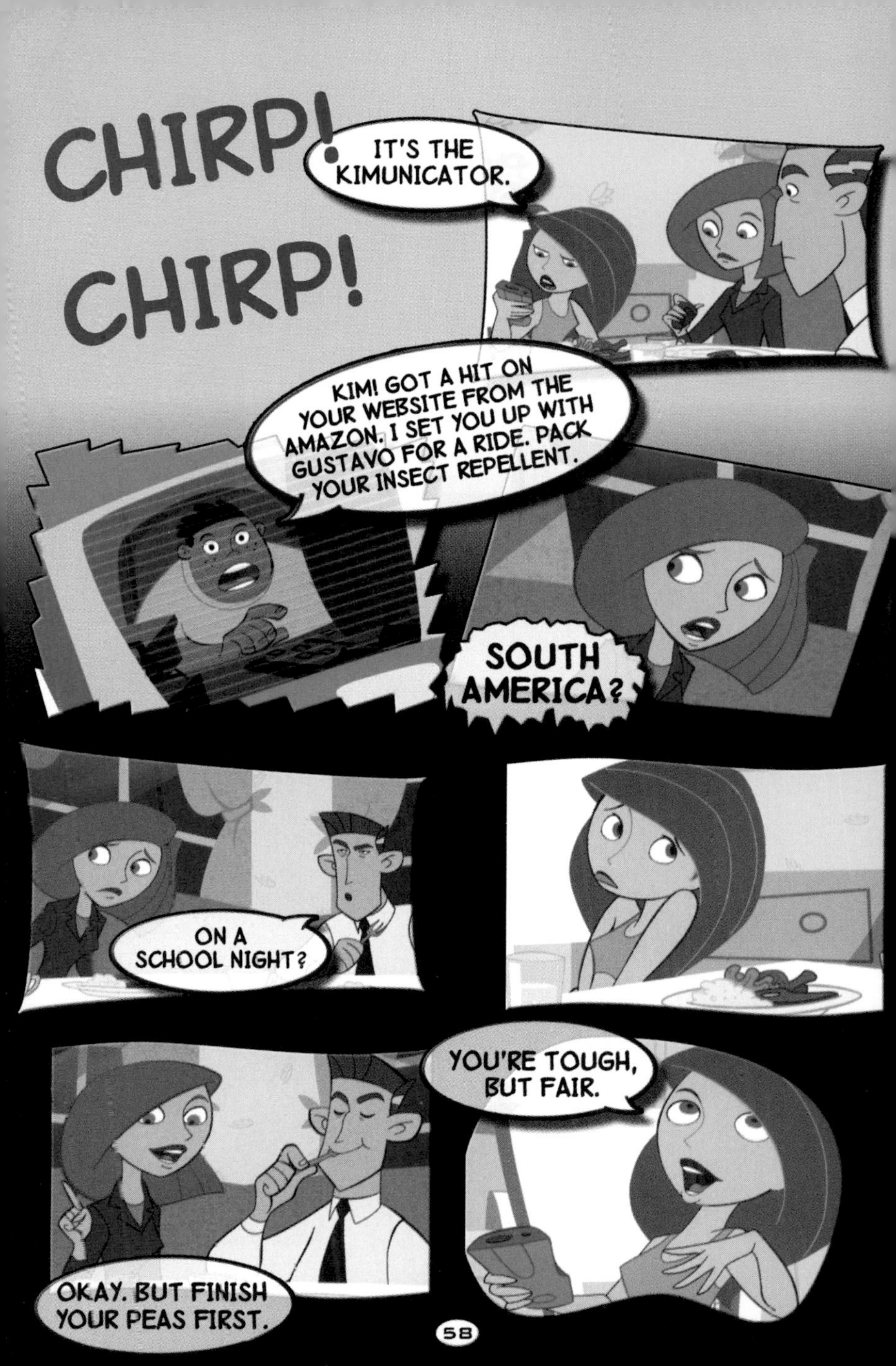
CHIRP!
IT'S THE KIMUNICATOR.
CHIRP!
KIM! GOT A HIT ON YOUR WEBSITE FROM THE AMAZON. I SET YOU UP WITH GUSTAVO FOR A RIDE. PACK YOUR INSECT REPELLENT.
SOUTH AMERICA?
ON A SCHOOL NIGHT?
OKAY. BUT FINISH YOUR PEAS FIRST.
YOU'RE TOUGH, BUT FAIR.

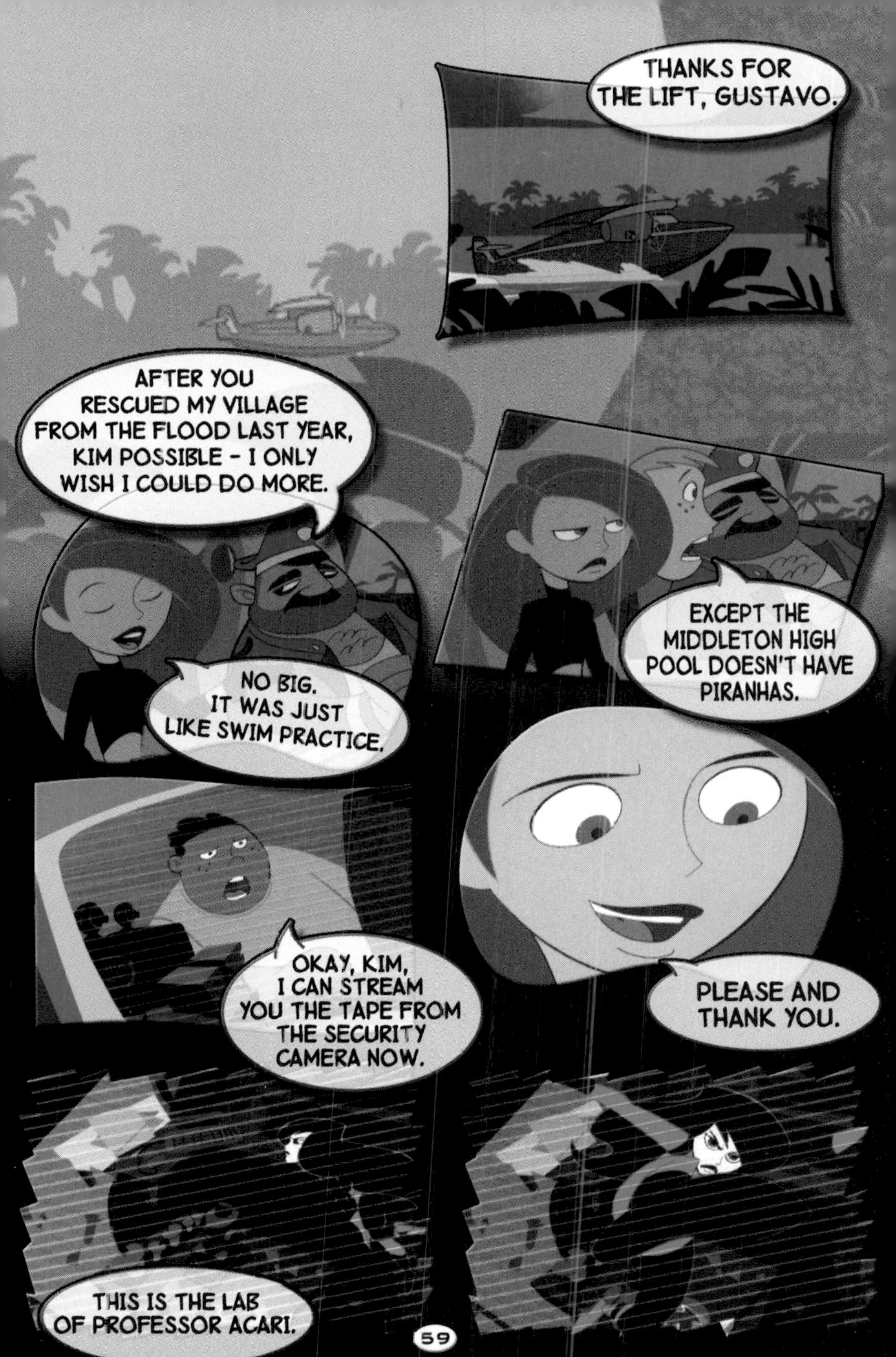
THANKS FOR THE LIFT, GUSTAVO.
AFTER YOU RESCUED MY VILLAGE FROM THE FLOOD LAST YEAR, KIM POSSIBLE - I ONLY WISH I COULD DO MORE.
NO BIG. IT WAS JUST LIKE SWIM PRACTICE.
EXCEPT THE MIDDLETON HIGH POOL DOESN'T HAVE PIRANHAS.
OKAY, KIM, I CAN STREAM YOU THE TAPE FROM THE SECURITY CAMERA NOW.
PLEASE AND THANK YOU.
THIS IS THE LAB OF PROFESSOR ACARI.

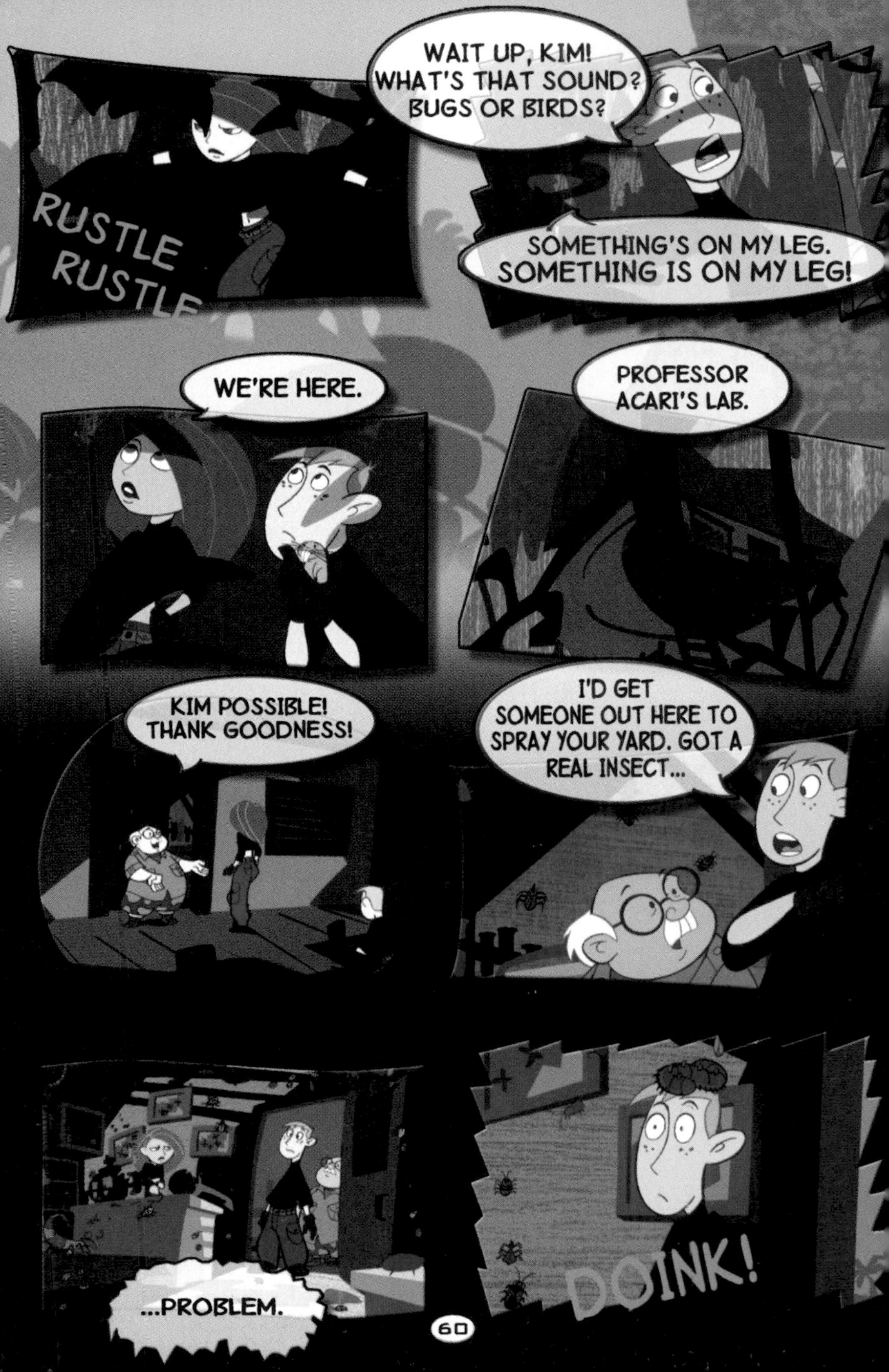
RUSTLE RUSTLE
WAIT UP, KIM! WHAT'S THAT SOUND? BUGS OR BIRDS?
SOMETHING'S ON MY LEG. SOMETHING IS ON MY LEG!
WE'RE HERE.
PROFESSOR ACARI'S LAB.
KIM POSSIBLE! THANK GOODNESS!
I'D GET SOMEONE OUT HERE TO SPRAY YOUR YARD. GOT A REAL INSECT...
...PROBLEM.
DOINK!

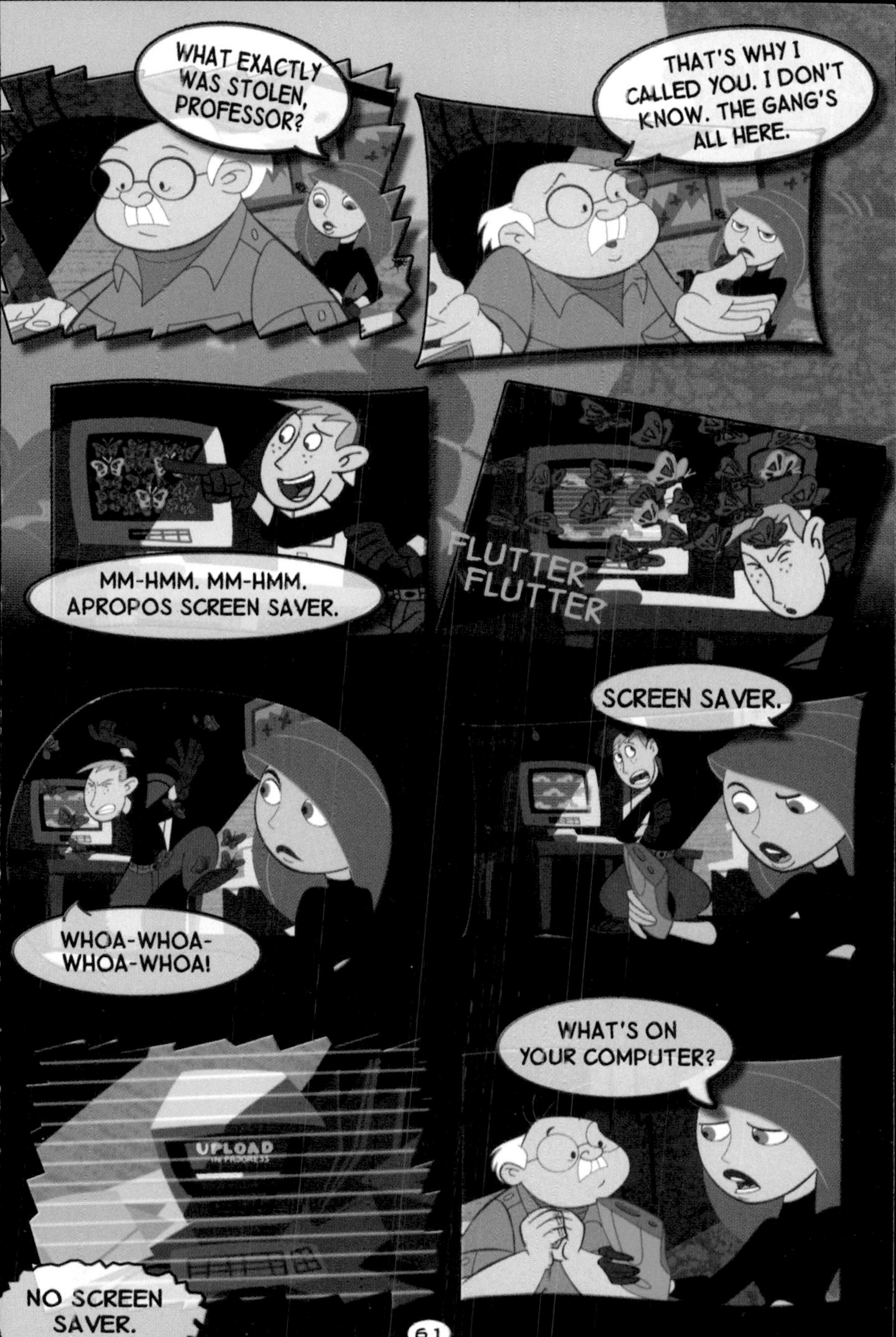
WHAT EXACTLY WAS STOLEN, PROFESSOR?
THAT'S WHY I CALLED YOU. I DON'T KNOW. THE GANG'S ALL HERE.
MM-HMM. MM-HMM. APROPOS SCREEN SAVER.
FLUTTER FLUTTER
WHOA-WHOA-WHOA-WHOA!
SCREEN SAVER.
UPLOAD
NO SCREEN SAVER.
WHAT'S ON YOUR COMPUTER?

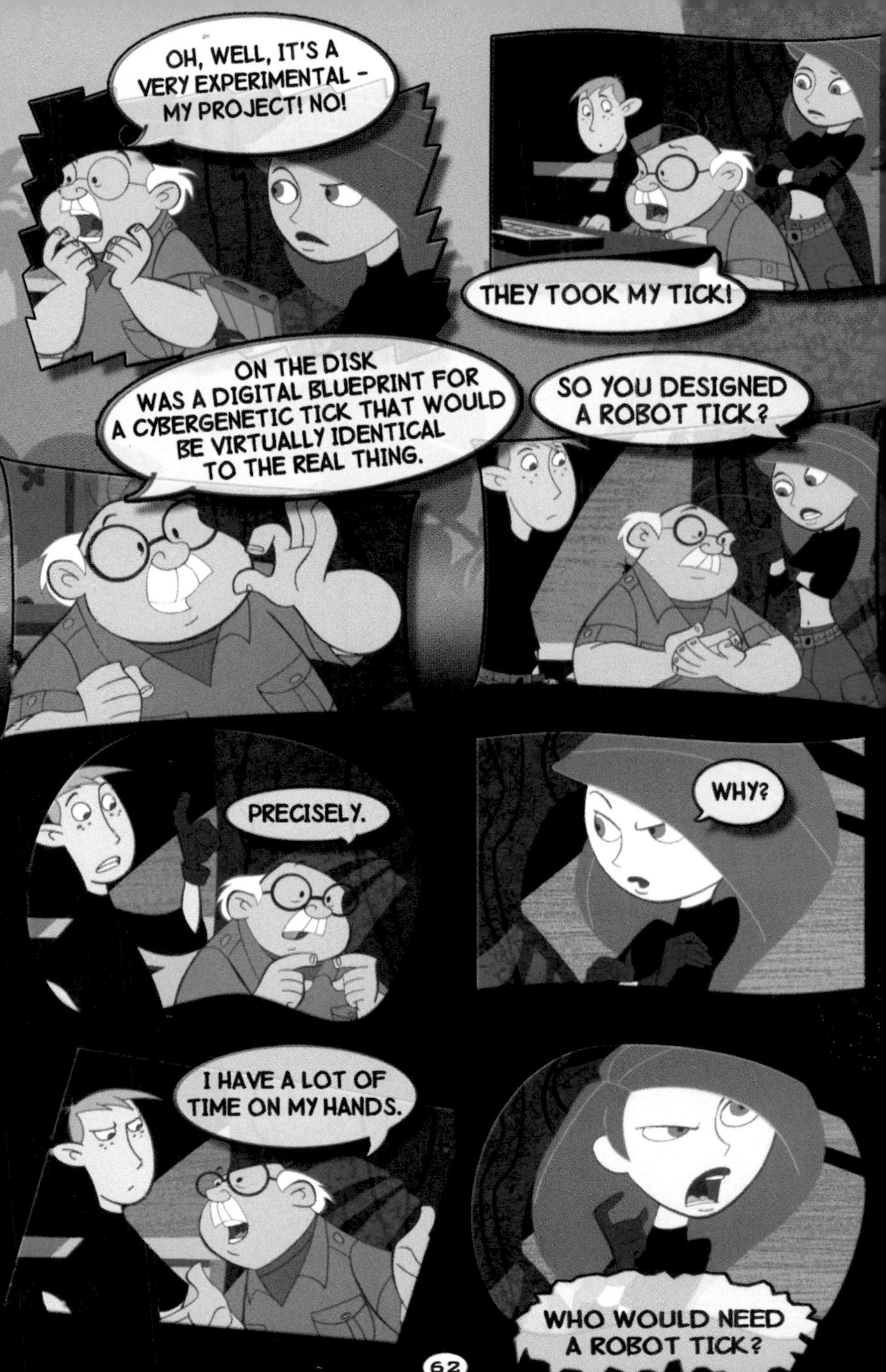
OH, WELL, IT'S A VERY EXPERIMENTAL - MY PROJECT! NO!
THEY TOOK MY TICK!
ON THE DISK WAS A DIGITAL BLUEPRINT FOR A CYBERGENETIC TICK THAT WOULD BE VIRTUALLY IDENTICAL TO THE REAL THING.
SO YOU DESIGNED A ROBOT TICK?
PRECISELY.
WHY?
I HAVE A LOT OF TIME ON MY HANDS.
WHO WOULD NEED A ROBOT TICK?

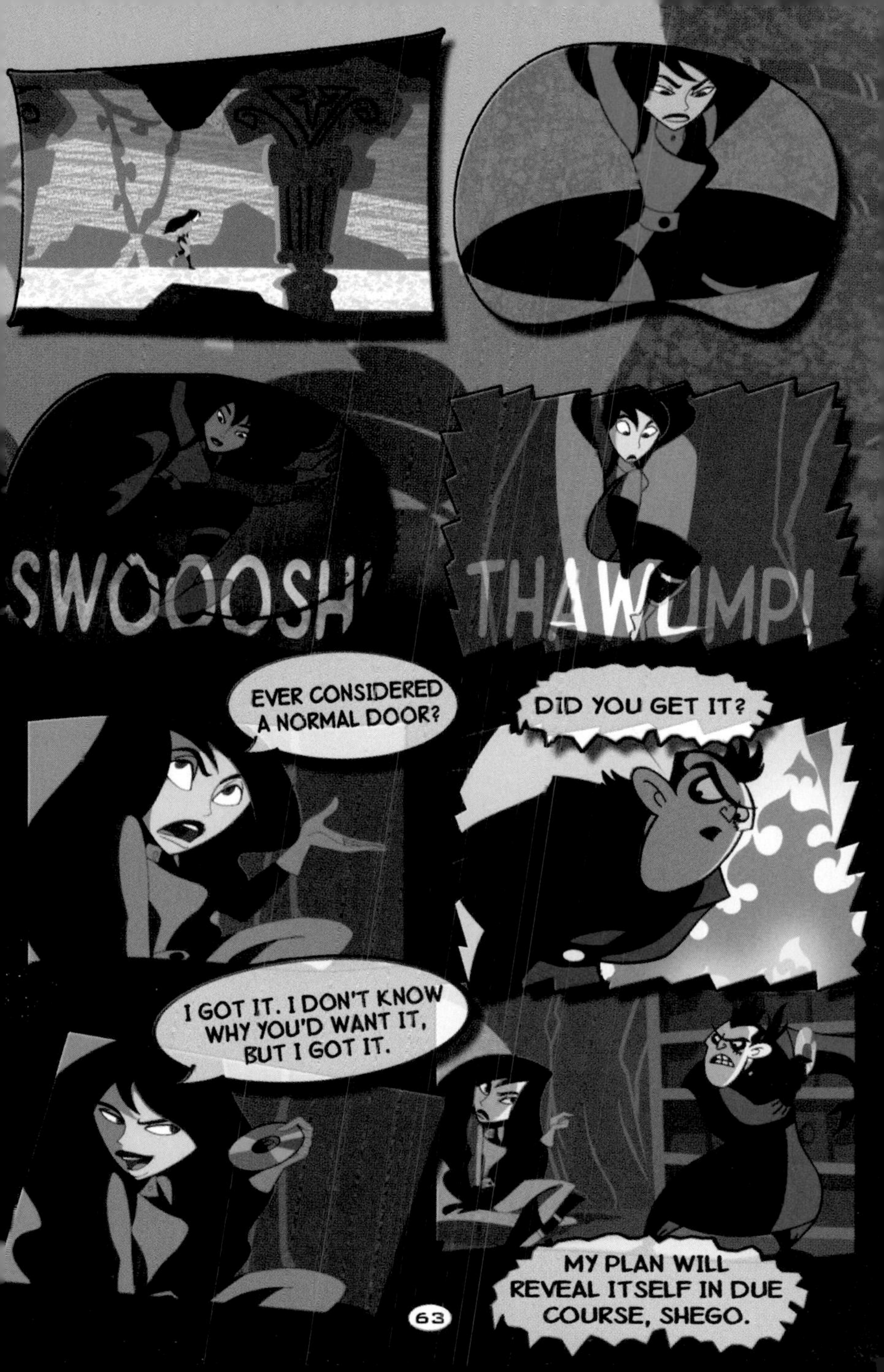
SWOOOSH!
THAWUMP!
EVER CONSIDERED A NORMAL DOOR?
DID YOU GET IT?
I GOT IT. I DON'T KNOW WHY YOU'D WANT IT, BUT I GOT IT.
MY PLAN WILL REVEAL ITSELF IN DUE COURSE, SHEGO.

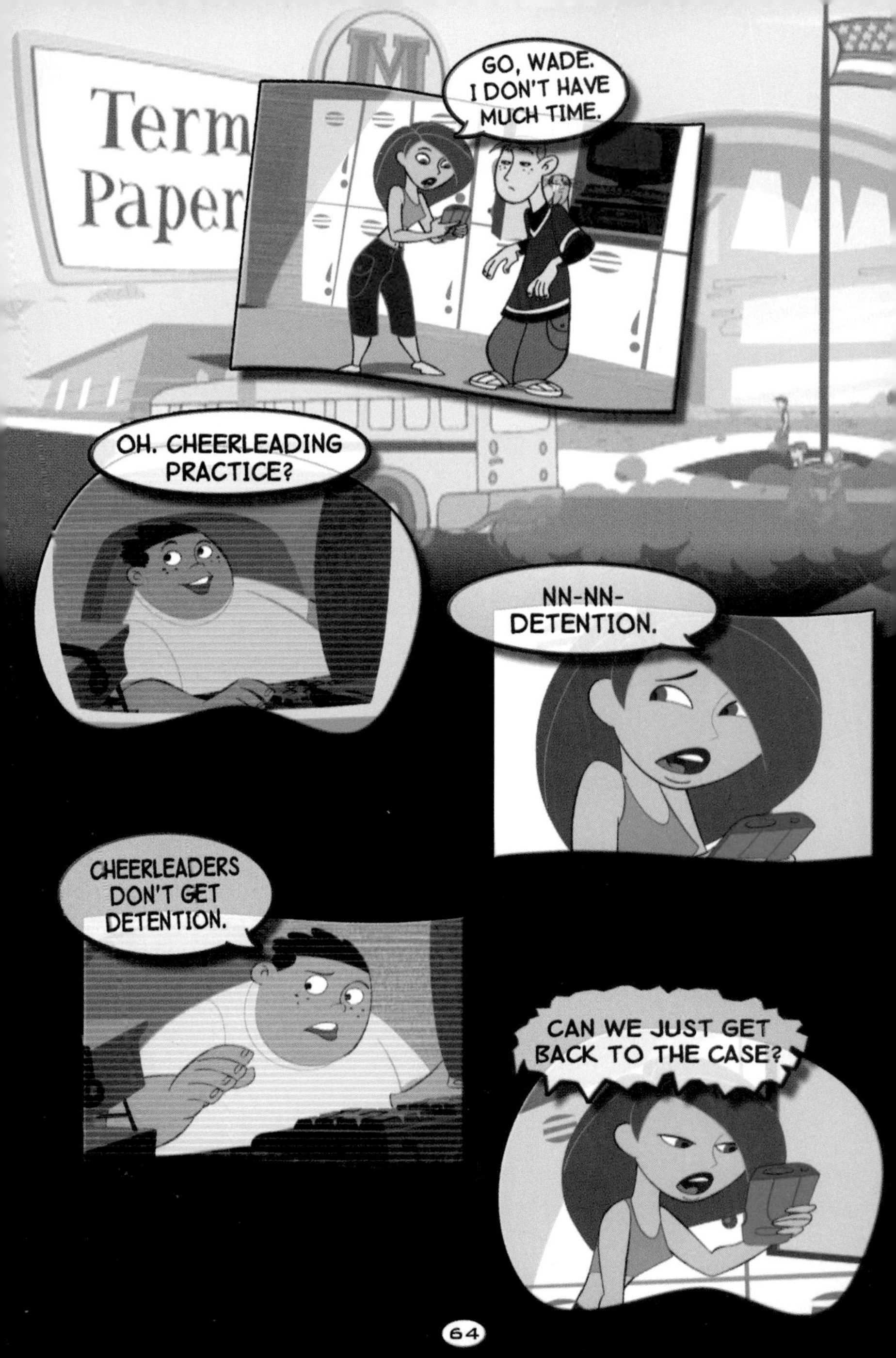
Term Paper
GO, WADE. I DON'T HAVE MUCH TIME.
OH. CHEERLEADING PRACTICE?
NN-NN- DETENTION.
CHEERLEADERS DON'T GET DETENTION.
CAN WE JUST GET BACK TO THE CASE?

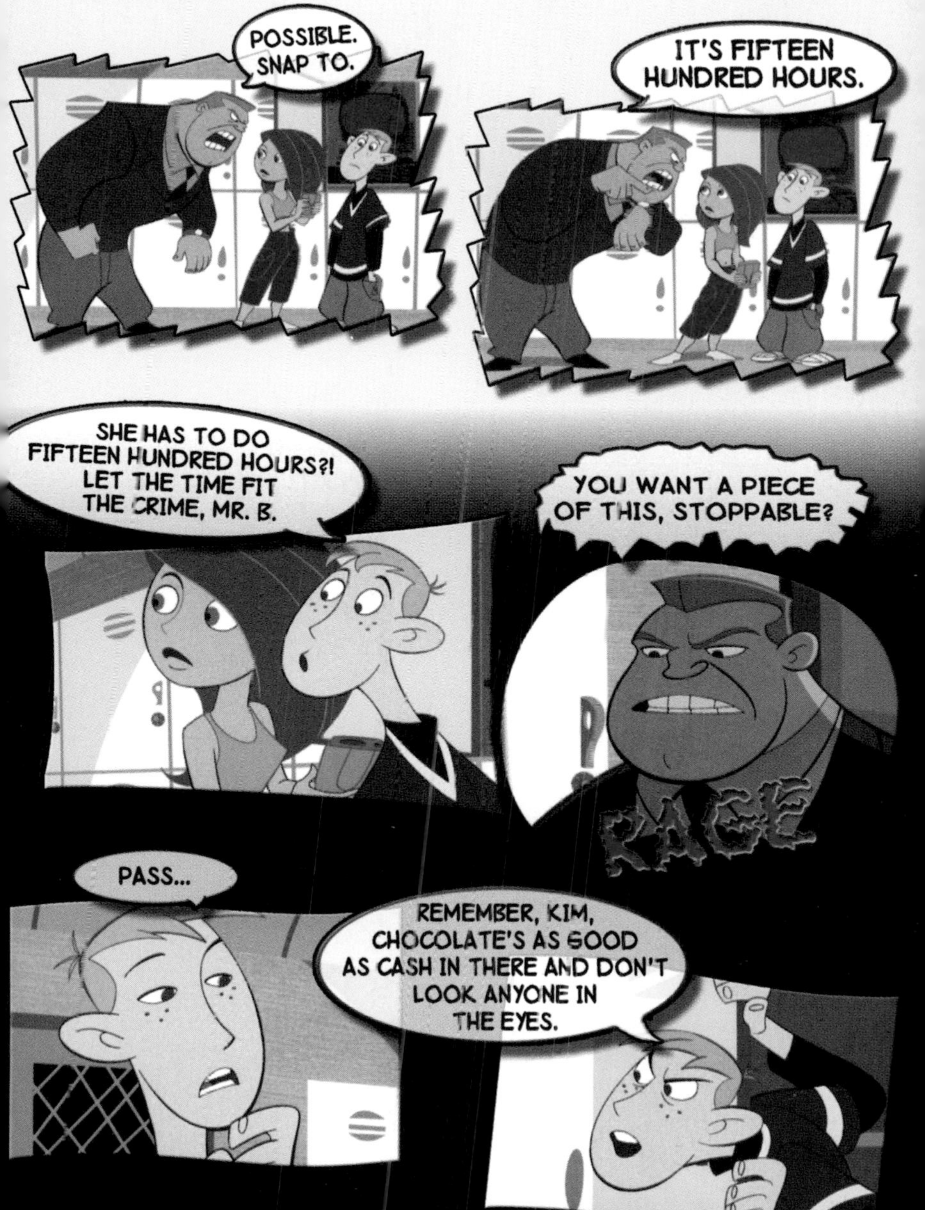
POSSIBLE. SNAP TO.
IT'S FIFTEEN HUNDRED HOURS.
SHE HAS TO DO FIFTEEN HUNDRED HOURS?! LET THE TIME FIT THE CRIME, MR. B.
YOU WANT A PIECE OF THIS, STOPPABLE?
RAGE
PASS...
REMEMBER, KIM, CHOCOLATE'S AS GOOD AS CASH IN THERE AND DON'T LOOK ANYONE IN THE EYES.

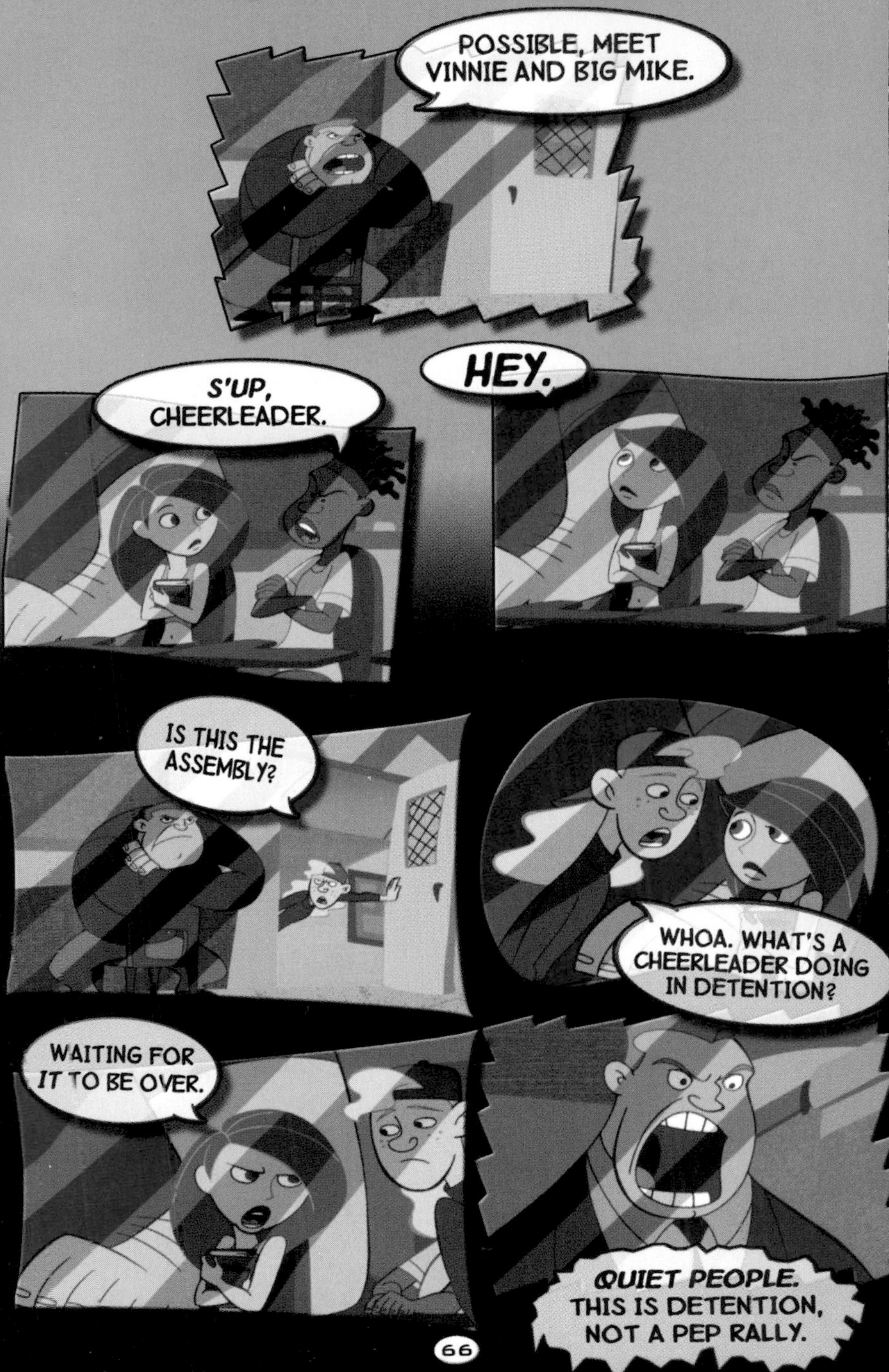
POSSIBLE, MEET VINNIE AND BIG MIKE.
S'UP, CHEERLEADER.
HEY.
IS THIS THE ASSEMBLY?
WHOA. WHAT'S A CHEERLEADER DOING IN DETENTION?
WAITING FOR IT TO BE OVER.
QUIET PEOPLE. THIS IS DETENTION, NOT A PEP RALLY.

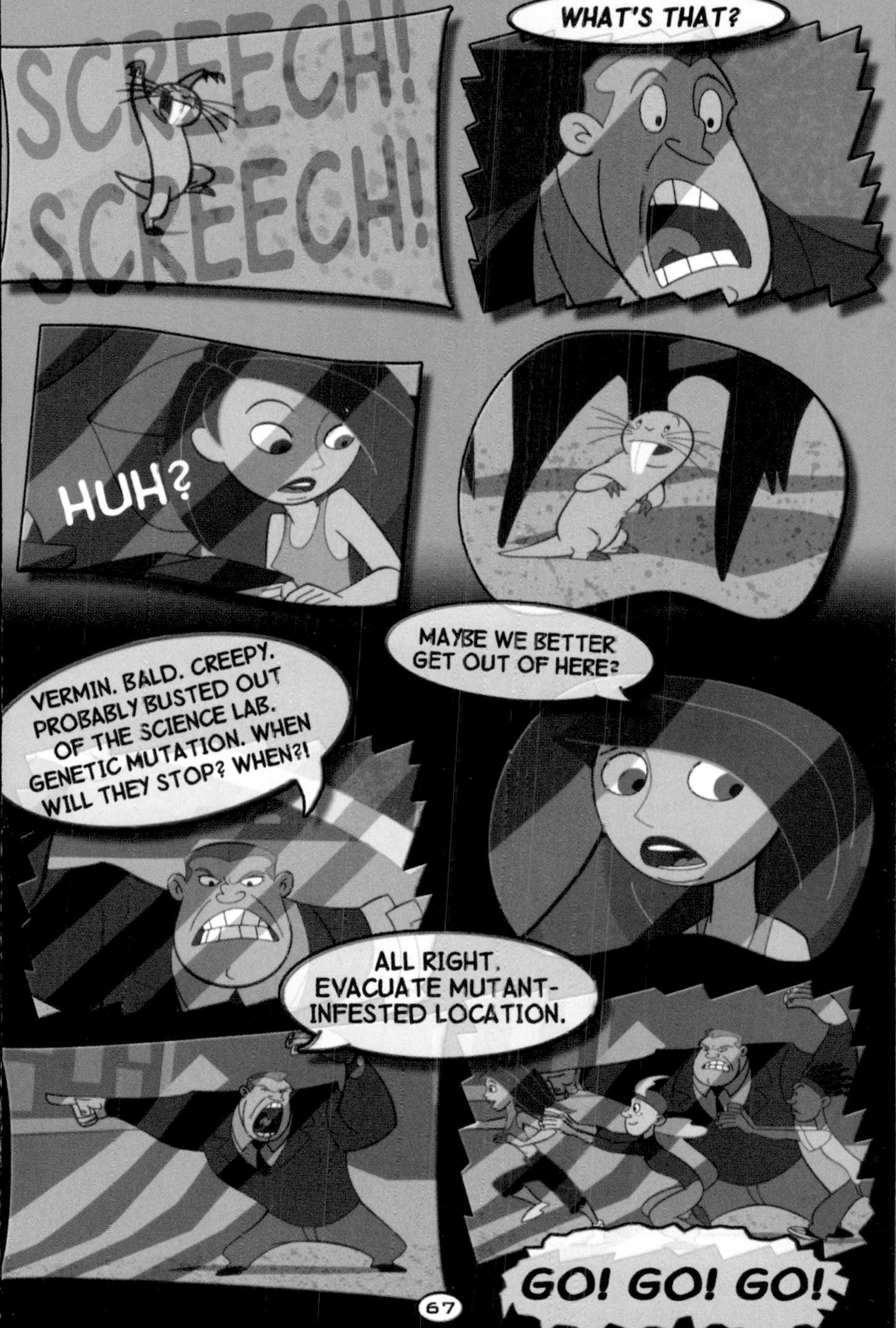
SCREECH! SCREECH!
WHAT'S THAT?
HUH?
VERMIN. BALD. CREEPY. PROBABLY BUSTED OUT OF THE SCIENCE LAB. GENETIC MUTATION. WHEN WILL THEY STOP? WHEN?!
MAYBE WE BETTER GET OUT OF HERE?
ALL RIGHT. EVACUATE MUTANT-INFESTED LOCATION.
GO! GO! GO!

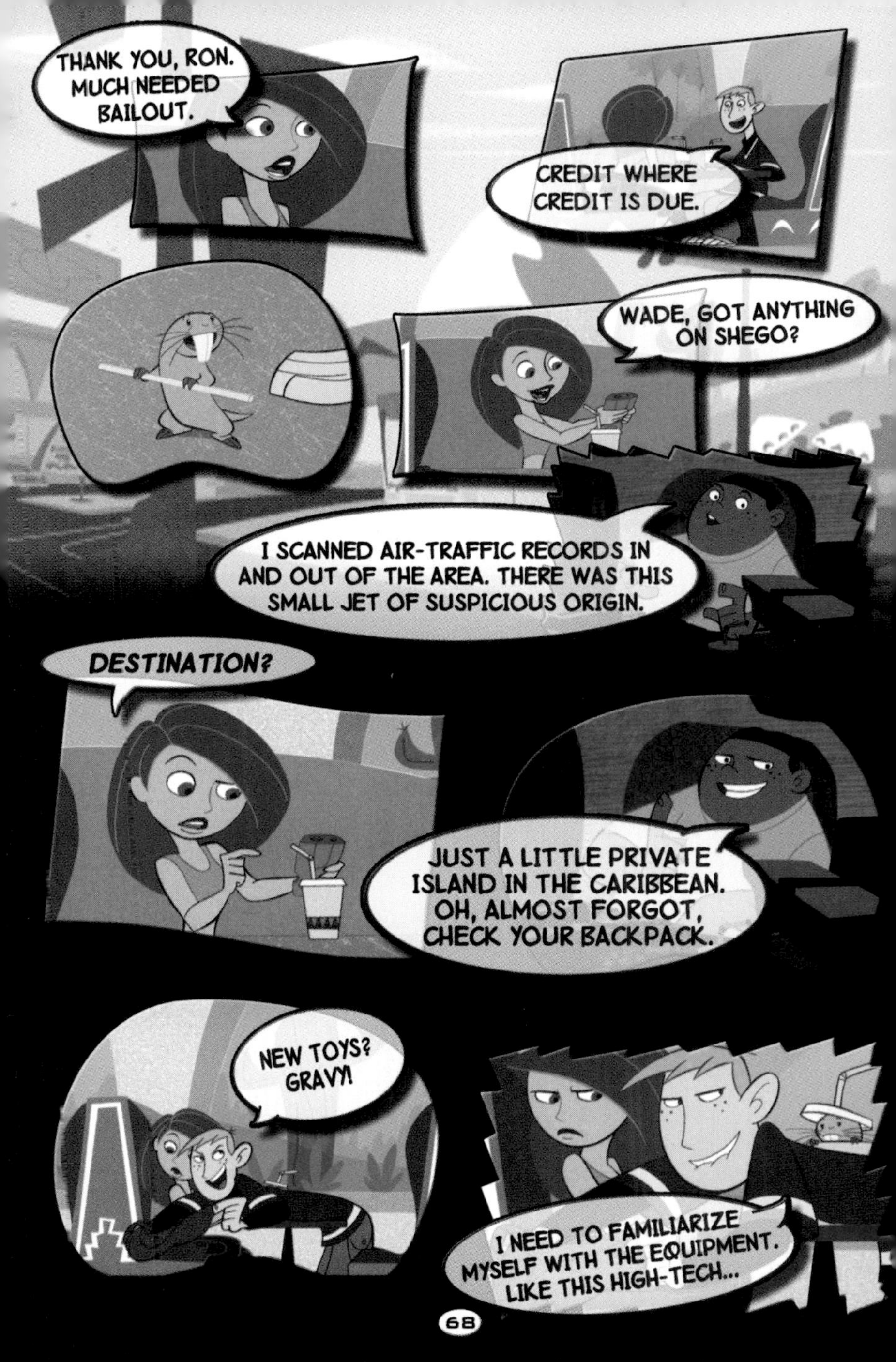
THANK YOU, RON. MUCH NEEDED BAILOUT.
CREDIT WHERE CREDIT IS DUE.
WADE, GOT ANYTHING ON SHEGO?
I SCANNED AIR-TRAFFIC RECORDS IN AND OUT OF THE AREA. THERE WAS THIS SMALL JET OF SUSPICIOUS ORIGIN.
DESTINATION?
JUST A LITTLE PRIVATE ISLAND IN THE CARIBBEAN. OH, ALMOST FORGOT, CHECK YOUR BACKPACK.
NEW TOYS? GRAVY!
I NEED TO FAMILIARIZE MYSELF WITH THE EQUIPMENT. LIKE THIS HIGH-TECH...

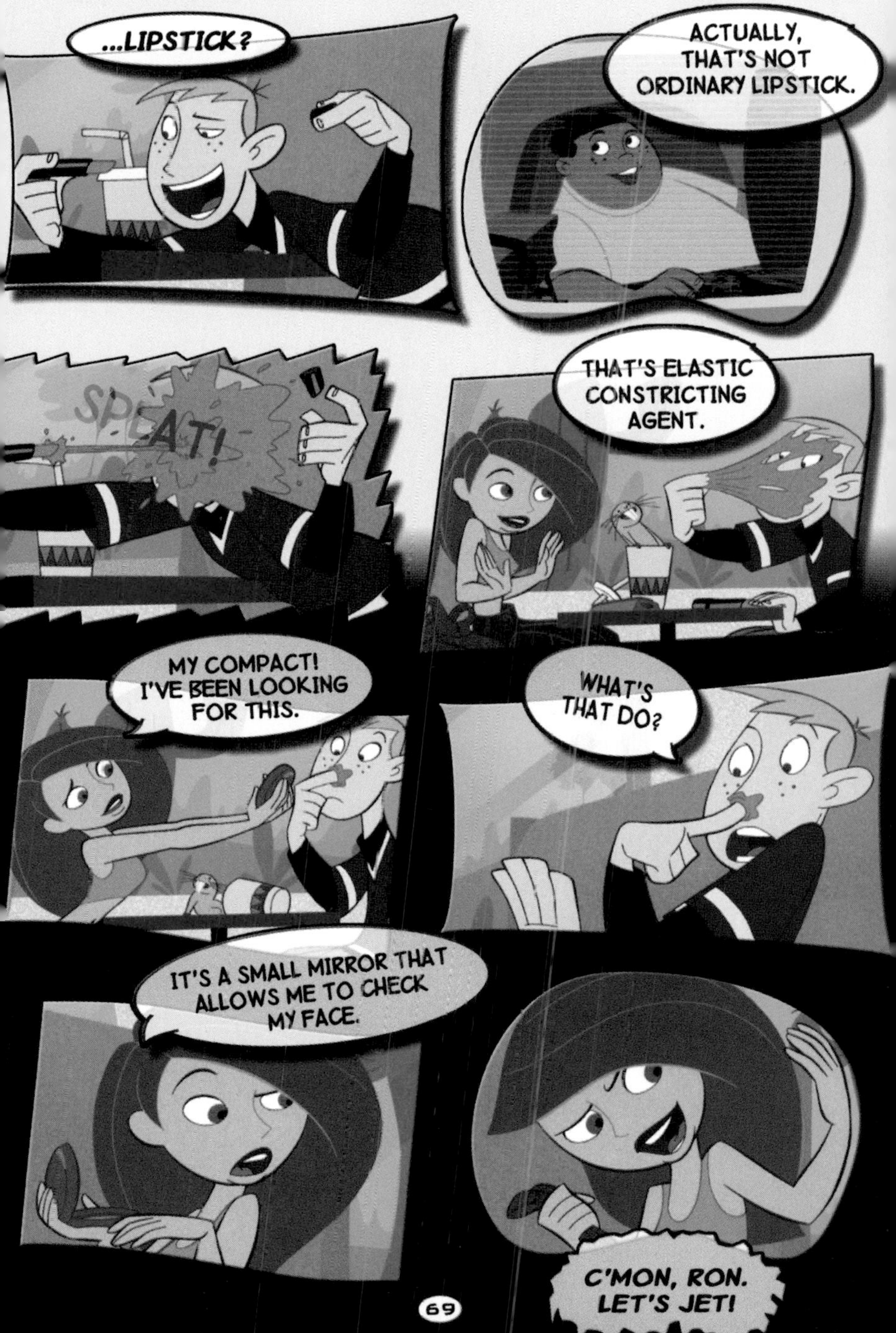
...LIPSTICK?
ACTUALLY, THAT'S NOT ORDINARY LIPSTICK.
SPLAT!
THAT'S ELASTIC CONSTRICTING AGENT.
MY COMPACT! I'VE BEEN LOOKING FOR THIS.
WHAT'S THAT DO?
IT'S A SMALL MIRROR THAT ALLOWS ME TO CHECK MY FACE.
C'MON, RON. LET'S JET!

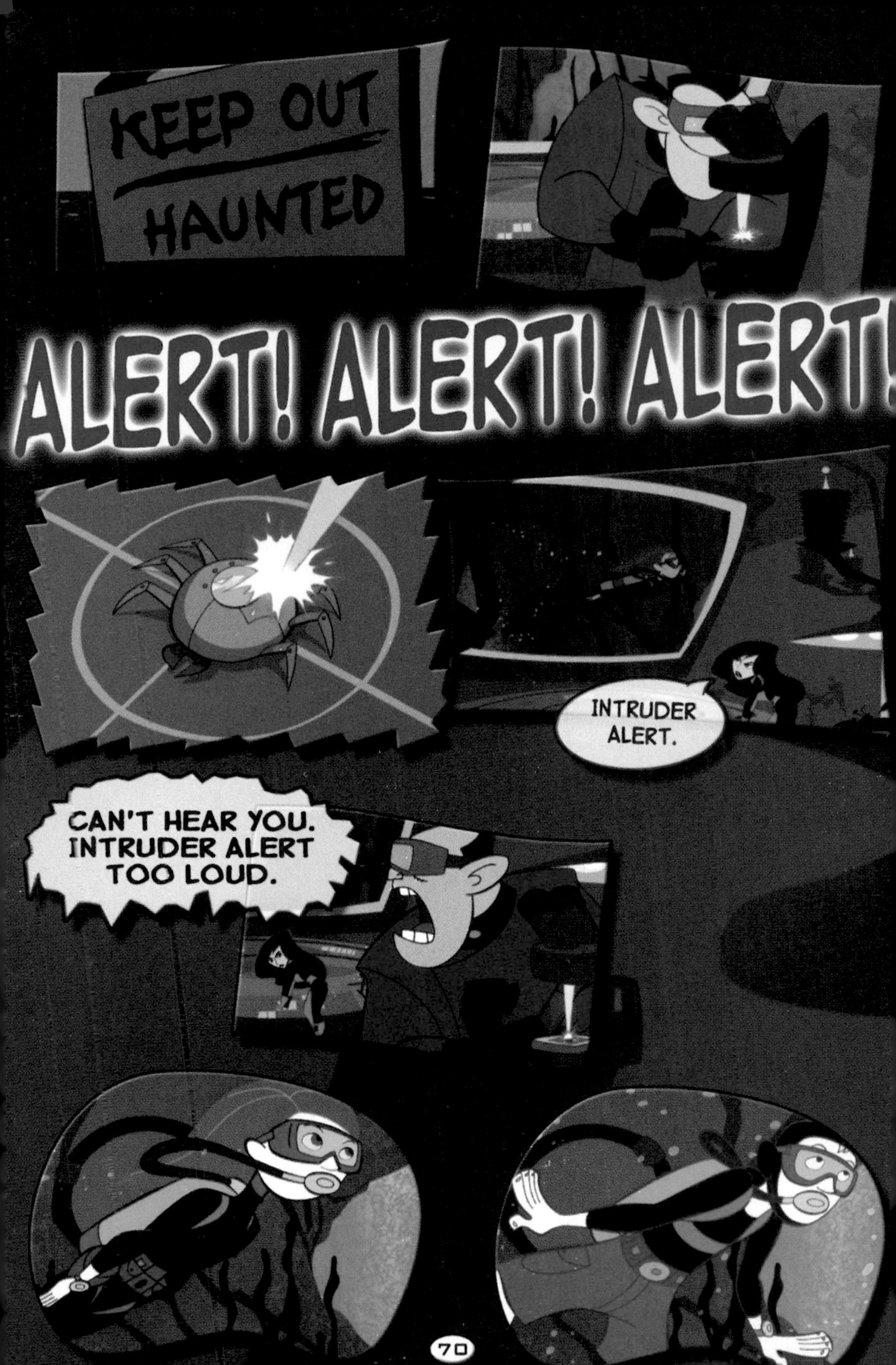
KEEP OUT
HAUNTED
ALERT! ALERT! ALERT!
INTRUDER ALERT.
CAN'T HEAR YOU. INTRUDER ALERT TOO LOUD.

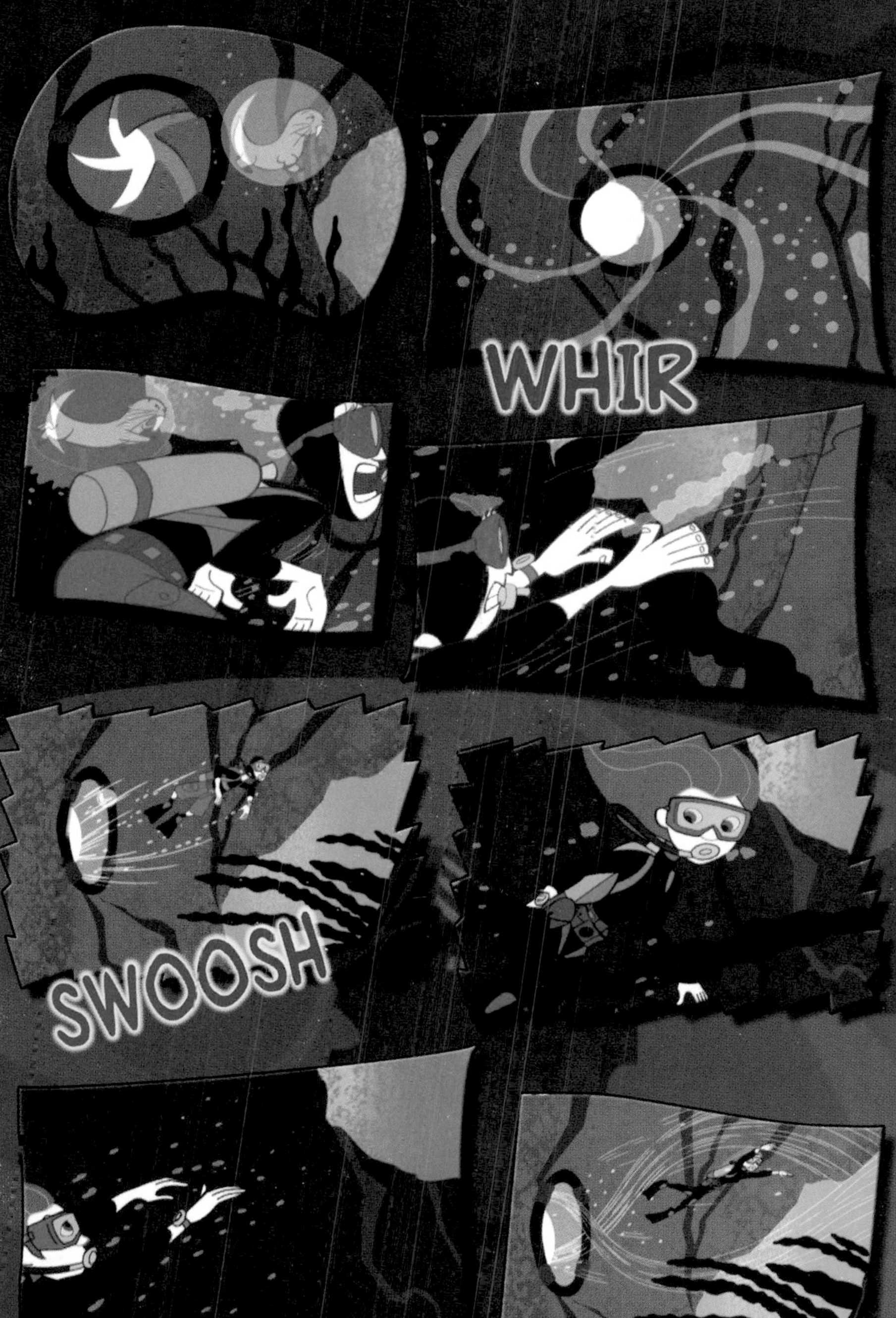
WHIR
SWOOSH

WELL, IF IT ISN'T THE WORLD-FAMOUS TEEN HERO KIM POSSIBLE AND HER CHUM...

ENOUGH CHITCHAT. MY PETS ARE FAMISHED. PERHAPS YOU TWO COULD STAY—

FOR LUNCH?

I WASN'T GOING TO SAY THAT.

OH DUDE, YOU WERE SO "FOR LUNCH."

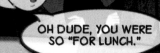

FINE! YES! THEN STAY FOR LUNCH!

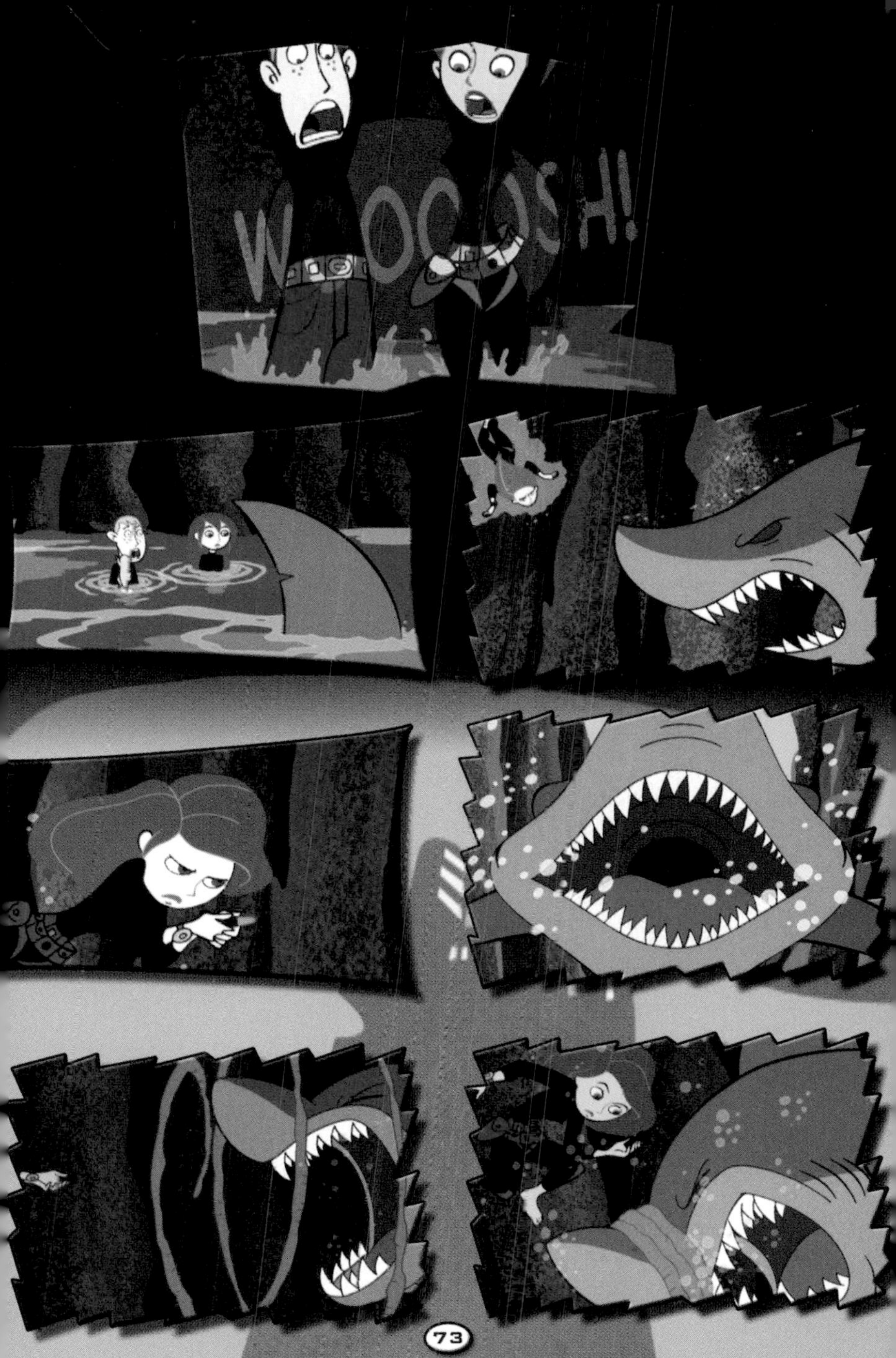
WOOOSH!

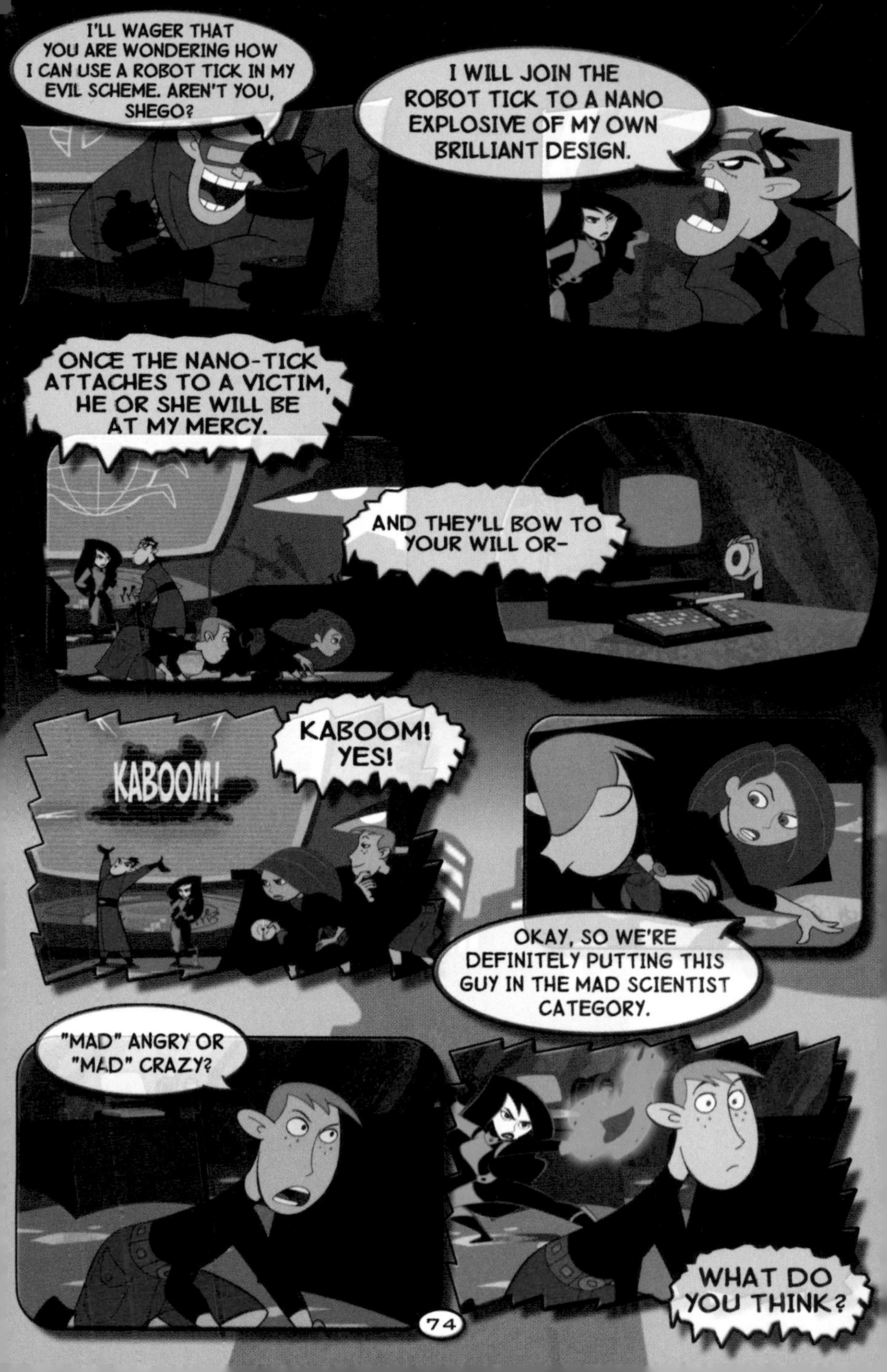
I'LL WAGER THAT YOU ARE WONDERING HOW I CAN USE A ROBOT TICK IN MY EVIL SCHEME. AREN'T YOU, SHEGO?
I WILL JOIN THE ROBOT TICK TO A NANO EXPLOSIVE OF MY OWN BRILLIANT DESIGN.
ONCE THE NANO-TICK ATTACHES TO A VICTIM, HE OR SHE WILL BE AT MY MERCY.
AND THEY'LL BOW TO YOUR WILL OR-
KABOOM!
KABOOM! YES!
OKAY, SO WE'RE DEFINITELY PUTTING THIS GUY IN THE MAD SCIENTIST CATEGORY.
"MAD" ANGRY OR "MAD" CRAZY?
WHAT DO YOU THINK?

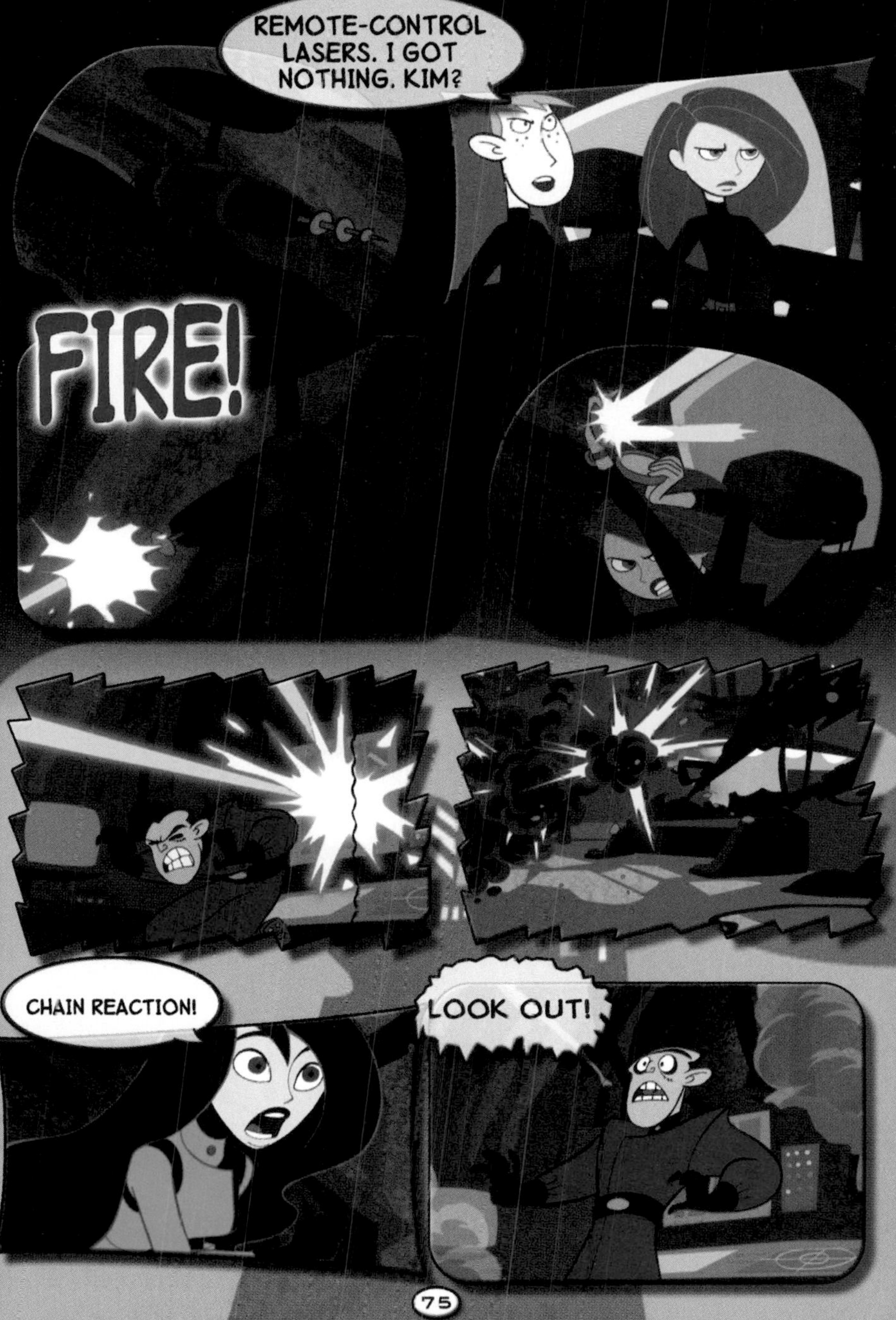
REMOTE-CONTROL LASERS. I GOT NOTHING. KIM?
FIRE!
CHAIN REACTION!
LOOK OUT!

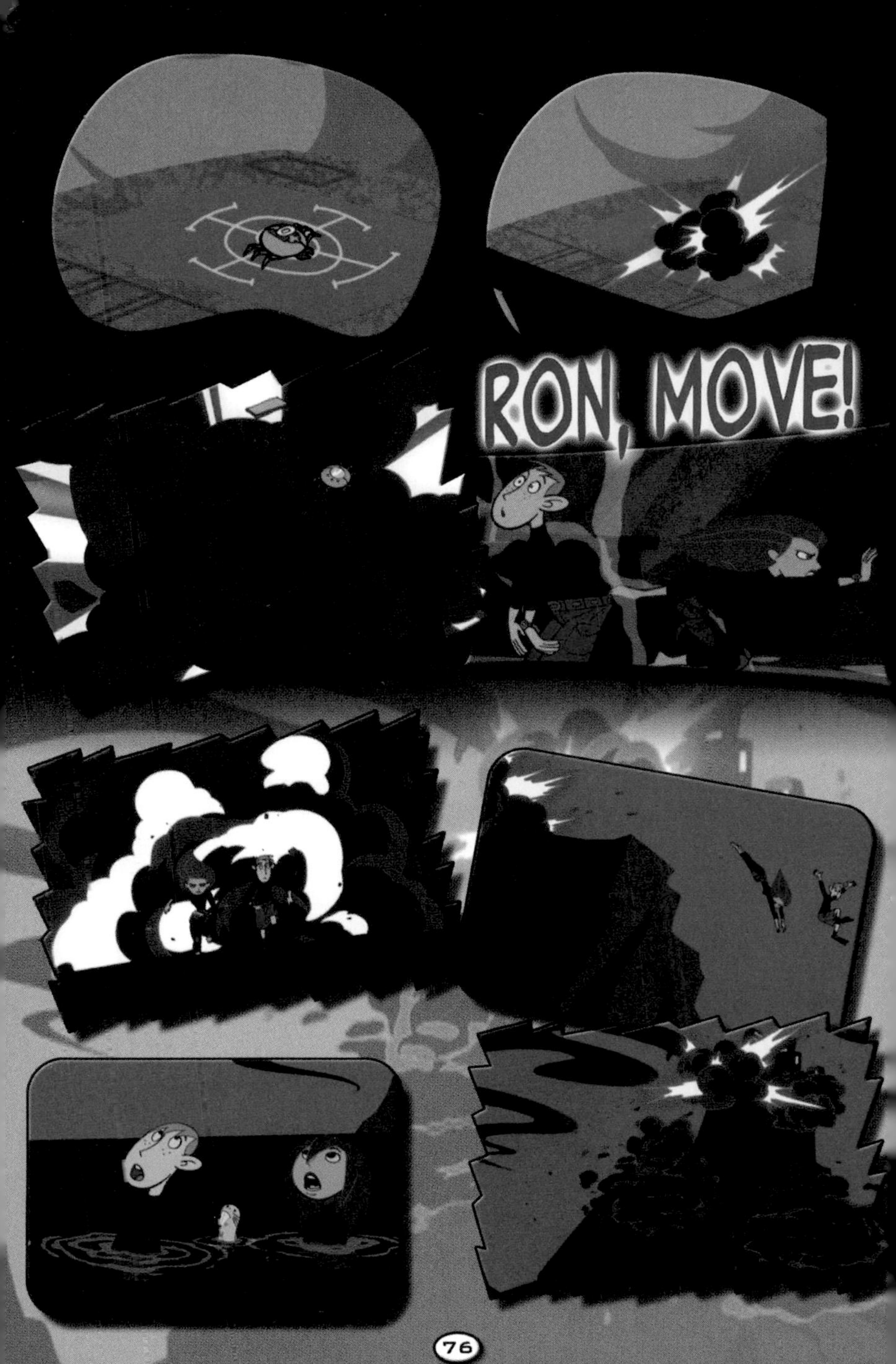
RON, MOVE!

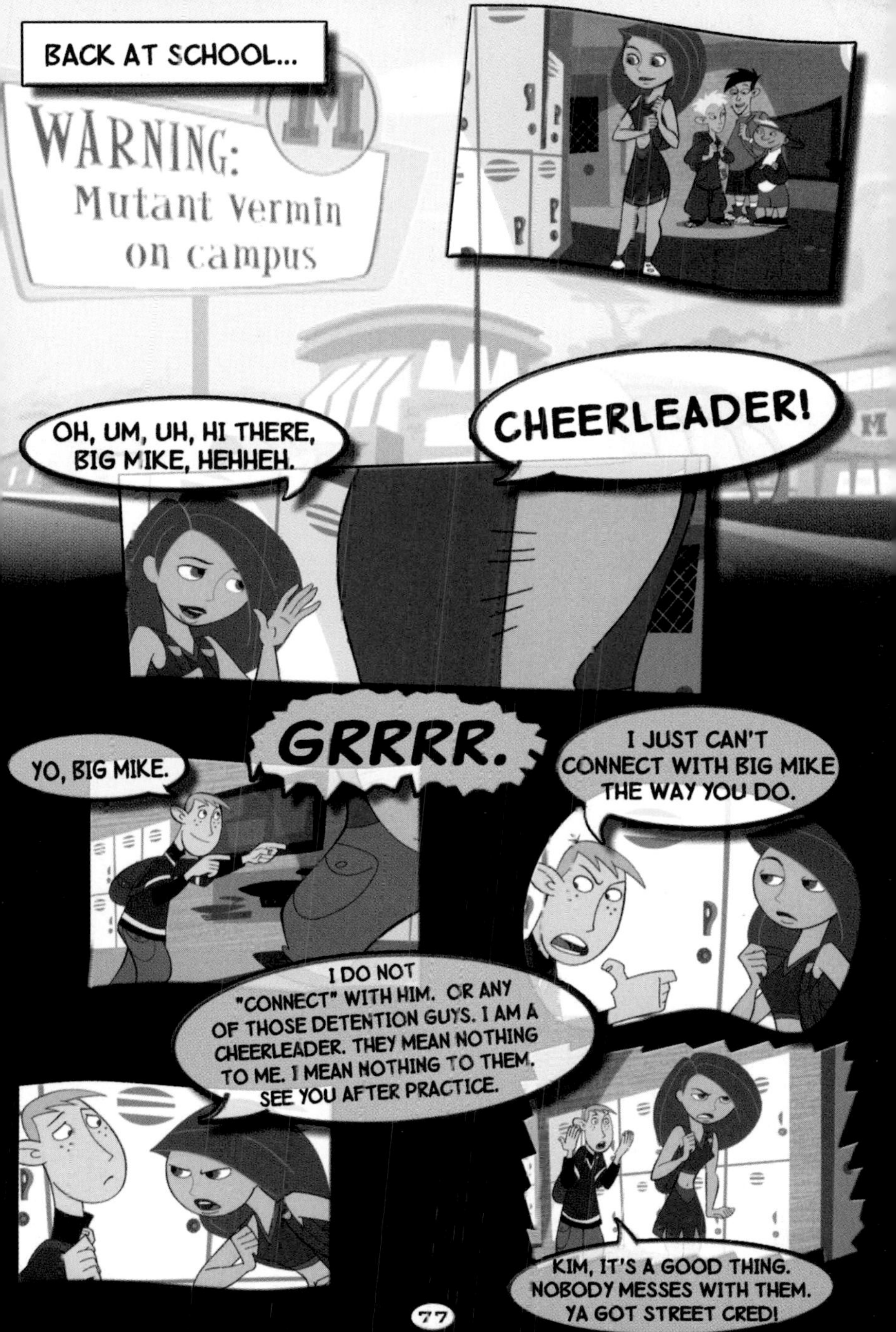
BACK AT SCHOOL...
WARNING: Mutant Vermin on campus
OH, UM, UH, HI THERE, BIG MIKE, HEHHEH.
CHEERLEADER!
YO, BIG MIKE.
GRRRR.
I JUST CAN'T CONNECT WITH BIG MIKE THE WAY YOU DO.
I DO NOT "CONNECT" WITH HIM. OR ANY OF THOSE DETENTION GUYS. I AM A CHEERLEADER. THEY MEAN NOTHING TO ME. I MEAN NOTHING TO THEM. SEE YOU AFTER PRACTICE.
KIM, IT'S A GOOD THING. NOBODY MESSES WITH THEM. YA GOT STREET CRED!

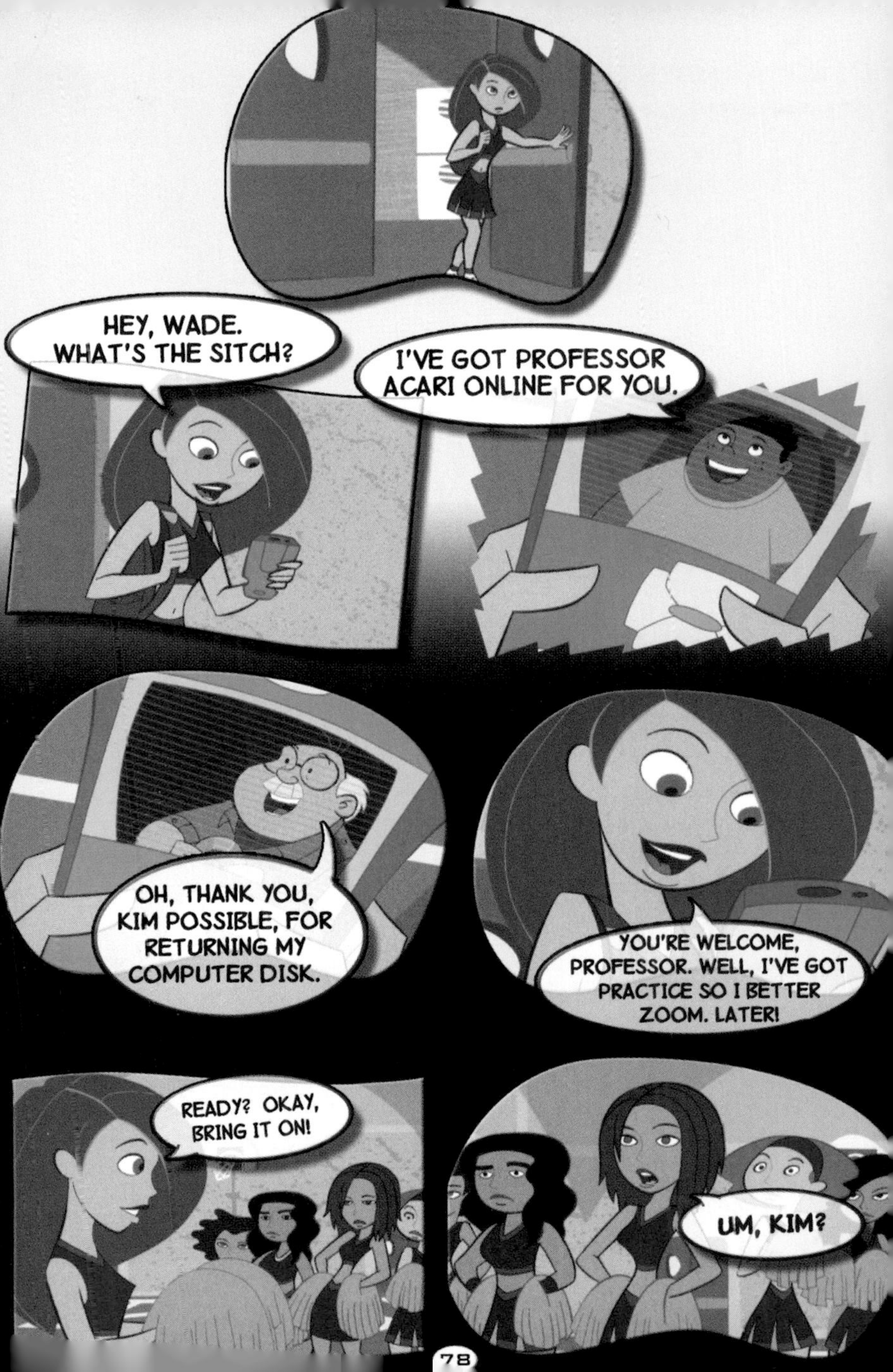
HEY, WADE. WHAT'S THE SITCH?
I'VE GOT PROFESSOR ACARI ONLINE FOR YOU.
OH, THANK YOU, KIM POSSIBLE, FOR RETURNING MY COMPUTER DISK.
YOU'RE WELCOME, PROFESSOR. WELL, I'VE GOT PRACTICE SO I BETTER ZOOM. LATER!
READY? OKAY, BRING IT ON!
UM, KIM?

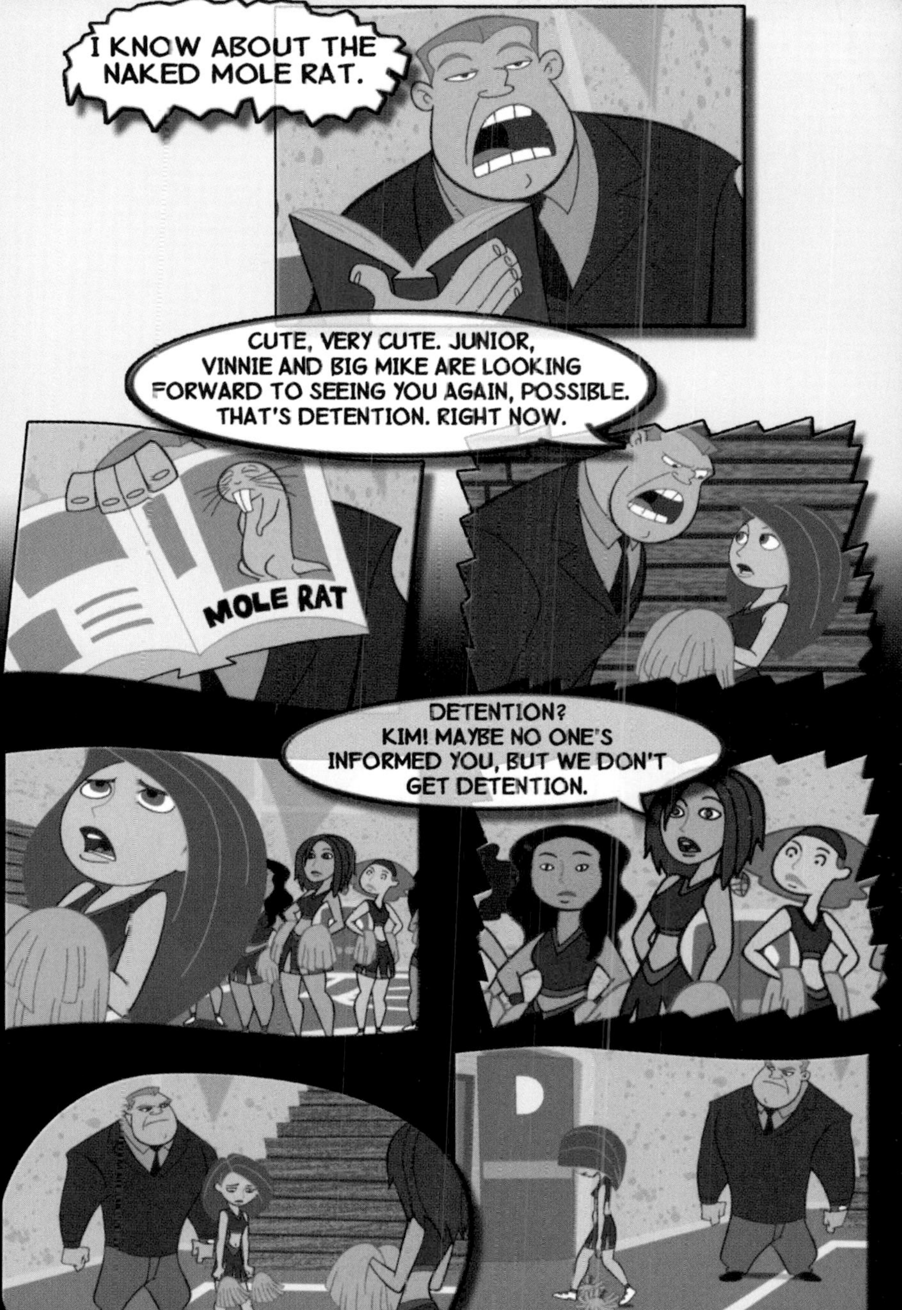
I KNOW ABOUT THE NAKED MOLE RAT.
CUTE, VERY CUTE. JUNIOR, VINNIE AND BIG MIKE ARE LOOKING FORWARD TO SEEING YOU AGAIN, POSSIBLE. THAT'S DETENTION. RIGHT NOW.
MOLE RAT
DETENTION? KIM! MAYBE NO ONE'S INFORMED YOU, BUT WE DON'T GET DETENTION.

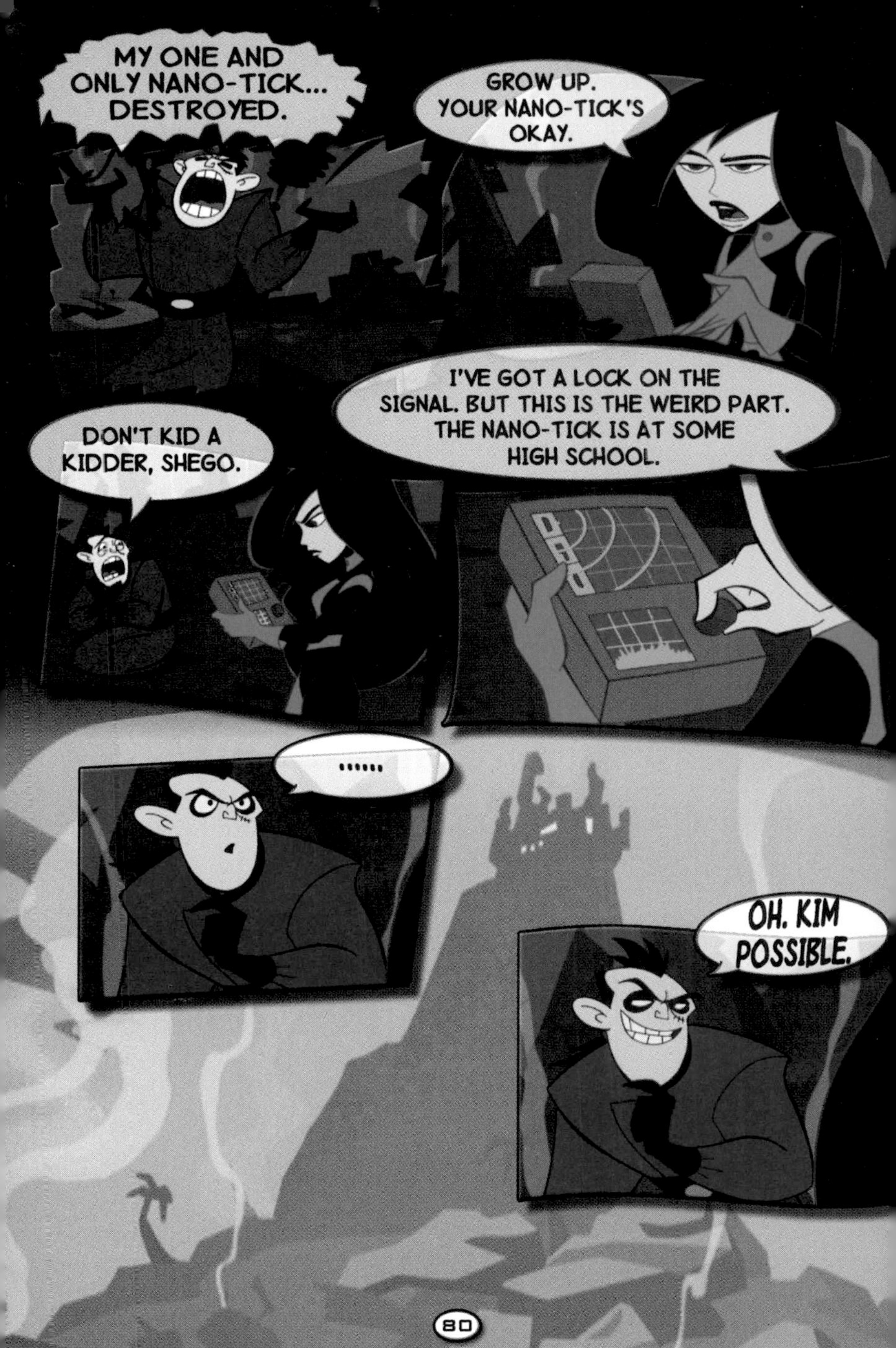
MY ONE AND ONLY NANO-TICK... DESTROYED.
GROW UP. YOUR NANO-TICK'S OKAY.
DON'T KID A KIDDER, SHEGO.
I'VE GOT A LOCK ON THE SIGNAL. BUT THIS IS THE WEIRD PART. THE NANO-TICK IS AT SOME HIGH SCHOOL.
......
OH. KIM POSSIBLE.

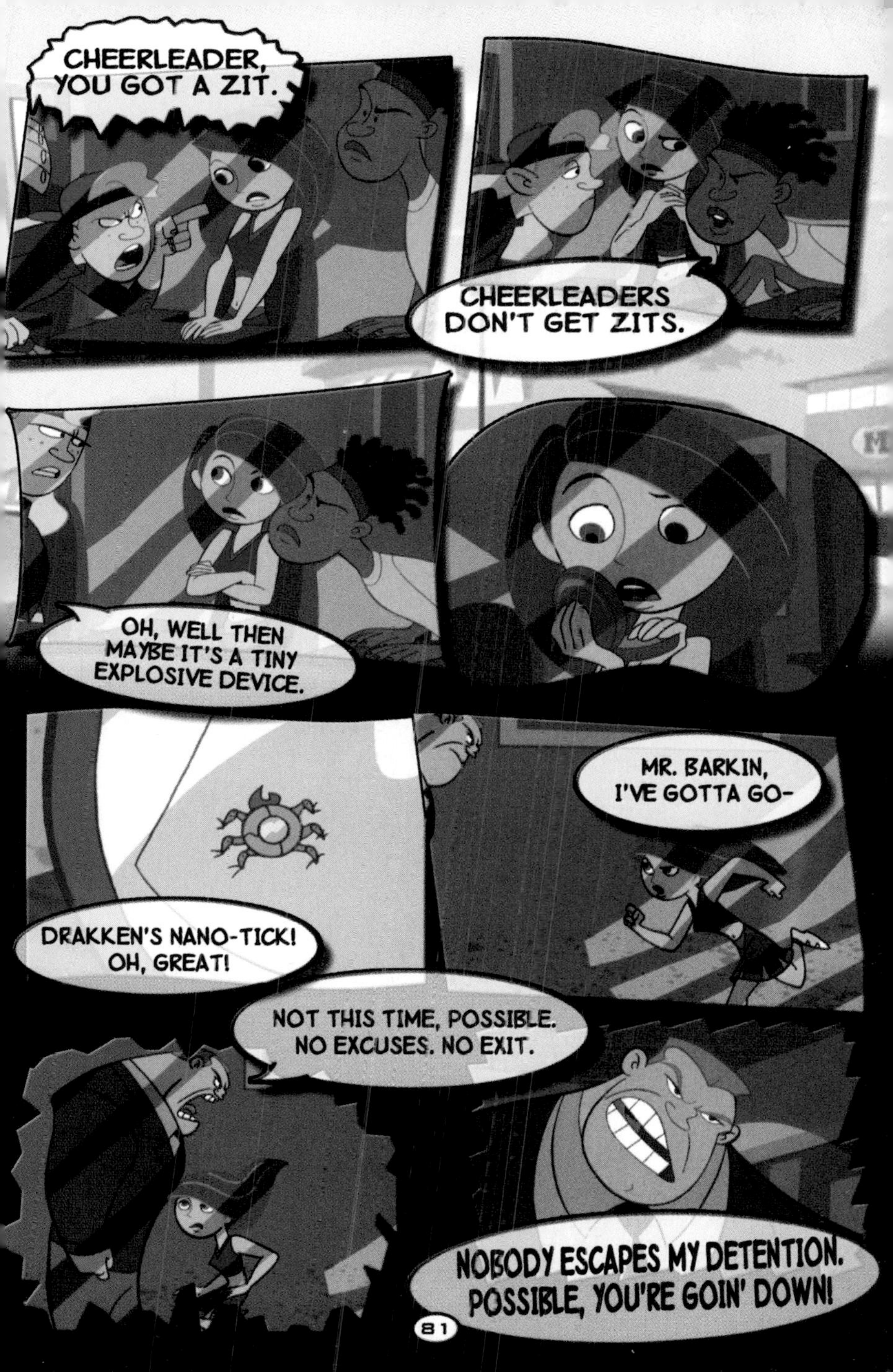
CHEERLEADER, YOU GOT A ZIT.
CHEERLEADERS DON'T GET ZITS.
OH, WELL THEN MAYBE IT'S A TINY EXPLOSIVE DEVICE.
DRAKKEN'S NANO-TICK! OH, GREAT!
MR. BARKIN, I'VE GOTTA GO-
NOT THIS TIME, POSSIBLE. NO EXCUSES. NO EXIT.
NOBODY ESCAPES MY DETENTION. POSSIBLE, YOU'RE GOIN' DOWN!

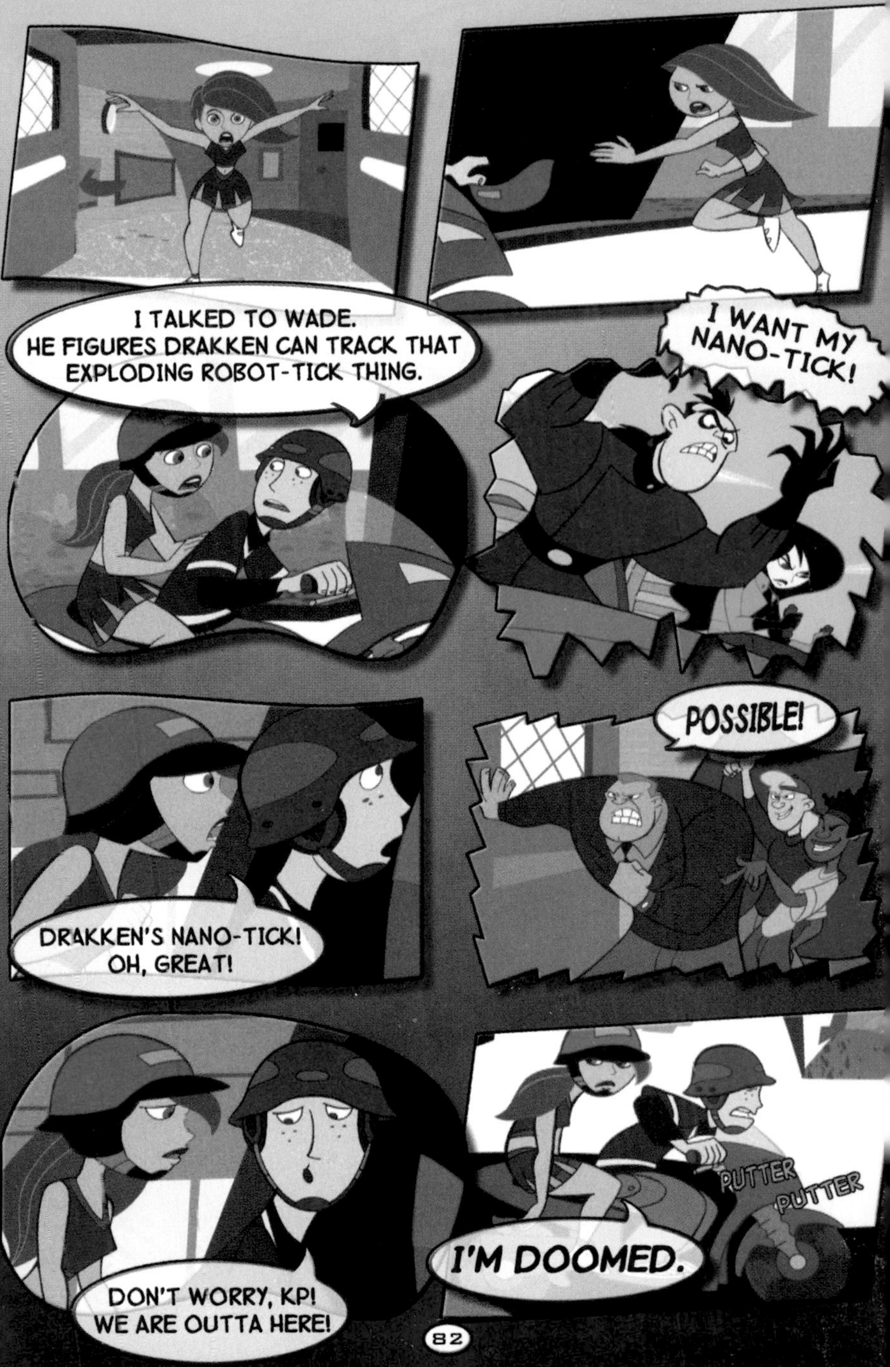
I TALKED TO WADE.
HE FIGURES DRAKKEN CAN TRACK THAT EXPLODING ROBOT-TICK THING.
I WANT MY NANO-TICK!
DRAKKEN'S NANO-TICK! OH, GREAT!
POSSIBLE!
DON'T WORRY, KP! WE ARE OUTTA HERE!
I'M DOOMED.
PUTTER
PUTTER

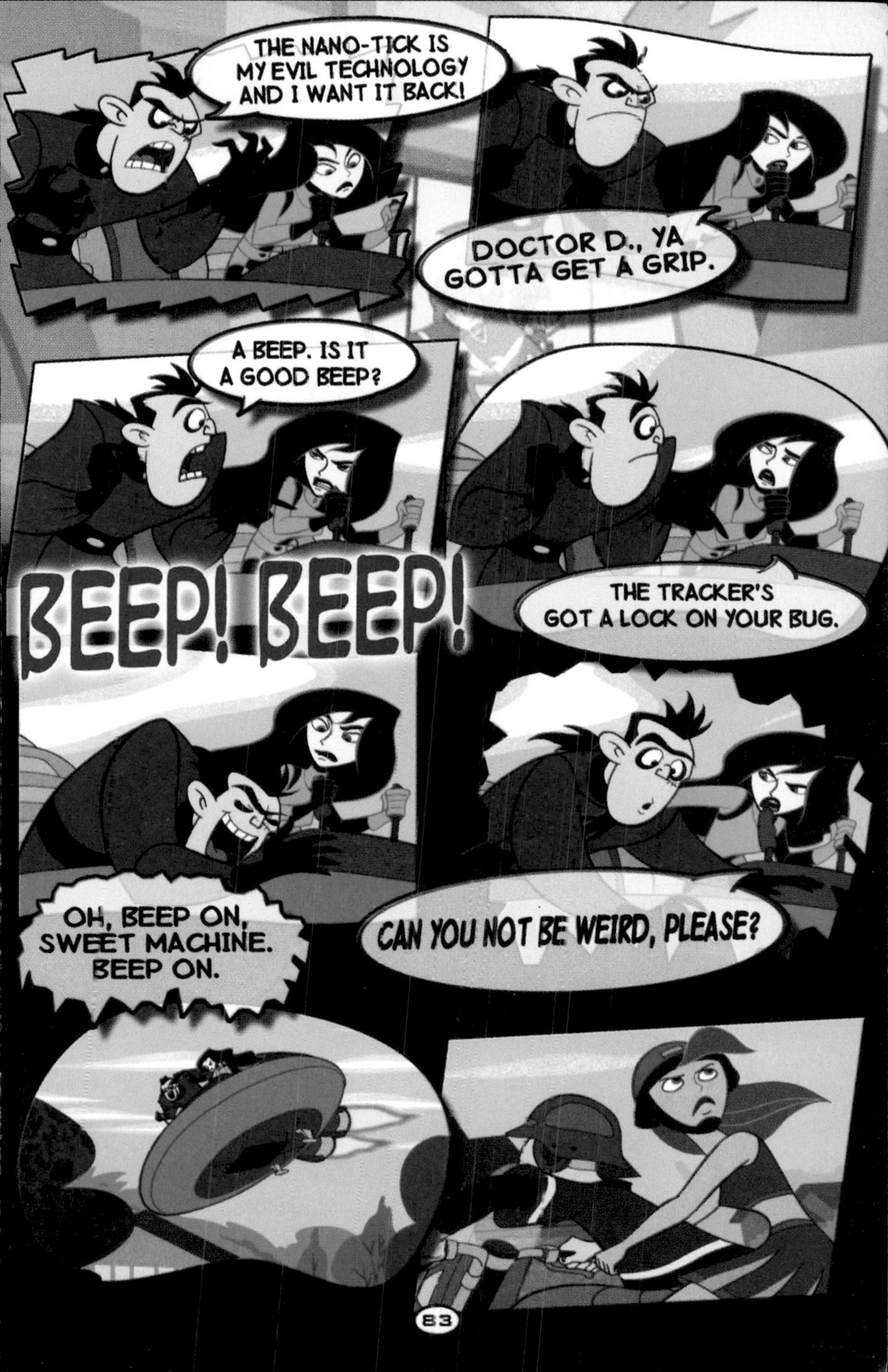
THE NANO-TICK IS MY EVIL TECHNOLOGY AND I WANT IT BACK!
DOCTOR D., YA GOTTA GET A GRIP.
A BEEP. IS IT A GOOD BEEP?
BEEP! BEEP!
THE TRACKER'S GOT A LOCK ON YOUR BUG.
OH, BEEP ON, SWEET MACHINE. BEEP ON.
CAN YOU NOT BE WEIRD, PLEASE?

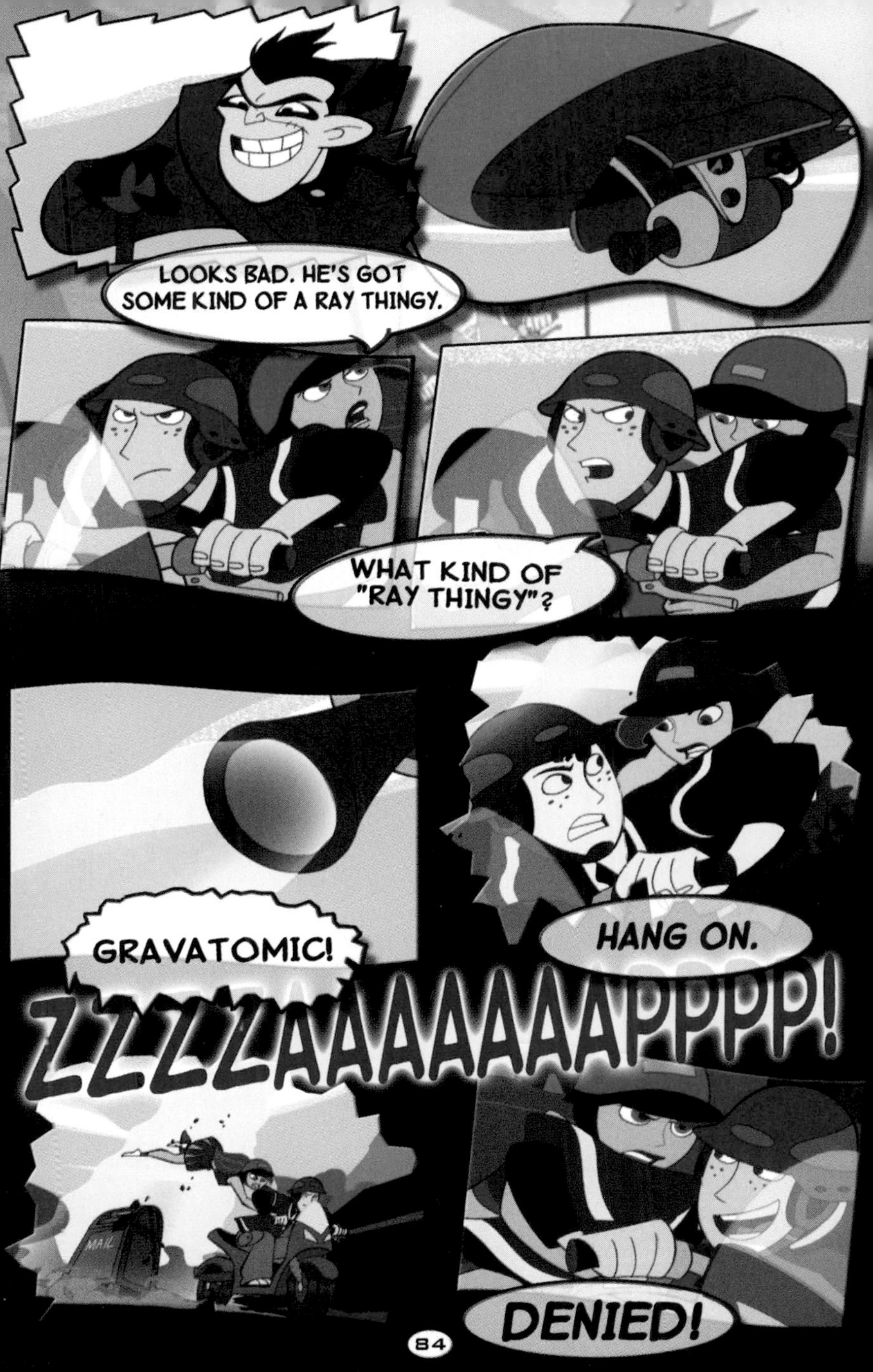
LOOKS BAD. HE'S GOT SOME KIND OF A RAY THINGY.
WHAT KIND OF "RAY THINGY"?
GRAVATOMIC!
HANG ON.
ZZZZAAAAAAAAPPPP!
MAIL
DENIED!

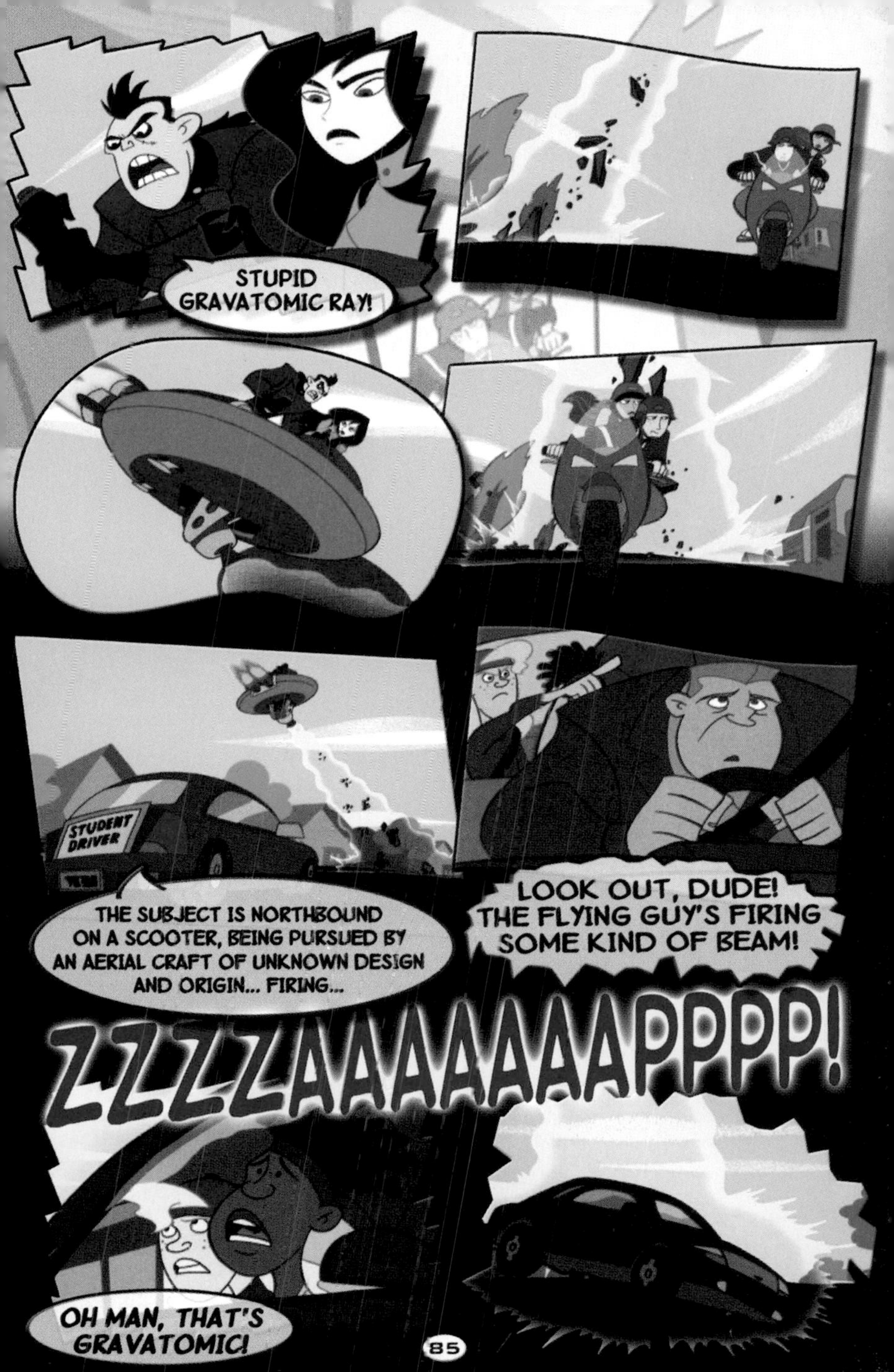

STUPID GRAVATOMIC RAY!
STUDENT DRIVER
THE SUBJECT IS NORTHBOUND ON A SCOOTER, BEING PURSUED BY AN AERIAL CRAFT OF UNKNOWN DESIGN AND ORIGIN... FIRING...
LOOK OUT, DUDE! THE FLYING GUY'S FIRING SOME KIND OF BEAM!
ZZZZAAAAAAAPPPP!
OH MAN, THAT'S GRAVATOMIC!

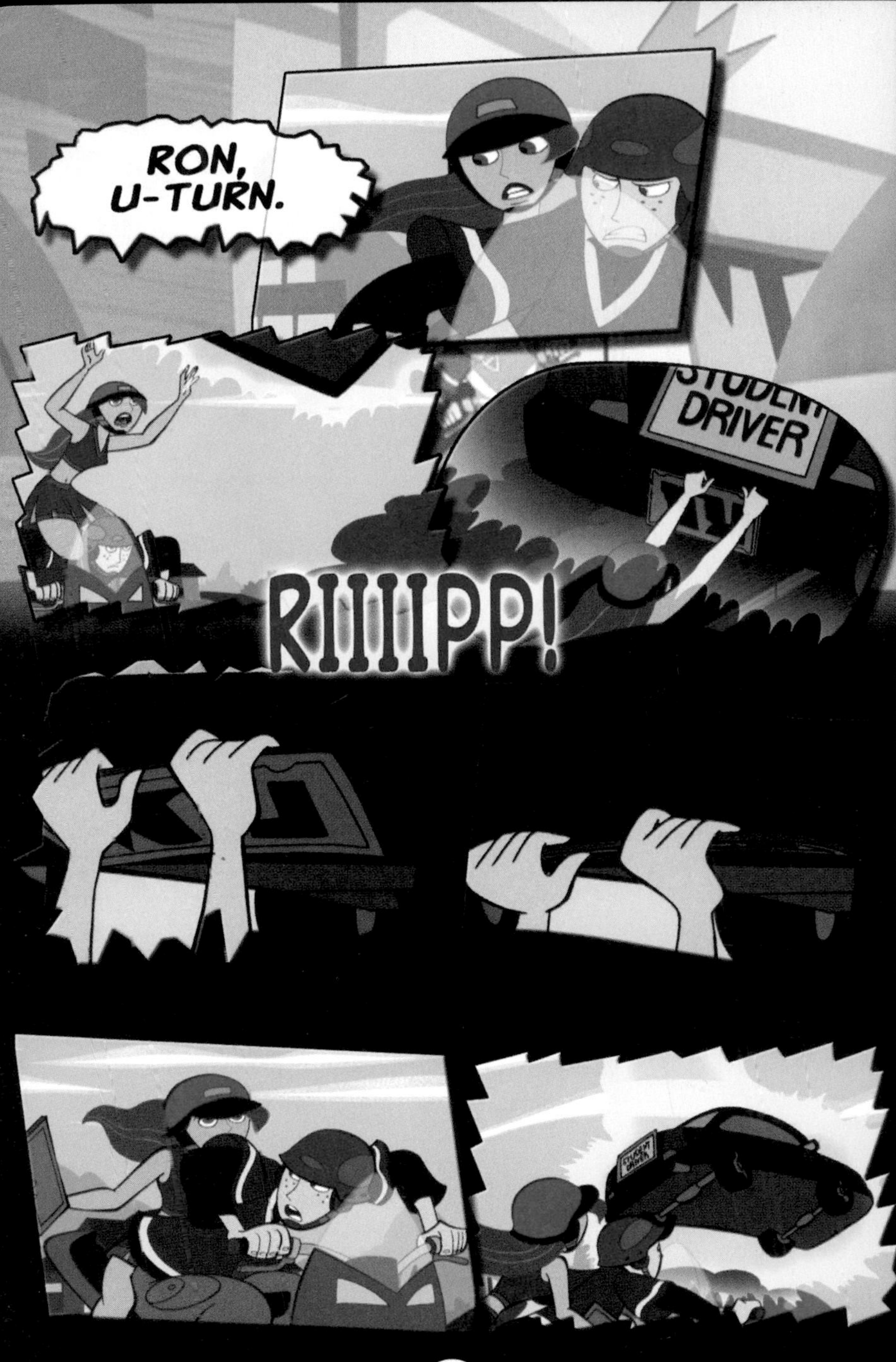
RON, U-TURN.
STUDENT DRIVER
RIIIPP!

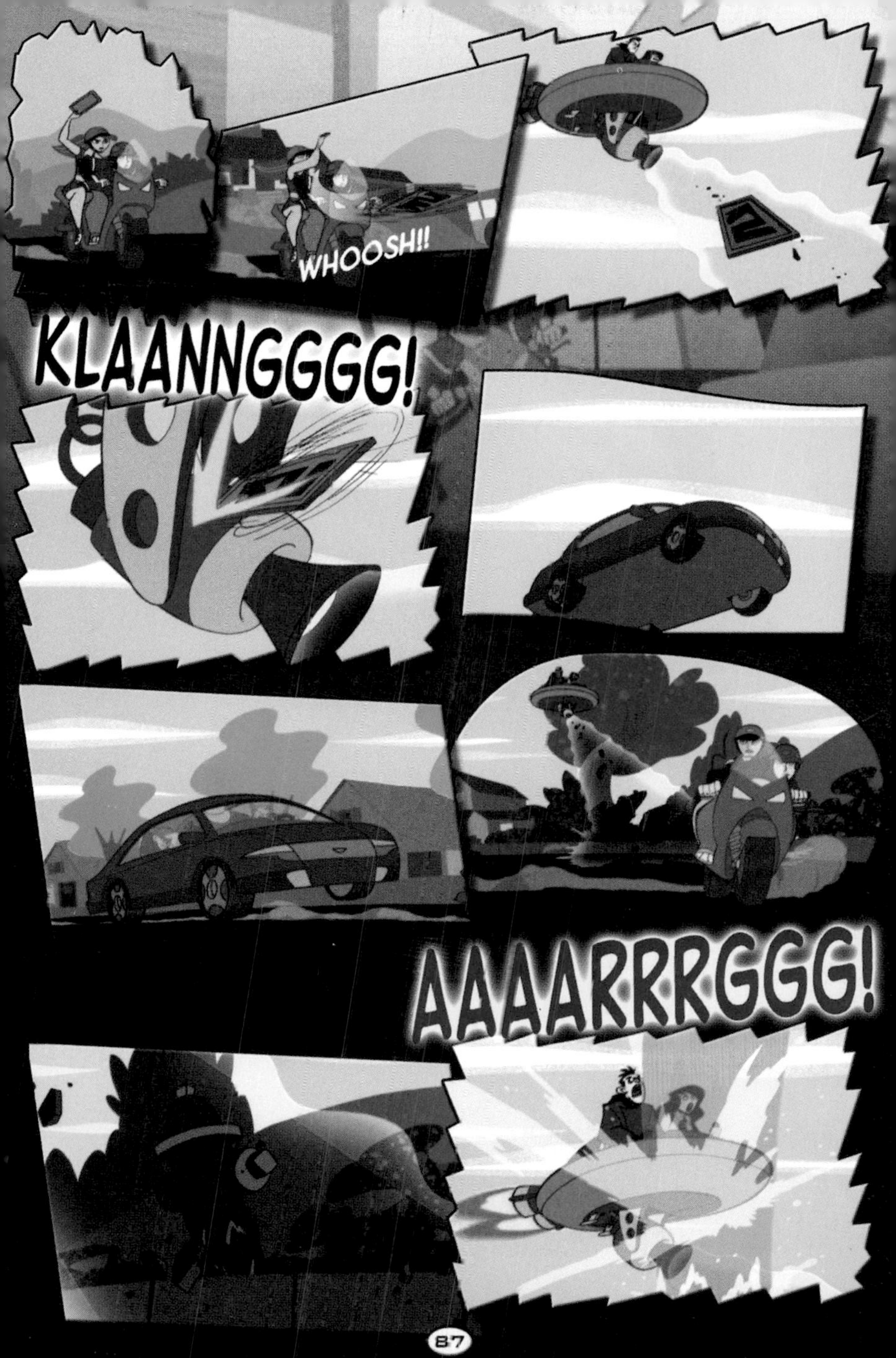
WHOOSH!!
KLAANNGGGG!
AAAARRRGGG!

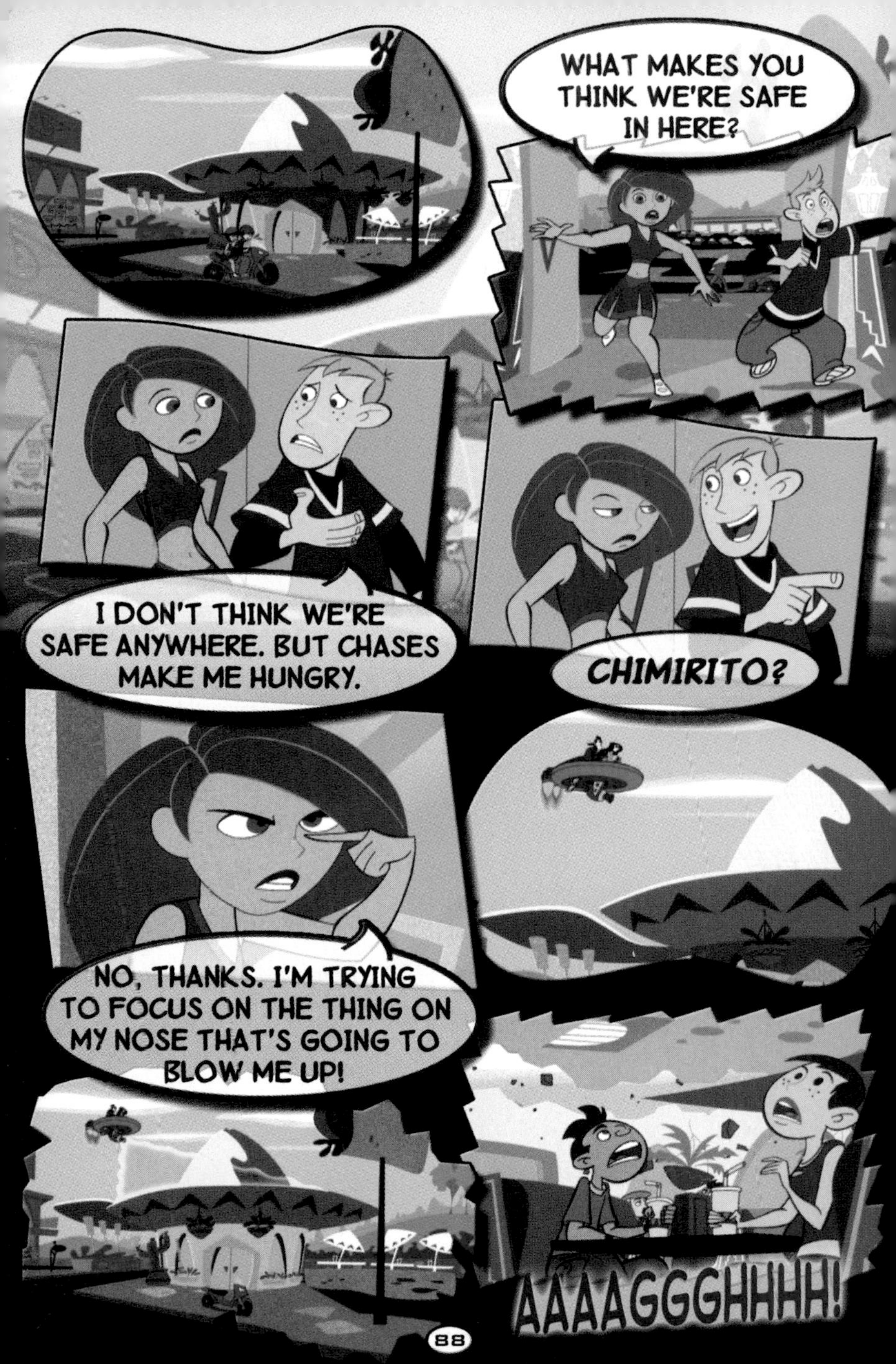
WHAT MAKES YOU THINK WE'RE SAFE IN HERE?
I DON'T THINK WE'RE SAFE ANYWHERE. BUT CHASES MAKE ME HUNGRY.
CHIMIRITO?
NO, THANKS. I'M TRYING TO FOCUS ON THE THING ON MY NOSE THAT'S GOING TO BLOW ME UP!
AAAAGGGHHHH!

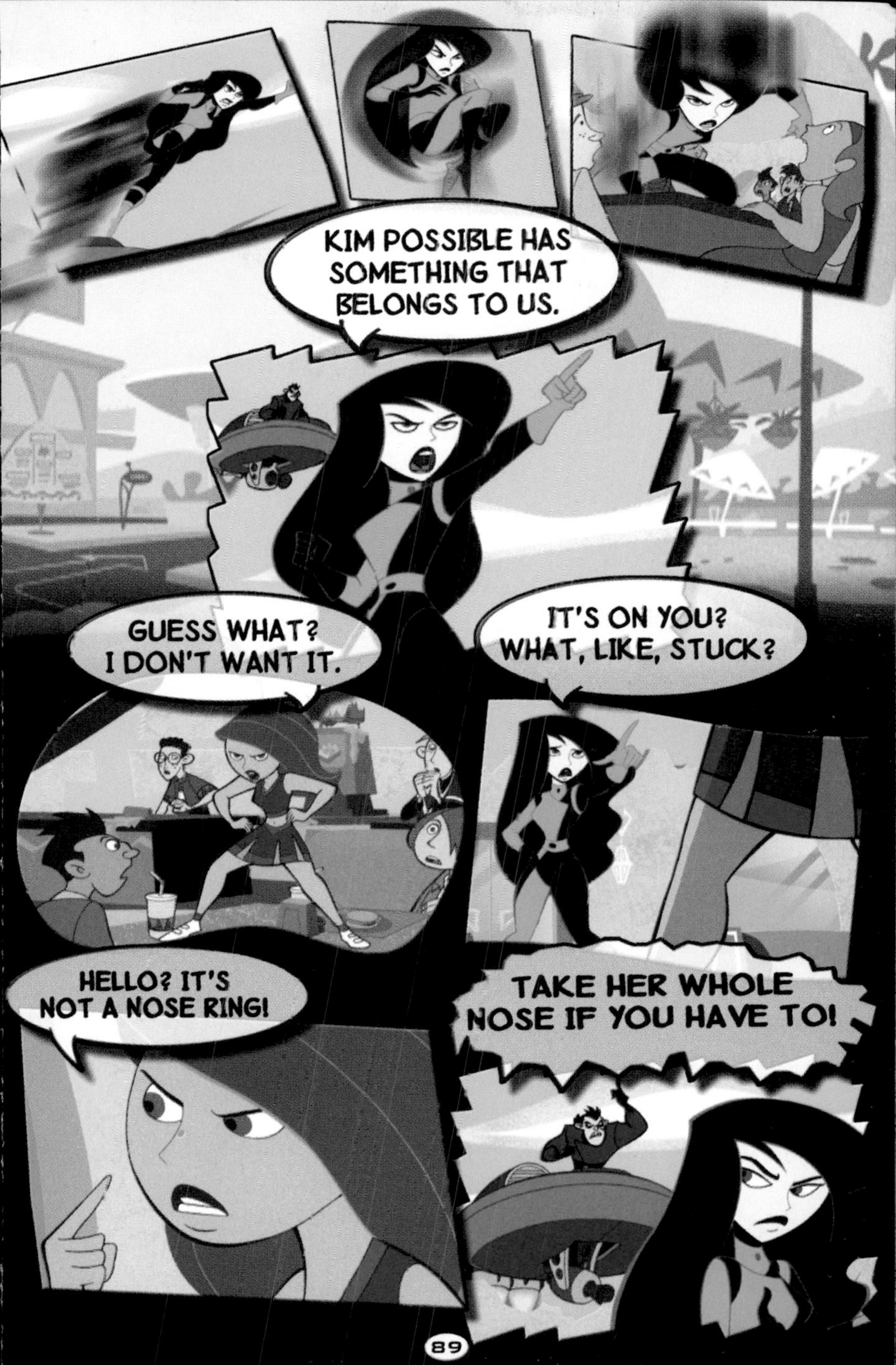
KIM POSSIBLE HAS SOMETHING THAT BELONGS TO US.
GUESS WHAT? I DON'T WANT IT.
IT'S ON YOU? WHAT, LIKE, STUCK?
HELLO? IT'S NOT A NOSE RING!
TAKE HER WHOLE NOSE IF YOU HAVE TO!

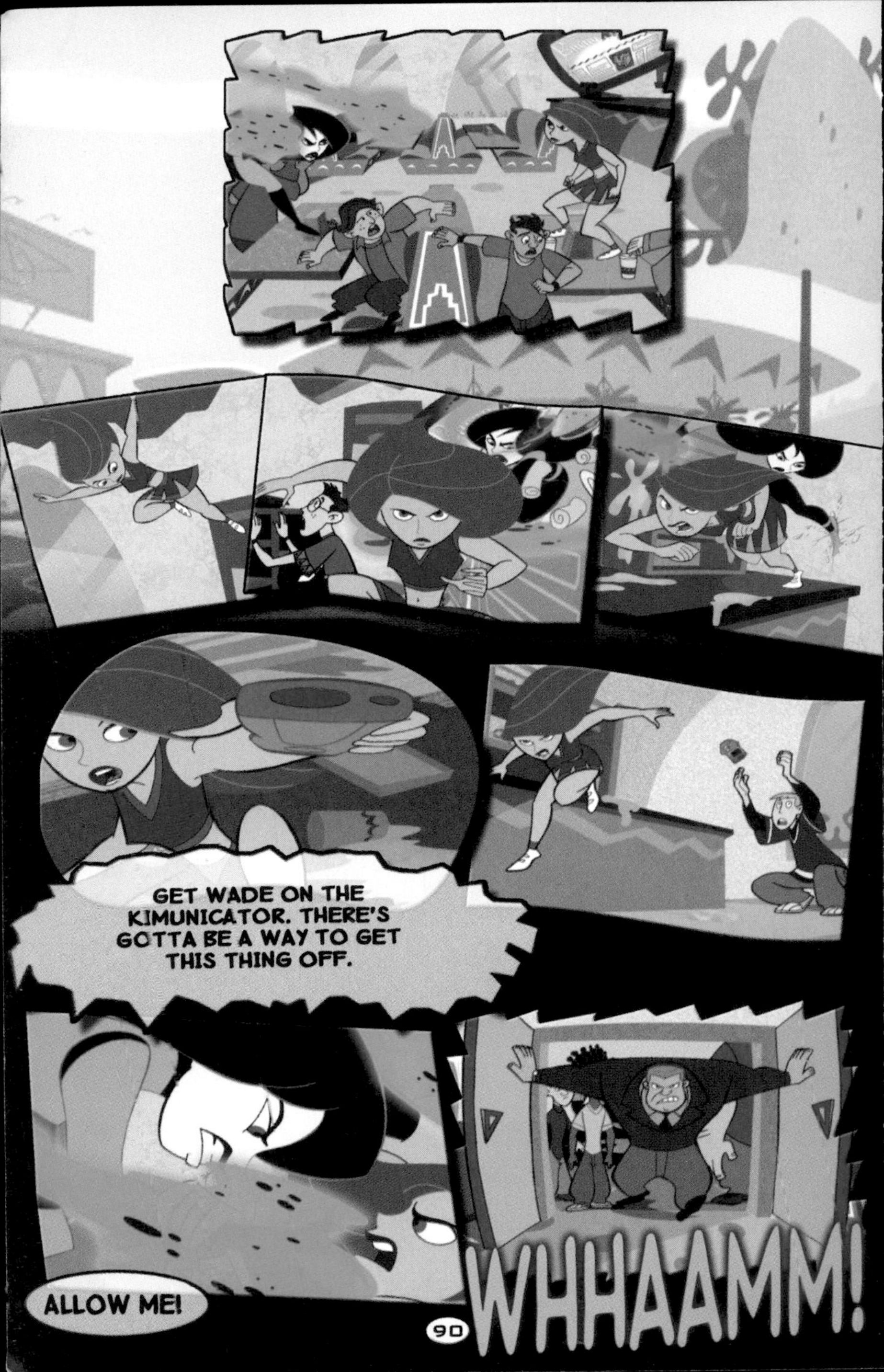
GET WADE ON THE KIMUNICATOR. THERE'S GOTTA BE A WAY TO GET THIS THING OFF.
ALLOW ME!
WHHAAMM!

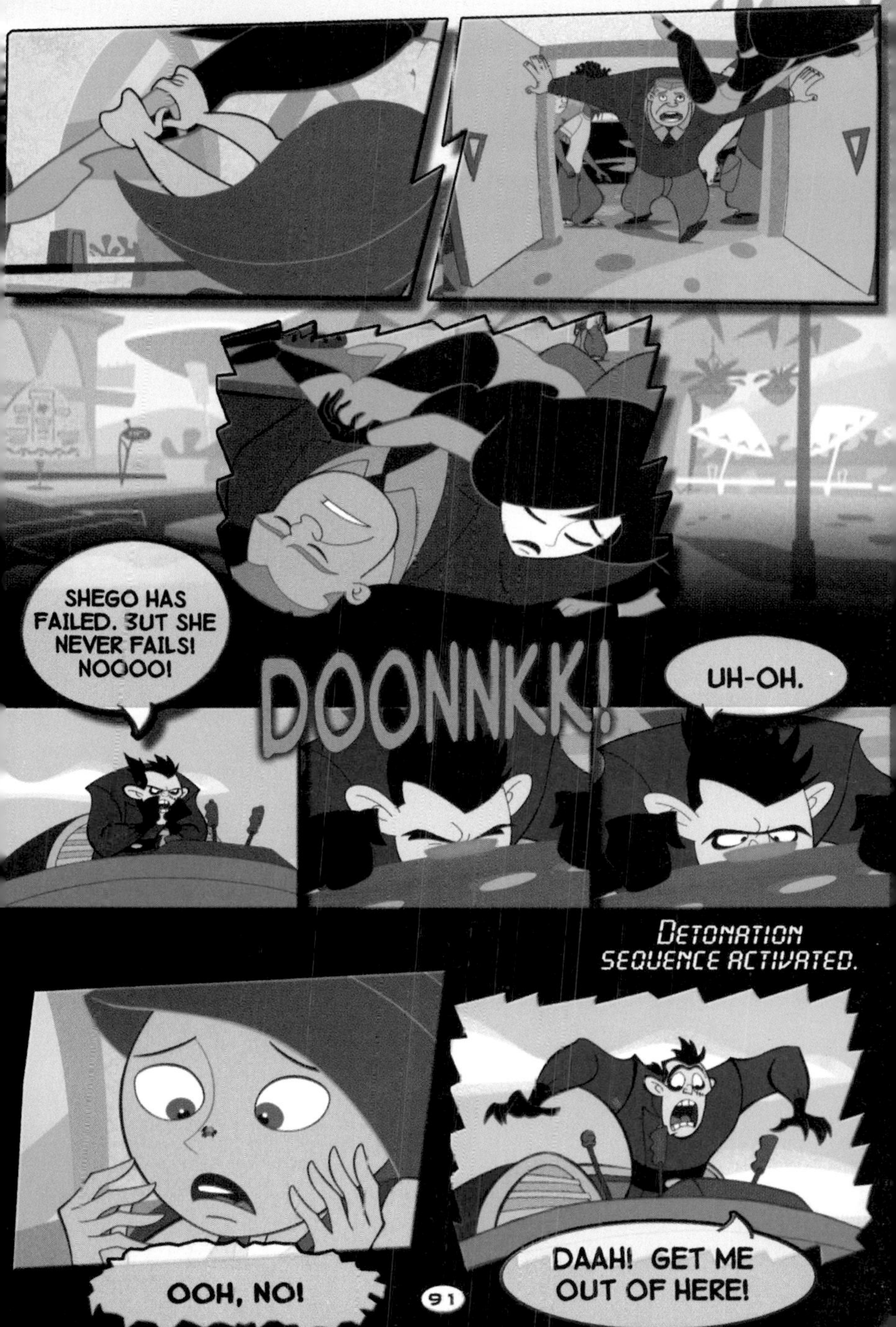
SHEGO HAS FAILED. BUT SHE NEVER FAILS! NOOOO!
DOONNKK!
UH-OH.
DETONATION SEQUENCE ACTIVATED.
OOH, NO!
DAAH! GET ME OUT OF HERE!

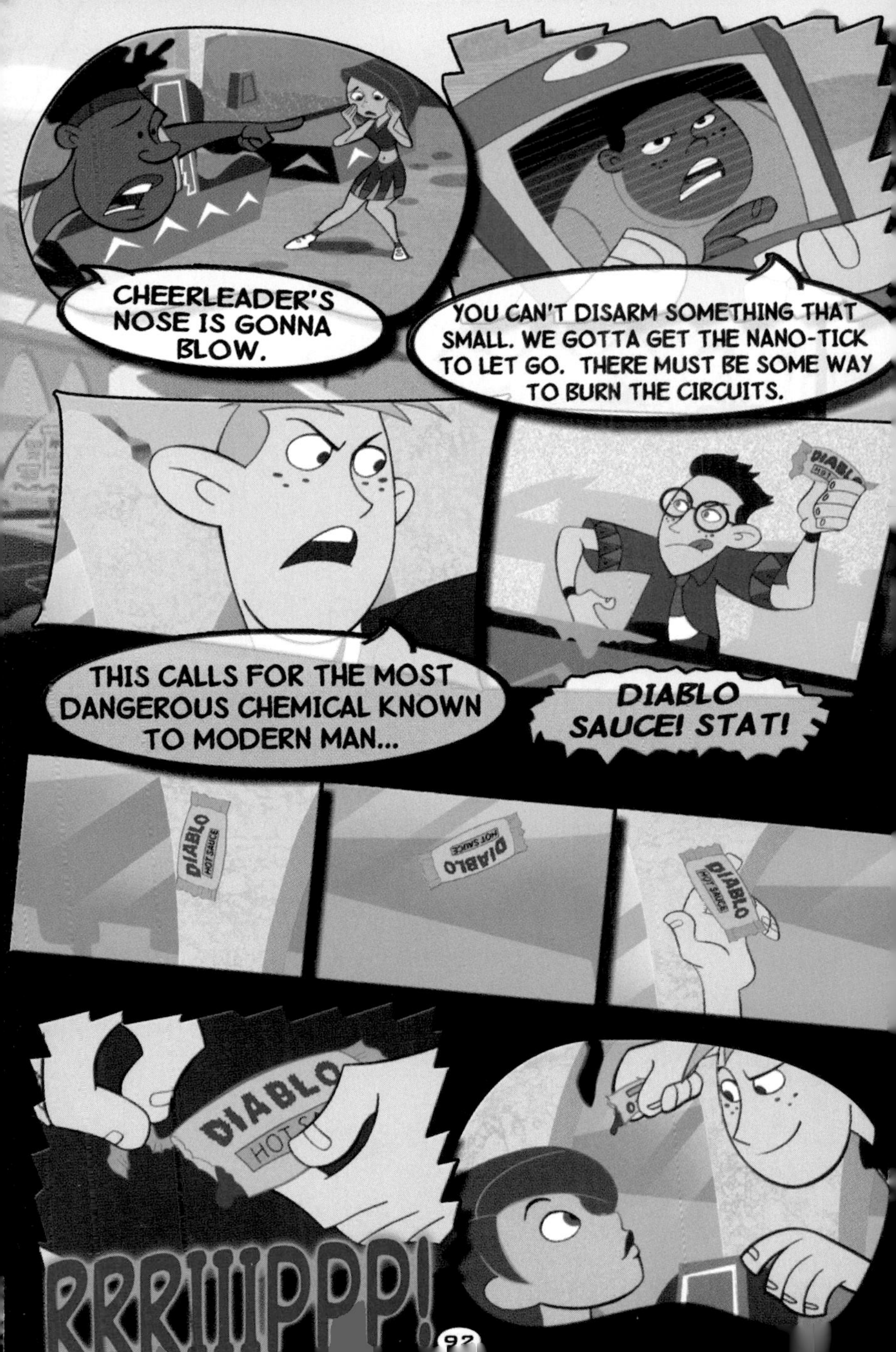
CHEERLEADER'S NOSE IS GONNA BLOW.
YOU CAN'T DISARM SOMETHING THAT SMALL. WE GOTTA GET THE NANO-TICK TO LET GO. THERE MUST BE SOME WAY TO BURN THE CIRCUITS.
THIS CALLS FOR THE MOST DANGEROUS CHEMICAL KNOWN TO MODERN MAN...
DIABLO SAUCE! STAT!
DIABLO HOT SAUCE
DIABLO HOT SAUCE
DIABLO HOT SAUCE
DIABLO
RRRIIIPPP!

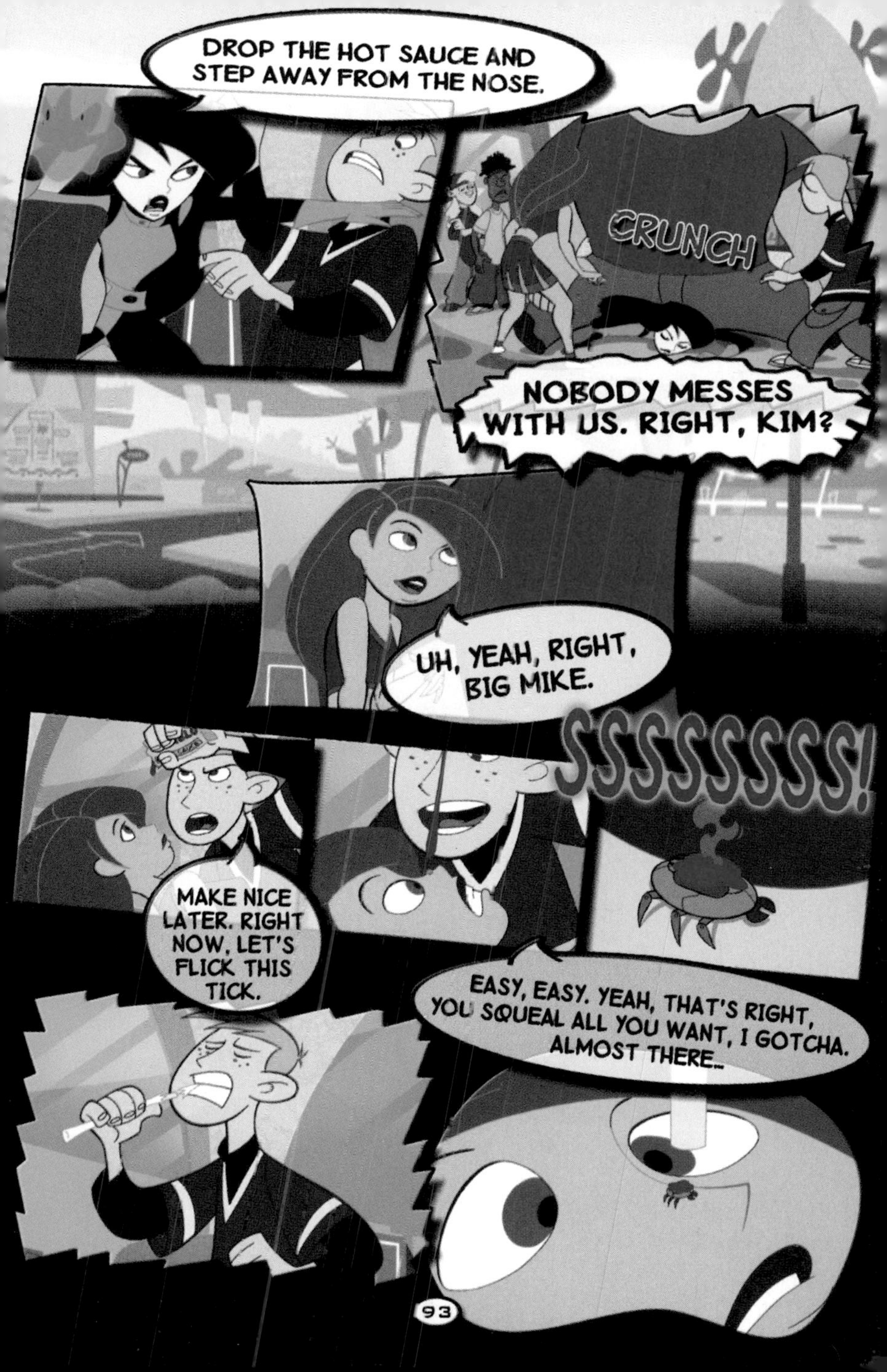

DROP THE HOT SAUCE AND STEP AWAY FROM THE NOSE.
CRUNCH
NOBODY MESSES WITH US. RIGHT, KIM?
UH, YEAH, RIGHT, BIG MIKE.
MAKE NICE LATER. RIGHT NOW, LET'S FLICK THIS TICK.
SSSSSSSS!
EASY, EASY. YEAH, THAT'S RIGHT, YOU SQUEAL ALL YOU WANT, I GOTCHA. ALMOST THERE...

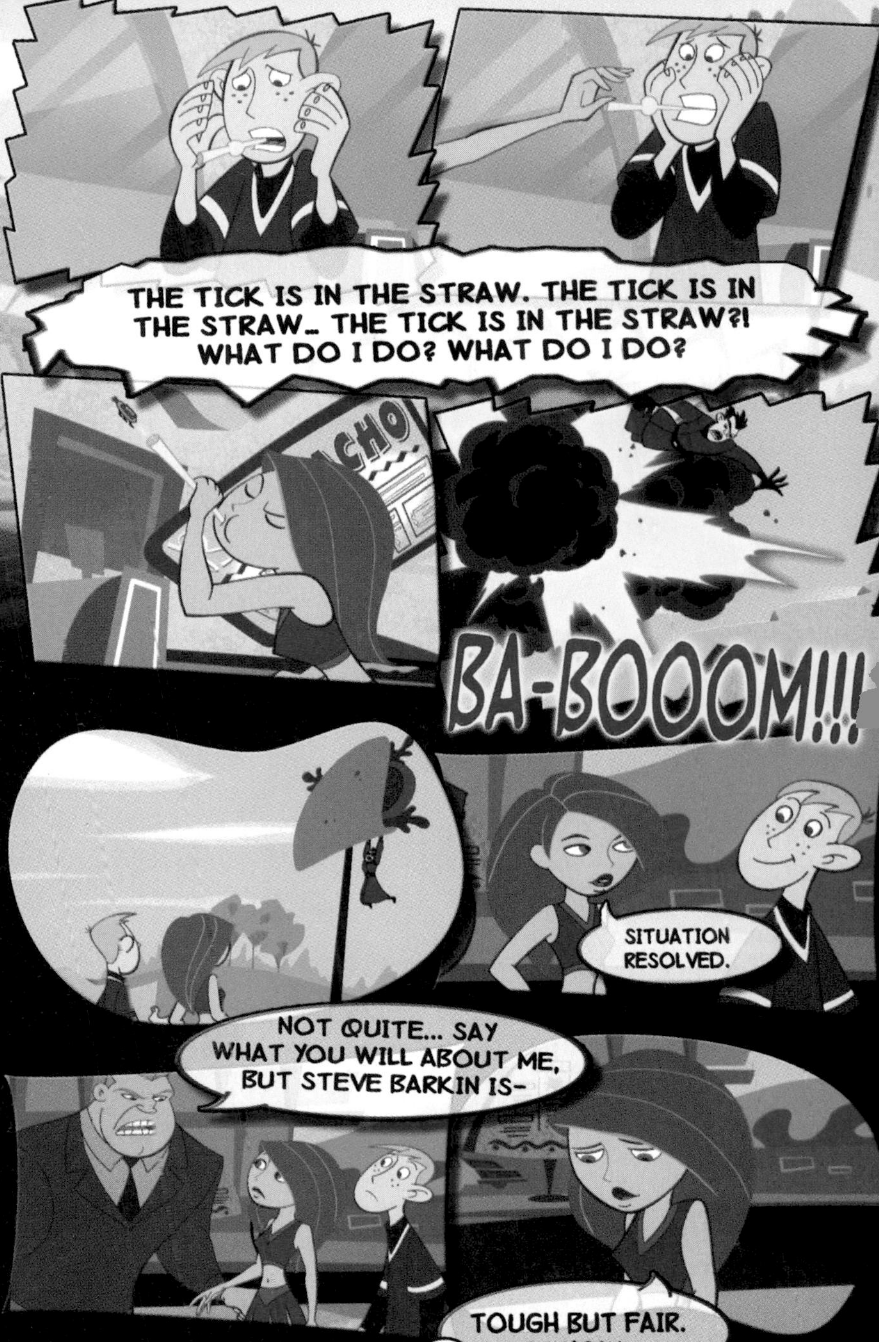
THE TICK IS IN THE STRAW. THE TICK IS IN THE STRAW.. THE TICK IS IN THE STRAW?! WHAT DO I DO? WHAT DO I DO?
BA-BOOOM!!!
SITUATION RESOLVED.
NOT QUITE... SAY WHAT YOU WILL ABOUT ME, BUT STEVE BARKIN IS-
TOUGH BUT FAIR. I KNOW.

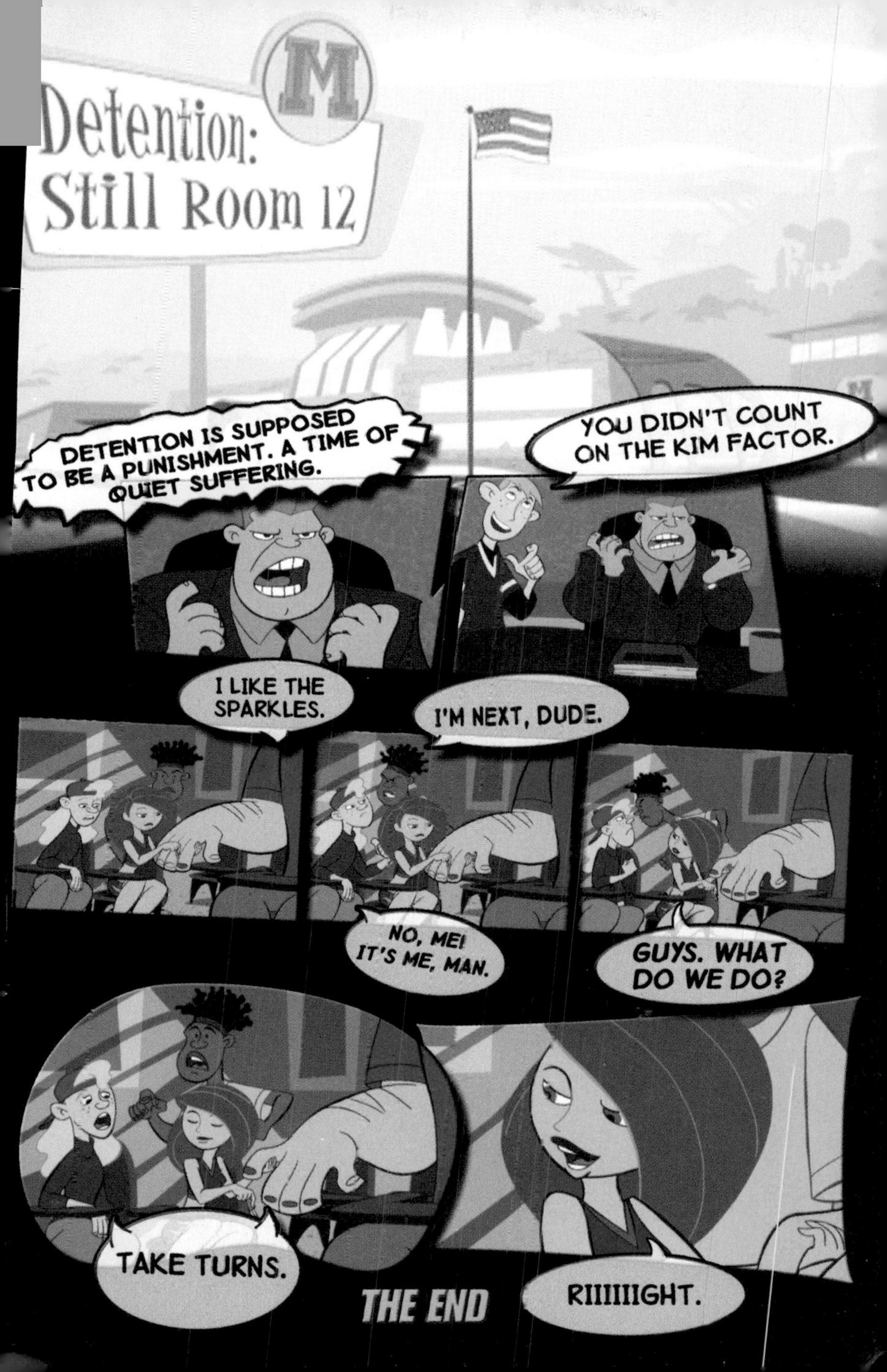
Detention: Still Room 12
DETENTION IS SUPPOSED TO BE A PUNISHMENT. A TIME OF QUIET SUFFERING.
YOU DIDN'T COUNT ON THE KIM FACTOR.
I LIKE THE SPARKLES.
I'M NEXT, DUDE.
NO, ME! IT'S ME, MAN.
GUYS. WHAT DO WE DO?
TAKE TURNS.
RIIIIIIGHT.
THE END

Disney's
KiM POSSIBLE
©Disney

Cine-Manga™ Volume 2
coming soon from TOKYOPOP®